PENGUIN BOOKS

AMAZONIAN

Dea Birkett is a distinguished travel writer and broadcaster. Her first book, *Jella: A Woman at Sea*, won the Somerset Maugham Award. Her latest is the much-acclaimed *Serpent in Paradise*. She has recently joined an Italian circus.

Sara Wheeler is a travel writer and broadcaster. Her books include *Terra Incognita: Travels in Antarctica* and *Travels in a Thin Country*, the story of a journey through Chile. She lives in central London.

THE PENGUIN BOOK OF
WOMEN'S NEW TRAVEL WRITING

Amazonian

Edited by Dea Birkett and
Sara Wheeler

PENGUIN BOOKS

PENGUIN BOOKS

Published by the Penguin Group
Penguin Books Ltd, 27 Wrights Lane, London w8 5tz, England
Penguin Books USA Inc., 375 Hudson Street, New York, New York 10014, USA
Penguin Books Australia Ltd, Ringwood, Victoria, Australia
Penguin Books Canada Ltd, 10 Alcorn Avenue, Toronto, Ontario, Canada m4v 3b2
Penguin Books (NZ) Ltd, 182–190 Wairau Road, Auckland 10, New Zealand

Penguin Books Ltd, Registered Offices: Harmondsworth, Middlesex, England

First published 1998
10 9 8 7 6 5 4 3 2 1

Grateful acknowledgement is made to Ben Okri for permission to quote from
'Ode to an English friend', from *African Elegies*, published by Jonathan Cape

The moral right of the authors has been asserted

Set in 10.5/13.5 pt Monotype Garamond by Intype London Ltd
Printed in England by Clays Ltd, St Ives plc

CONTENTS

INTRODUCTION

There's a monstrous tribe which lives in our imaginations. They wear corsets and long tweed skirts, are armed with parasols and consider hairpins *de rigueur* even up the Amazon. They rampage through jungles, swatting flies and dispensing prejudices, their manifold items of luggage borne behind them by a snaking file of natives. Safely installed back at home, they retire to the parlour and produce volumes such as *To Lake Tanganyika in a Bath Chair* (Annie Hore, 1896), *Peregrinations of a Pariah* (Flora Tristan, 1835) or the epic *On Sledge and Horseback to Outcast Siberian Lepers* (Kate Marsden, 1893). This is the tribe of women travel writers: bold, benign and clearly barking.

The better-known 'male travel writer' belongs to an entirely different species. For a start, they have not become extinct. Paul Theroux, Eric Newby, Jonathan Raban – still very much with us, writing books of sober literary endeavour and standing shoulder to shoulder with proper writers.

We have found that even when people are confronted by a real, live woman travel writer, they still get us wrong. In the time allowed for questions after a lecture we are regularly asked, 'Was that before you sailed round the world or after?' even though neither of us has ever done any such thing. The inference here is that to qualify as travel writers women must achieve astonishing and record-breaking feats. Either that, or we're trying to get our hands down some man's trousers. One of us was once asked by the president of a distinguished geographical institution, 'What made you go to Chile? Was it a guy?'

Since Herodotus wrote about his Egyptian travels in the fifth century BC or Etheria, the first-known woman travel writer, took a three-year pilgrimage through the Holy Land from 381 to 384, all the journeys have been done. Tell us about the most remote spot on planet earth and we'll tell you who's written a book about it. There are no longer any empty spaces on the map. Over the past decade aspiring travel writers have tackled this problem by completing old journeys in new ways: if someone had canoed up the Amazon, the next person had to canoe back down it in the other direction, and the person after that had to do it both ways with one hand tied behind their back.

Enough! The hapless reading public don't want to read about a blindfold attempt on Everest simply because no one has tackled the mountain blindfold before. Similarly, a sweat-soaked and life-threateningly dangerous journey no longer justifies a travel book. We've had a surfeit of willies in the jungle. Wilfred Thesiger, doyen of the roughie-toughie school and, at his best, a heartbreakingly beautiful writer, said recently that if he had gone across the Empty Quarter (the Great South Desert of Saudi Arabia) by camel when he could have gone by car 'it would have been a stunt'. The only point of doing it by camel, he said, was that it could be done *only* by camel.

When you travel, you are divorced from the familiar aspects of your life and you become the static, the familiar, the known spot on the landscape around you. One of the most frequently quoted travel maxims is Horace's line about the person who runs across the sea changing his skies, not his mind. It follows, then, that the writer's inner journey is the most important part – and certainly the most interesting part – of any travel book. It doesn't make any difference where you go; it's your interpretation of it that matters. Apsley Cherry-Garrard, who wrote a classic book about an Antarctic journey, said that the important thing was 'the response of the spirit'.

The writer's creative imagination has always been crucial to the success or failure of a travel book. All the great travel writers in the golden age between the wars had it in abundance: Robert Byron, Norman Douglas, Evelyn Waugh, Peter Fleming, Graham Greene. But now that writers have been everywhere, this feature – the inward-looking eye – is more important than ever. More important than anything else. The journeys writers make are slip roads to the private colonies of the imagination. Good writers look at an Alpine meadow and see more than aspirin-white peaks and forget-me-nots. Maud Parrish, a sprightly American traveller born in 1878, put it like this in her book *Nine Pounds of Luggage*: 'Some see life in black-and-white; others – and they're the lucky ones – in old-gold hues.'

Travel writing has made a new departure. A generation of writers who push the limits of the genre has emerged from the old adventure school. Julia Blackburn's *The Emperor's Last Island* and Bruce Chatwin's *The Songlines* draw upon biography, memoir and – in particular – fiction. Chatwin's *In Patagonia* opens with one of the most famous lines in travel writing: 'In my grandmother's dining-room there was a glass-fronted cabinet and in the cabinet a piece of skin.' Chatwin later admitted privately that this was a fabrication. There was no grandmother, and no piece of skin. As Robyn Davidson wrote, 'The writers of travel books reimagine what happened. They turn real people into characters ... It's not that they make it up, it's that they *make* it.' Travel writers have become more literary and less literal. This fusion of biography, memoir and fiction – let's call it New Travel Writing – is among the richest literature around.

In this new writing, it is the psychological journey that is paramount. 'The most foreign country,' Alice Walker wrote, 'is within.' Good travel books take readers out of themselves, and in the opposite direction too. We, the authors, don't have to have done anything ridiculously daring, or to have heroically suffered great acts of violence. It's what we thought and how we reacted that matter; it's not *what* we see, but *how* we see. The long red line drawn across continents – the Cape-to-Cairo kick – has been replaced by an emotional journey. And women have a head start here: the emotional terrain is traditionally seen as the territory of women writers. In *Three Guineas* Virginia Woolf put it like this: ' As a woman I have no country . . . As a woman my country is the world.'

If the emotional journey is the most important, it is that which has to be unique. At last, we can all go to the same place. We just have to write something different about it. We describe our unique relationship with that place. In her book *Clouds from Both Sides*, published in 1986, the mountaineer Julie Tullis wrote, 'The challenge is to myself and not to the mountain.'

Many writers celebrate the transforming power of travel. After all, on the road we can shed our old selves, try out new identities, often literally dress up. One of us – a thirty-five-year-old mother from the southern counties – recently joined an Italian circus and toured Italy, donning a gold-sequined G-string, a pair of putty-coloured fishnet tights, a huge white ostrich-feather headdress, and not much else. We could never have joined its British counterpart; transforming at home, in front of friends and family, would have been far too embarrassing. Crossing geographical boundaries allows us also to trespass into the possibility of having other lives away from that place called home. In New Travel Writing the story of transformation is often the central theme. (In our books, this is especially so.) To a certain extent it is the oldest story. Fairy-tales and children's stories are about transformation: Cinderella, the Prince and the Pauper . . . These new stories of transformation draw on our very earliest dreams.

There has always been stout opposition to women acting out these desires. 'A woman's place is in the home' is one of the best-known sayings in the language. Threatened by the growing number of single Victorian women who were stepping through their garden gate and heading for distant lands, in 1893 *Punch* published a poem called 'To the Royal Geographic Society'.

> A lady an explorer? A traveller in skirts?
> The notion's just a trifle too seraphic:
> Let them stay and mind the babies, or hem our ragged shirts;
> But they mustn't, can't and shan't be geographic.

When we began travel writing ten years ago, there were no separate shelves in the bookshops for travel literature and few role models. Dervla Murphy had been pioneering away since the publication of *Full Tilt* in 1965 and Robyn Davidson had been the only woman to win the Thomas Cook Travel Book Award (with her remarkable *Tracks* in 1980). When one of us approached a publisher, timidly suggesting that we wanted to write a travel book, we were told, 'It's a pity you weren't raped by fifteen Arabs.' Women write bodice-rippers or literary fiction. Our travel stories were unashamedly tame, intimate, domestic even – but we felt that they were, none the less, good stories, and that they fitted alongside the adventurers on the bookshelves. A decade later, we're there – and each year a few more join the band of what we call the Amazonians.

For women, the possibility of becoming something other is particularly attractive. The spur behind those oft-parodied Victorian lady travellers was the desire to abandon the embroidery in a corner of the darkened parlour and take a more powerful role. Many were delighted on their travels to be referred to and treated as men. Mary Kingsley, tramping through West Africa in the 1890s, said, 'I am a most ladylike person yet constantly I am called "Sir".'

Sometimes, dreaming is enough. Mary Morris tells the following story in her 1991 book *Wall to Wall*:

It was my mother who made a traveller out of me, not so much because of the places where she went as because of her yearning to go. She used to buy globes and maps and plan dream journeys she'd never take while her 'real life' was ensconced in the PTA, the Girl Scouts, suburban lawn parties ... Once, when I was a child, my parents were invited to a Suppressed Desire Ball. You were to come in a costume that depicted your secret wish ... The night of the ball, my mother descended the stairs. On her head sat a tiny, silver, rotating globe. Her skirts were the oceans, her body the land, and interlaced between all the layers of taffeta and fishnet were Paris, Tokyo, Istanbul, Tashkent. Instead of seeing the world, my mother became it.

New Travel Writing isn't all written by women. Jeremy Seal, Rory Maclean, Charles Nicholl, Nik Cohn and others are all dissolving presumptions about what counts as a travel book. But women have undeniably been influential. And because of this, we decided to make a collection of their vibrant new writing.

Everyone we approached was eager to be part of the book. But not all writers are pleased to have 'travel' tagged to their name. Jonathan Raban and Paul Theroux both insist on being called simply 'writers' (which they are, of course) rather than 'travel writers' (which they are as well). Bruce Chatwin turned down the cheque from the Thomas Cook Travel Book Award, insisting that *The Songlines* was simply a novel. Contemporary travel literature has been dismissed as 'a false genre created by publishers to market books'. In *Amazonian* we want to celebrate the fact that travel writing can now break down boundaries, rather than erect them. That is why we invited novelists, journalists and an actor to contribute, as well as travel writers.

All those writers who have rejected the tag of travel writer, we invite you to rethink. New Travel Writing is crossing frontiers, challenging literary territories, taking risks. This is just the start of its journey.

Editors' Top Ten
Our all-time favourites

DEA BIRKETT

Return to Laughter, Elenore Smith Bowen
The Emperor's Last Island, Julia Blackburn
The Towers of Trebizond, Rose Macaulay
Old Glory, Jonathan Raban
Tracks, Robyn Davidson

SARA WHEELER

The Worst Journey in the World, Apsley Cherry-Garrard
The Road to Oxiana, Robert Byron
Love and War in the Apennines, Eric Newby
The Lycian Shore, Freya Stark
News from Tartary, Peter Fleming

DEA BIRKETT

Folkestone: A Love Affair

ENGLAND

Ten years ago, I decided to leave London. I drove along the south coast of England, looking for somewhere I might live. It had to be close to the sea, and it had to be somewhere I didn't know. That was difficult, because all the seaside towns I drove through were familiar to me – Littlehampton, Brighton, Bognor Regis, Eastbourne, Hastings, Greatstone-on-Sea. My English childhood and the seaside were fused; I either went there when I was young, begged to go there, dreamt about going there or read books that were set by the sea. If I had to draw a map of the journeys of my first five years, it would be dotted with red and gold carousels, bright plastic buckets, tiny animals made from molten glass and castles of sand. I have a black and white photograph of myself, aged around three or four, squinting against the wind, holding my mother's hand, wearing a ruched swimsuit (stretch fabric had not been discovered) with a cardigan over the top, standing on a beach as ribbed as a packet of Plasticine. Over thirty years later, this photograph, for me, encapsulates the essence of my childhood. Oddly, I remember little about the flats and houses I lived in when young, but I can conjure up vivid pictures of the places we went on holiday – Margate, St Mary's Bay, Westcliff-on-Sea. On holiday we ate sticky things, danced in the shallow ripples, took off our clothes. The rough rub of the beach on my bare skin is the first sensation I can remember.

One day, in search of this unknown seaside town, I drove 150 miles, all the way from Swanage to Selsey, with the English Channel on my right. I couldn't find the name of a town I had never heard of before. Every place I had visited – or imagined that I might have visited – a long, long time ago. Then I reached Folkestone.

I had no recollection of ever having visited Folkestone, or having read about it. Only seventy-five miles down a motorway from London, it was a working port with a ferry to France – a place to pass through on the way to somewhere else, not settle in. It could not be called picturesque. Nuzzling in the hollow of a chalk cliff, it was wrapped by a fraught one-way road system which fenced it off from the countryside beyond. Just outside the ring road, looking London-wards with its back to the water, was the mighty complex of the yet-to-be-opened Channel Tunnel, larger than Folkestone itself. Within the inner circle of the town, slot-machine arcades rattled, cafés exuded the suffocating smell of overcooked food, a few souvenir shops stocked Folkestone tea-towels, a joke shop sold shiny plastic puddles of dog shit (while real poo sat like day-old sausages on the pavement outside) and a small, sad pedestrianized shopping centre was being slowly boarded up. Saga – the holiday company which caters for the over-sixties – had its headquarters on the edge of the one-way ring road, although it never sent holidaymakers to Folkestone. The closest a Saga customer could come was Eastbourne, sixty miles along the coast, which had also been part of my childhood itinerary.

I was leaving behind a rented flat in the centre of London, not far from the river, which I shared with my boyfriend. I wanted to start anew, redefine myself as someone other than the Londoner I had always been. I needed somewhere I had never heard of; I also needed somewhere that offered to reawaken that sensuality I saw in the black and white photograph. For that, it seemed, I needed the sea.

I bought a house on the edge of town, on the hill above the port.

It was a proper house, far larger than anything I could have afforded in London, with three bedrooms and a large back garden that would need looking after. I couldn't see the sea from any of the windows, not even those in the attic room, but if I walked to the end of the road, just a few doors along, I could catch the tips of the waves and judge their height. Some days, I could see France – a ridge of cliff – but only if it was neither too dull nor too bright. People in Folkestone said that the weather came from France, so if there were grey clouds teetering over the French cliffs it would be raining in Folkestone soon, once the showers had crossed the Channel. The same never seemed to be said about the sun; only bad weather was provided by the French.

Folkestone had been the first, vital link between London and Paris. At noon on 1 August 1843, an enterprising South Eastern Railway company had launched the paddle steamer *City of Boulogne* on the Folkestone–Boulogne route. The French capital could be reached from London within fourteen hours, and Folkestone became the closest point on the British mainland to the cafés of Montmartre. Writers and artists began to be attracted to the seaside town. Charles Dickens took rooms in the swanky white Georgian terraces on Leas Cliff, overlooking the harbour. Joseph Conrad, who lived on nearby Romney Marsh, set the suicide scene in *The Secret Agent* on the Folkestone ferry's wooden decks.

Now, for all its proximity to the rest of Europe – only twenty-six miles away, closer than any other point in Britain – Folkestone looked inward. The ferry went four times a day to another country, but if my neighbours took it, it was on a 'Flyer', nicknamed the boomerang cruise. For just one pound you could board the boat, sail across the Channel and buy duty-free, all without having to disembark in France. You simply came straight back on the same boat. At first I sniffed at the thought of crossing the water without touching French soil, but within a few weeks of moving to Folkestone I made my first Flyer trip. I went on one regularly every month after that, stocking up on cheap Belgian lager and litre-bottles of gin.

I revelled in Folkestone's inward-lookingness. In London I could get anything I wanted, meet anyone I liked. I wanted to shake my cosy assumptions about what was important. I wanted to move somewhere where everything that had become valuable to me was considered pretty near worthless. Launch parties, column inches, contacts, who you were seen drinking with in Soho – I no longer wanted to care. I wanted to be somewhere that no longer cared either. Folkestone was just perfect. I had found somewhere that was satisfied with and secure about itself. The people of Folkestone not only rejected France; they rejected London too. So close, they chose to stand apart, and I wanted to stand next to them.

I had been in Folkestone only a couple of weeks when I experienced my first moment of soaring joy. There was a man who came round to wash my windows. He didn't have a ladder or any cloths, but he did have a bucket, as if equipped to build sandcastles rather than wipe down windows. He also had a small radio, which he held right up against his ear whether he was walking along the street, standing on the doorstep or up a ladder. It was tuned to Invicta, the local commercial radio station, which mixed pop music and chat.

He would ask to come in to fill up his bucket at the kitchen sink, borrow a cloth and use my ladder for the upstairs windows. He was very clumsy, partly because he did everything with one hand, the other being occupied clutching the radio against his ear. Whenever he filled the bucket at the sink, squeezing in some washing-up liquid, he'd knock over the plates and mugs stacked on the draining board. Once, I found him hurriedly stuffing huge shards of broken glass into his pocket, trying to hide the tumbler he'd smashed. I'm not sure why I let him wash my windows, as he didn't do it very well and the washing-up liquid made them very streaky, but I always said yes. As well as listening to his radio and cleaning the windows, he would chat, and that is probably why I kept him on. I was paying him to stay in my company.

He was doing the back windows when he asked, 'What does your boyfriend do?' Kevin had just left for the London flat after visiting for the weekend.

'He's a journalist.'

'Who's he work for? The *Folkestone Herald*?' He climbed down the ladder, barely holding on even with his free hand.

'No, the *Guardian* mostly.'

The window cleaner shook his head. 'No,' he said, full of pity, 'it must be very difficult to get a job on the *Folkestone Herald*.'

My heart roared. *That*, I thought, is why I'd come to Folkestone, to shake the complacency of being surrounded by fellow *Guardian* readers. I had found a place, so close to home, where what I had always considered important and interesting counted for nothing at all. This was really travelling.

As I settled into Folkestone, I grew to love it more and more. I enjoyed the cocky self-confidence of the town and, by implication, me as its citizen. I had shed the skin of the city; Folkestone made me feel sexy, like a fresh affair.

There were continual confirming instances of how right I had been to move there. When I went to the greengrocer and asked for an aubergine, the shop assistant in the blue and white tiny-checked nylon overall didn't know what I meant.

'Eggplant?' I tried. She shook her head. There were potatoes, greens and boiled beetroot. I hadn't had boiled beetroot since I was a child; I had never seen it in my local shop in London.

There were many cafés in town, but my favourite was called Paradise. It sold weak coffee with plastic tubs of non-milk-fat creamer; the cappuccino bars of Soho were far away and, I hoped, long behind me. I liked this café because the man who ran it always asked me how

I was ('All right, luv?'), and because of a handwritten sign he had pinned up over the counter: PARADISE CAN BE HIRED FOR PRIVATE FUNCTIONS. I decided that, for my fortieth birthday, I would hire Paradise.

Visiting a café became part of the rhythm of my days. In London, my time was counted out by how long it took to get somewhere, and when I had to be at that destination, this meeting. In Folkestone, I could walk anywhere very quickly, and wasn't meeting anyone, anyway. The day was launched with a blast from the ferry's horn, announcing the eight o'clock sailing. If the morning was misty, the foghorn at the tip of the breakwater would wail dully, parting the air. I would go to my desk and imagine the boat setting sail, engines in reverse thrust, pushing away from the harbour wall. I'd get out my diary and plan my next Flyer, although I didn't really have to plan, as I had few arrangements.

Another spur to leaving London was to abandon journalism for more serious, sustained writing. I unplugged my phone, so the ephemeral world of London couldn't intrude. In Folkestone I wasn't going to be a mere scribbler of articles, a hack; I was going to be an author, writing books. I made the smallest room in the house into my office and bought the biggest desk I could find, which almost filled the room. That way, I could do nothing but write.

Living alone, with nothing to determine what I did but my own desires, creating a pattern for the day, with milestones placed through it, became increasingly important. I leaned on other people's rhythms like skeletons about which I built the flesh of my day. First came the ferry's horn, after which I would write for a couple of hours, longhand, on the unused side of used paper, then wait for the man who lived opposite to have his lunch.

His home was the smallest and prettiest in the street. Each window – there were only two, one up and one down – was bordered with green plastic window boxes suspended in black wrought-iron holders.

In the window boxes were rows and rows of pink and white flowers, permanently in full bloom, as they were all plastic. His rug-sized front garden had a little green-roofed wishing well in it with a notice attached: NO FISHING. All around the well were rose bushes, from which sprang another notice, hung on a tall wrought-iron stand. Letters were burnt into the wooden plaque, JUST IN COTTAGE, so everyone in the street called the man Justin. I never knew his real name. Justin was often in his garden, pruning his roses, which must have been of some miraculous fast-growing, ever-lasting variety, because despite his fierce daily pruning there always seemed to be another slender branch left to cut back the next day.

Every morning, at around eleven-thirty, a late-middle-aged woman with wiry red hair walked up from the other end of the street carrying a dinner plate covered in silver foil in front of her, opened Justin's florid wrought-iron gate and let herself in to Just In Cottage with a key. A few minutes later she would come out of the house empty-handed and go back up the street. An hour or so afterwards she'd return, let herself in again and re-emerge with a plate, but no silver foil.

I had been watching this routine for months before a neighbour on my side of the road told me that the woman was Justin's ex-wife.

'Divorced now,' she whispered. 'She lives with her sister at the other end of the road.'

As Justin was retired, his former wife made him his dinner each day and brought it round for him. When he'd eaten it, alone, she'd come back to collect the empty plate.

Justin looked quite young to be retired, in his mid-fifties perhaps. I made a remark to this effect to the neighbour. 'Well, not *retired* exactly,' she mouthed. 'He was made redundant, from the ferries, when they cut back to one boat. He was a cook on the ferry.'

*

The end of Justin's early dinner marked the beginning of mine. A friend had told me that the German philosopher Kant, who never went abroad, took a daily stroll around his home town of Königsberg, to contemplate his thoughts and let his writing breathe. Perhaps I could learn from this. Each day in Folkestone I took a contemplative walk, heading towards a café.

A good place to eat was the Pig Out. What I liked best about it was the smell. It was of food that had been boiled – boiled chicken, boiled potatoes, boiled cabbage, boiled ham. Because of all the boiling, the Pig Out was always steamy, the windows thick with condensation, and a thin layer of water would cover my arms like sweat. When I went home, I carried the smell of boiled food back with me, lasting throughout the afternoon.

After eating, I'd look at the sea. Every day it would be a different colour, sometimes dull grey, sometimes bright green, as if each night it was swapped for another substance entirely. Sometimes it was calm, hiccuping against the harbour wall, but at other times it seemed senseless, to have lost its direction, wildly battering against the breakwater as if looking for a way out. Despite the weather, I would wear short sleeves and shorts if at all possible, eager to feel the sting of the wind.

Whatever the weather, there would always be ships, either sailing south, keeping to the far side of the Channel, towards the Bay of Biscay, or north towards Scandinavian waters. The ferry criss-crossed this traffic, slicing through the shipping lanes. Back at my desk, as the day closed, the seagulls screeched and I plugged the telephones back in. If anyone who didn't know me rang, they'd ask if I had a baby, thinking the sound of the gulls was a young child sobbing.

For three years I lived like this in Folkestone. There were demonstrations in Tiananmen Square, an earthquake in Mexico killed 2,000 people, a fatwah was issued against Salman Rushdie, Grenada was invaded, Ben Okri won the Booker Prize, Simone de Beauvoir died. I watched these events on my television every night on the ten o'clock news, supper on a tray on my lap. Still I heard the horn, watched Justin's lunch being delivered, went for a walk and stood in front of the sea. At weekends Kevin came down and we strolled along by the sea together. He told me about London and I told him the small stories of my week. The waitress at the Pig Out, who was married to the owner, had had a baby boy. His big brother wanted him to be called Schwarzenegger, but the parents had named him Matthew. Now his big brother called him 'boring Matthew', or 'Schwarz' for short. Kevin's life seemed large; mine was lost in detail – a child's remark scribbled down, how the seagulls danced on the grass to trick the worms. On Monday morning, when it was still dark, before the ferry's horn, he drove back up the motorway and my week began.

I wrote one book, then another. In the author's biography on the back flap, it read, 'She lives in Folkestone.' I felt that Folkestone and I were a relationship that would last.

It was the *Folkestone Herald* that broke the story that the ferry was to be closed down. For 150 years the Folkestone ferry had been carrying mail, passengers and freight over one of the most hazardous strips of water in the world. While other ports had modernized, Folkestone lagged behind; until 1972, cars were being hoisted on to the deck of the ferry by crane. At the expanding modern port of Dover, just six miles along the coast, superferries were carrying 600 cars at a time; the twenty-year-old Folkestone ferry carried just 200. In the new superferries, the crossing from Dover to Calais took almost half the time of that from Folkestone to Boulogne, despite the fact that it was several miles longer. But it wasn't until the imminent opening of the Channel Tunnel that the Folkestone ferry eventually foundered. On the last day of 1991 she made her final voyage. On board, a prospective Greek buyer was snapping up the last chance to see the ship in operation. Soon there would be no more link between the town and France. Folkestone would be able to contemplate only itself.

The withdrawal of the ferry service shouldn't have bothered me. I rarely went to France anyway; just on the Flyers. But I no longer heard the horn in the morning, the first milestone of my day, and when I looked at the sea I knew I couldn't cross it. There was no possibility of getting away.

Each morning, hearing that horn, I had vicariously travelled myself. I had told myself that if the whim had taken me, I could within two hours replace boiled ham at the Pig Out with sidewalk cafés, croissants and croque monsieurs. I had felt wonderfully intimate with another world. Now there was no pretence; I could not escape. Folkestone had to provide everything I wanted.

Every day I was in Folkestone was no longer an active choice. Folkestone, stranded, began to turn sour. In truth, the coffee in Paradise tasted really bad. I was fed up with boiled ham and cabbage. As the Iron Curtain dissolved, there was no one with whom I could discuss it. Then one day I saw the window cleaner walking through the shopping centre, radio against his ear, tuned in to the *World at One*. In a sea of indifferent shoppers, he seemed to be straining to hear what was happening beyond the one-way ring road. But rather than finding his new interest in the wider world heartening, it sickened me: only the window cleaner cared.

I fell out of love with Folkestone quickly. I became irritated with the town. Quirks and failings which I had once found charming now annoyed me, much as a trait in a lover which initially delighted and tickled transforms into an irritating habit – the way he always pushes his fingers through his hair, how he pulls on his socks before getting dressed, the way he tends to walk with his hands in his pockets. Those small things which were once part of the tender parcel of loving now turned against that love and destroyed it. I was no longer boastful of Folkestone; I was embarrassed. I began to tell people that I just went there for weekends. Of course, the person I was really telling was myself; I was articulating my new hope.

I began to notice things I hadn't seen before. Had that house two doors along always been boarded up? Hadn't the dog shit on the pavement got a lot worse lately? Had the litter always been that bad on the beach? I didn't see the town's shortcomings as other people did; I saw them as far worse. It was as if I'd not only had the blinkers removed from my eyes but also been given a microscope through which to inspect every inch. There were cracks and flaws everywhere. Then, one day, I wasn't even able to buy a copy of the *Guardian*; my local newsagent had decided that sales were so low he would no longer bother to stock it. These oddities and omissions that had attracted me to the town in the first place were now pushing me away. The time for Folkestone had passed.

I now visit Folkestone very rarely. I no longer feel irritated, embarrassed or annoyed by the place. I just feel sad. Once I loved this town, was excited by it, flaunted it, proud that our names were linked, that we belonged together. Where has that affection gone? Sometimes I long for it again, long to feel tingled by the sea air, to be exulted by the agonized cries of the gulls. But I know I will never hire Paradise; I must find some place else.

GINNY DOUGARY

Something Else

THE DESERTS OF ARABIA AND THE ARCTIC

Hot

I was born in a small town called Ahmadi in the Middle East. My father was a senior executive of the Kuwait Oil Company and my mother had the equivalent of a full-time job as the wife of an important man, entertaining guests and opening bazaars. We lived in a large bungalow, glass-fronted along one side, from which one could view my mother's nostalgic efforts to create an English country garden in the desert.

Ahmadi itself was an attempt to plant a version of home for a community of foreigners. Every house was a bungalow, every family was British or American, and everyone was an employee of the KOC. Oil was the only reason to be there.

Even as a child, I was aware that there was something odd about the place. It felt too small and inward-looking, surrounded by the vastness of the desert. There was an underlying impression of impermanence, as though it were waiting for something to supersede it. When the sand storms came, the *shamal*, we would barricade ourselves behind the shutters, slamming them over the mosquito-meshed windows, and listen to the sound of giants hurling handfuls of tacks against the walls. I imagined that our low-lying houses would be buried under the sand and Ahmadi would disappear for ever.

Much later, when our family had moved to London, I discovered that it was only a matter of time before the Americans and the Brits would be obliged to hand over oil operations to the Kuwaitis. Perhaps, in the way that children do, I had absorbed the idea that this was only a temporary posting. Home for all of us was always going to be somewhere else.

Ahmadi bore no resemblance to the country we visited on my father's annual leave. It was more Middle America than Little England. My friends at the Anglo-American school had names like Chuck and Hank and wore lurid-patterned Bermuda shorts. We watched Westerns in the community cinema and drank Pepsi-Cola floats. There were twisting competitions at the Hubara Club, where our mothers played mah-jong or bridge. Trick or Treat at Hallowe'en was a big deal. Our driver was a Kuwaiti who wore his *dishdasha* robe and *gutra* headdress with Robert Mitchum sunglasses and drove a Buick which had smoky pop-star windows. At the souk, stalls of brightly coloured saris and inlaid boxes of sugared almonds and pistachio nuts were flanked by others selling *The Archies* and *Superman* comics. *The Beano* and *Bunty* might never have existed.

There were plenty of reasons to feel like an outsider in Ahmadi, and that was part of its appeal. I was thoroughly at ease being a foreigner in a foreign land, one step removed from reality. My childhood was an adventure, sampling different cultures, trying to decipher the different codes: why some things were allowed and some not, depending on who you were. I was not aware then that a sort of apartheid existed. The Americans and the British held senior positions in the company, while the junior jobs tended to be filled by Indians. They lived in a separate area, in more modest bungalows, with a club, a school and a swimming pool of their own: a mirror image of the white chiefs' compound.

The chiefs all had domestic servants and, as if to reinforce the status quo, they too were Indian. Our cook, Fernandez, and the ayahs, Mayli and later Gracie, called my parents Sahib and Memsahib. Fernandez used *Mrs Beeton's Cookbook*. He was very fond indeed of his calico piping bag. Shepherd's pie would come deconstructed: a mound of mince and a fluffy moat of potato, sculpted into turrets and minarets. Blancmange was a riot of cochineal, as sugary pink as the Indian sweets he used to sneak me, with whorls of artificial cream forming a necklace around the plate.

After eating with my family, I would join what I thought of as my other family in their quarters behind the house. I loved it there, on the other side of the courtyard. The contrast between their living conditions and ours was, I suppose, appalling. But I was only aware then of their pleasure, and mine, in my being there.

The room was a cross between a temple and a kitchen, with a bed in one corner. There was a Madonna on one wall and a picture of a strange figure with many legs and arms on another. It was always dark and the most sheltered place I knew from the sun. I can still see Mayli clearly: hair as shiny as vinyl pulled back into a bun, strong brown arms jangling with delicate glass bangles as she kneaded vegetable pulp – always with one hand – into a ball with flour and spices, and lobbed it into the pan. She would call me her 'little chickadee', like my father called my mother, and giggle.

I'm not sure that my parents were aware of quite how much time I spent with the servants on the other side of the divide. It was one of those areas which one instinctively knew was a bit touchy, just as I knew not to ask my father why there was a secret cupboard full of alcohol, kept under lock and key, in the kitchen. And I would never have dreamt of asking why he had all those magazines full of naked ladies underneath the drawer of chocolate supplies in his dressing room, since why was I looking there anyway?

There is something about spending your childhood in a faraway foreign place which invests that time with a dreamlike quality, a sort of preternatural vividness. Your past is quite particularly another country, with no outward signposts to guide you back. So when as an adult you come to revisit those early years, they are full of incidents which seem almost implausible in their exoticism and strangeness; it is hard to distinguish between what was make-believe and what was real. And since all contact with the characters who were so important to me as a child was lost when we left Kuwait, there are no witnesses to corroborate or deny my stories.

Some of the memories are my own, some are second-hand but so richly woven into my imagination that I can convincingly claim ownership of them. My favourite story as a child was the one where my mother and father were driven far out into the desert, to dine seated on Persian rugs under the star-laden skies. The guests were outnumbered by the servants, who stood like sentinels in a circle around them. I always pictured their host as a fabulous Rudolph Valentino figure, draped in white cotton robes, smouldering eyes – beneath his headgear – inviting my mother to tango on the cool sand. It must have been the way that she told it.

Other memories are more impressionistic still: a blurry, black and white cinematic reel of memory, spliced-together segments of past time. There is a picture of my father, looking like Bogey in a boxy suit and serious shades, talking to Red Adair – the world's most famous firefighter – the oil well alight behind them. I can look at that photograph and feel the heat on my skin. The diabolic flames rising out of the desert – fifty feet in the air, twenty feet wide – raging for months; my father's fear and awe. The next time I saw those flames was in news footage in 1991, alongside maps of Kuwait, prominently displayed in Britain's broadsheet newspapers, with a tiny black dot and the words Al Ahmadi. My birthplace had become a key target in the Gulf War.

My family returned to England when I was ten. We arrived in London in 1966, in the middle of the school year. My father was very ill and my mother had been told to prepare herself for the worst. Life shrank. My vigorous father, Mr Bonhomie, became a cantankerous presence in a dressing gown. The gleam in his eyes disappeared, along with the immaculate white shirts and important suits. My mother looked permanently distracted and tried to remember how to cook and clean.

My sister, ten years older than me, a bobby-dazzler of a Chelsea Girl with her Vidal Sassoon bob, feather boa and little-girl smocks, would occasionally appear and shake our gloomy house down. After her visits, the gloom would seem even more impenetrable. My father retreated into himself and sat in the dark with his tumbler of whisky. He could not tolerate any noise, including laughter. All those years I had hardly seen him; now that I had him to myself, I was to be seen and not heard.

This 'home' didn't feel like home at all. It was a horrid nowhere, a limbo-land of waiting: waiting for me to go to school, waiting to see if my father was going to die. My mother fixed me up with a governess. She wore prim shirtwaisters with exuberant necklaces. I soon learned to manipulate her weakness for talking about herself. We would put aside our books and she would tell me stories about her other life in a hot country: of teaching in a village in Africa, of wild music and dancing in bars where her face was the only white one, and – most thrillingly reprehensible of all – of her lovers. We were linked by the sense that our past was more real than our present.

I watched other children play from my bedroom window. Saturdays were always the same. I listened to *Junior Favourites* on the radio, and could soon sing all the words of 'The Ugly Duckling'. My mother would take me to St James's or Hyde Park to feed the birds. Afterwards we would eat stale teacakes in the cafeteria, then head home for *Doctor Who* and *The Monkees*.

I thought about Ahmadi a lot. I missed my ayah and my friends, and forgot that it had sometimes been tough being the boss's daughter. But it was the absence of Arabic-ness – a quality I had hardly noticed when I was there – which made me feel most cast adrift. The keening wail of the muezzin calling the worshippers to prayer which filled the air; the sight of the gardeners kneeling on their *gutras*, heads down on the parched grass, at different times of the day. It was as though some vital ingredient in a dish had been forgotten. England tasted bland.

That autumn I went to school. My dear father was given a reprieve. And our family slowly embarked on the transition from expats to pats. Ahmadi faded, and with it went my childhood.

I don't know what it is that makes people want to travel. Some say that it's in the blood, or that it's a desire to escape, or to reinvent yourself. Expats – they say – are always disgruntled, never feeling that they truly belong in either their country of adoption or the one they left behind. But I am happy not to belong. It feels like my natural habitat.

My birth was more adventurous than most. My father drove my mother down the dirt track to the temporary maternity hospital: a Nissen hut with a corrugated-tin roof and half a dozen beds. The desert stretched out as far as you could see. My mother – groaning in labour – only had time to take in the Bedouins tending their goats outside their makeshift shacks, which looked as small and mean to her as dog kennels, and then I was born.

A few years earlier, she had transferred from the London office of KOC to the company's headquarters in Kuwait. She was intending to stay only for twelve months, but she met and married my father. Her first marriage had broken down and her daughter, my half-sister, was left in the care of my mother's parents until the year was up. My father had escaped from Edinburgh to seek his fortune in the oil-rich Middle East. Did I inherit the desire to reinvent myself in different cultures from them?

By the time I was in my early thirties, I had lived only a third of my life in England. And a pretty rum third at that. Boarding school might as well have been another country, with its own arcane dress code, rules and private language. A little world within a town whose natives viewed us 'gels', in our scratchy greengage uniforms, with suspicion. As soon as I left university, where on the first day I had met the scruffy flaxen-haired boy who was to become my husband, I wanted to be off – teaching English as a foreign language in somewhere as far from England as possible. Africa, like my old governess, Egypt maybe, but never quite Kuwait.

Talked out of it by my parents, whose own wanderlust was spent, on the grounds of it not being 'sensible', I stayed in London and got what was considered a proper job. Two years later, my husband and I moved to New York, where he sold vegetables from a stall in Harlem, and I sold vintage clothing in a shop in Greenwich Village, and then to Sydney, where we both worked as journalists. I could hear my parents' sigh of relief from the other side of the world. We came home when our first child was three months old. My father had been told that he didn't have long to live and this time there was to be no reprieve.

I had always been snooty about the idea of a mid-life crisis. When men left their wives or jobs or bought huge motorbikes and attempted to transform themselves into teenage tearaways, I looked down from a great height and pronounced airily, 'Oh dear. How pathetic. How predictable. How unimaginative.' There was no female equivalent because women, of course, were far too sensible to go off the rails.

Then I hit forty and something unsettling began to happen. I had everything that I thought I had ever wanted and yet I was as bolshy and unsatisfied as an adolescent. Every new challenge – embarking on a novel, rebuilding the house – only took me further into this unfamiliar, edgy hinterland. It made no sense at all. If I loved my husband and my beautiful sons, how come I wanted an adventure that did not include them?

I played with the idea of fishing out my tatty 1950s dresses and going dancing all night. I drank too much with strangers into the early hours in bars in Soho. I wanted to be me at nineteen, with no responsibilities or career or cares in the world.

This was definitely uncharted territory. My husband is my best friend, but he couldn't help. I wanted some sort of confirmation that it was all right, that what I was experiencing was only to be expected in a woman of my age. But no reassurance was forthcoming. There was a smattering of new novels by middle-aged women who seemed to be exploring this theme, their heroines walking out of their lives and families at forty, into the bright unknown. I was intoxicated by the idea that a woman didn't have to put up with being unhappy, that she could just remove herself from the frame. Get up and go, without being struck down by lightning. But this was fiction. What about real life?

I started to make cautious inquiries among the women I knew and was surprised by what I found. Each of their stories was different, but there was a common thread: time was running out, there were fewer years ahead than behind, and to think too much about the future made them feel disorientated, as though they might lose their footing and fall.

I was most wary of broaching the subject with my oldest friend – always the voice of robust reason, less given to morbid introspection than anyone I know. But she too, I discovered, was in a new, hard place. For the first time in her life, she said, there was nothing to look forward to. In her teens, there had been the freedom of university, then the challenge of a first job, exploring London, the first big relationship, the wedding, setting up home, the birth of her children. And now . . . well, we sighed melodramatically, there seemed to be little else on the horizon but illness, divorce and death.

In my case, the restlessness was compounded by something else. My life had been a ten-year cycle of change, and now another decade was drawing to a close. This was the longest time I had spent in the same job, the same house, the same country. My husband and I had talked about moving to Dublin or France, or even back to Australia, but decided not to because of our sons. How strange. All this time I believed that I had relished the travelling I did as a child, yet I chose to deny my own children the same opportunity. What I wanted for them was to grow up with a solid, unshakeable sense of their roots; to have a consistent idea of Home. I wanted them to be happy to belong. We chose to stay on.

I was in limbo-land again, waiting for something to happen. Only this time I had no idea what it was to be.

It was – the smallest of epiphanies – a short paragraph in a glossy magazine about a woman who had hitchhiked her way, from base to base, across Antarctica. The words and the accompanying photograph of an ice-blue dreamscape, like a beautiful hallucination, made my heart race. All the bustling noises around me sounded muffled, as though they came from some far-off place. I was shot through with excitement. How thrilling to think that a woman, on her own, could make an imprint on that immense snow-white continent – a place which had always been associated with a particularly rugged sort of male heroism. The horizon suddenly seemed limitless; a world, after all, in which everything was possible.

This sudden kinship was as curious as it was unexpected. I am by no means a gung-ho type. I have not owned a sensible pair of shoes in my life. I dislike camping. I scream if I see a snake. And snowy holidays have never appealed.

But it is surely possible to have an adventurous spirit without being a conventionally adventurous person. In the early 1980s, I had travelled a huge distance from Sydney to Pine Gap, an eerie cluster of white domes rising out of the red earth of Australia's Northern Territory. Eight hundred-odd women had gathered from all over Australia to highlight the presence of an American intelligence base, which had been identified by the Russians as a prime nuclear target.

We were joined by several Aboriginal tribes, including members of the Pitjantjara, some of whom had walked all the way from Western Australia. The site the Americans had chosen, as far away as possible from the public's gaze, was on sacred land. I had erected my own tent, managed to use the basic toilets without flinching, and got hot and sweaty and dirty – and had rarely felt so alive.

I couldn't get the image of that shimmering icescape out of my head. I bought every available book on the polar regions. I found myself irresistibly drawn to novels which incorporated the word 'snow' in their titles – and what a lot of them there suddenly seemed to be. I watched Michael Palin's travels from Pole to Pole with my sons, and natural history videos with titles such as *Life in the Freezer*. My family started to make jokes about my 'obsession'.

Christmas came and went. We built a snowman on the Common, but he had melted by the afternoon. After one grindingly domestic Sunday, I was suddenly struck by what it was that attracted me so profoundly to the white wastes. It was the absolute absence of clutter. A space as still and silent and empty as my everyday life was full of movement, chaos and noise. There was something liberating about the thought of all that nothing. The paradox, at once anaesthetizing and invigorating, of a chilly oblivion.

That evening, going through the newspapers, I read about a group of British women who were about to embark on the first all-female expedition to the North Pole. I highlighted the name of the sponsors. One of the bonuses of being a journalist is that your job can sometimes allow you to pursue your dreams, and my editor agreed that this was a story worth pursuing. By the following night, I was booked on a plane to the Arctic.

Cold

The total flying time to Resolute Bay, on the tip of Cornwallis Island in the furthest reaches of Canada's far north, is fifteen hours, and with three changes of plane and a one-night stopover you have several days in transit – from here to there, with the temperature dropping and the landscape emptying – to focus on where you are going.

At Calgary airport, we are greeted by an ancient cowgirl with platinum curls and an extravagantly fringed scarlet costume. 'Wel-come,' she says to each passenger who files past. 'Wel-come.' We descend the escalator accompanied by the sound of birds twittering and assorted farmyard noises and reach the lobby, where there are sepia photographs of pioneers in front of wigwams and faded pictures of the Rockies, and at least a dozen equally faded cowboys and cowgirls, all unpaid volunteers, who can tell visitors everything they need to know about the history of their home town.

On to Edmonton, which boasts the biggest shopping mall in the world. It is midnight our time. I spend the night near the airport in Leduc, which got lucky with oil in 1947. I got unlucky with my motel, which boasts a twenty-four-hour bar. There is a smell of vomit outside the entrance, which the woman on reception valiantly tries to identify as skunk. I find it impossible to sleep. Neon light floods my room, the bedding is threadbare, the mournful hoot of trains too nearby, and an interminable fight lasts long into the night, the thwack of fist meeting flesh, between several men and a woman whose voice rises plaintively, and nonsensically, again and again, 'But I *live* here. I *live* here.' And I am a long way from home.

Next morning the dining room is packed with men. Some of them are locals, others are trophy hunters: big-gutted guys with gentle faces, heading north to shoot grizzly bear, musk ox, caribou. They have to pay a lot of money for their pleasure. A licence to kill costs $15,000 alone. They get to take the heads to decorate the walls of their halls back home, but are obliged by law to leave the skins and meat to the Inuit.

At last we fly out of Edmonton, on the shuttle plane for Resolute – as far north as you can fly in Canada on a conventional airline. The land below is ribbed and tufted in tasteful gradations of colour: sage green, olive, caramel, sludgy browns. The plane is full of hulking great men with beards, most of whom are bound even further north than Resolute for the lead and zinc mines of Polaris. The four North Pole women, in their bright red suits emblazoned with sponsors' names, are a source of considerable interest. Everyone seems to have heard about their expedition.

I am slightly dismayed to discover that theirs is only one of twenty-six expeditions this season. I am told this by a long-limbed hippie-ish young man from Minnesota sitting next to me who will be guiding a group of rich Americans – there is no other kind in the Arctic – to the Pole on dog-powered sleds. Perhaps this icy desert isn't empty at all, but a tundra teeming with tourists who call themselves explorers. A nice old boy in a trilby and shiny trousers tells me he has laid out $22,000 to fly from Vegas to the Pole. 'An adventure holiday of a lifetime,' he says.

When is an adventure holiday an expedition, I wonder, and vice versa? The answer, at least in part, is money. One you pay for yourself, the other is paid for you by your sponsors, who want publicity – and new angles are increasingly hard to come by, which is why the women are on to such a winner. The only way to make news on an adventure holiday is to die.

After Yellowknife, where we briefly disembark, the air begins to chill. When I next look down, the world is unrecognizable. We fly in over great snowy dunes and the frothing spume of the sea, the waves frozen in mid-crest – nature in icy, arrested motion. I am confronting the land which has invaded my imagination for all these months.

At Resolute airport, there is a brief and tearful reunion between the four women in Team Charlie, who have just been airlifted off the ice having completed their leg of the relay, and Team Echo, with whom I have flown out from England. Echo is the last of the five four-women teams which make up the expedition, and its members alone will have the privilege of planting the flag at the North Pole.

Resolute is the expedition's base camp. The women are driven to their temporary home in the Inuit settlement, of approximately 170 people, where they will be holed up with their trainer, a dour Cumbrian unaccustomed to female company. I am staying at the Narwhal Hotel, which is also unused to the presence of women. There are times, over the next few days, when I feel as though I have intruded into a jocks' locker room.

The Narwhal is in the 'other' Resolute, three and a half miles away from the Inuits, a completely separate community of about sixty-five permanent 'southerners' who work at the Polar Shelf scientific research project or for one of the local air services. As winter turns to spring, and five months of death-like darkness turn into twenty-four-hour daylight, there is an additional fluctuating population of explorers, tourists, trophy hunters and engineers bound for the mines and rigs which are dotted across the northern wastes.

Exploration, one might think, would be the ultimate travel experience. Yet it seems to me to be essentially anti-travel. The women who have landed in the Inuit hamlet are unlikely to meet any of its inhabitants. They have barely two weeks of training on the ice – learning how to navigate, operate the radio, haul sleds weighed down with more than 300 pounds of supplies over the jagged, shifting terrain – before they embark on their journey. Their gaze is set so far ahead that they cannot see what is around them. They are not interested in the place at all. A sort of myopia – or tunnel vision – is a prerequisite for survival.

In the early weeks of the expedition, two members of Team Alpha fell through the melting ice into the freezing water. The newspaper reports back home were full of 'Woman cheats death' headlines and 'My struggle for life, by Arctic adventurer'. Even a bona fide expedition can benefit from a brisk brush with the beyond to make it newsworthy. It helped that the woman who fell deepest – reportedly up to her neck – was a mother of triplets.

I do not think for one moment that the women have nothing to fear except fear itself. Or that it doesn't take tremendous nerve and grit for women like these – most of whom have never done anything intrepid before – to undertake such a journey. It must be terrifying to fall through the ice when you are on skis, harnessed to a massive weight, in the middle of nowhere. Echo, like the women before them, will be travelling 100-odd miles on foot with no machinery in one of the harshest and most unforgiving environments in the world. Whatever the back-up – and it is considerable, with two highly experienced female guides, an American and a Canadian, accompanying the British women all the way to the Pole, as well as a team of men at Resolute who are there specifically to meet all their needs – it is impossible to eliminate risk altogether.

My first evening follows the same pattern as my other evenings at Resolute, only it is marginally more disorientating as I haven't yet adapted to the idea of a permanent pastel sky. It's easy to stay up all night, when night looks like day. At around ten-thirty, I decide it's time for my evening meal. But I have long since missed dinner, which is served at the Narwhal, canteen-style, between six and seven. I go to bed in my cubicle room at three a.m., hungry, dog-tired and buzzingly awake, the white night pouring in through the flimsy tacked-up curtain.

Rupert 'Polar Pen' Hadow runs the travel company which has organized the women's expedition. In a neat contemporary twist, he and his friends – upper-class hooray-ish chaps, with nicknames – have assumed the role of handmaidens for this trip. He has volunteered himself as my personal guide in the Arctic, partly to placate the stern

Cumbrian trainer, who is not overjoyed about having his charges shadowed by a journalist on a four-day assignment. I will be allowed some time on the ice with the women and the rest in pursuit of my own small-scale adventure: building an igloo to sleep in, skidooing through a ravine and flying in a twin-Otter plane in the remote hope of spotting a polar bear.

The women are phenomenally fit, as they must be to commit themselves to such an undertaking. They have worked hard for months – dragging tyres around Dartmoor, pumping iron in the gym – to hone their bodies into lean survival machines. I arrive five minutes late for the first training session and already they are far away from Resolute, their distinctive red suits fanning out in an arc over the limitless white.

I try to catch up with them, but it's hopeless. This is my first attempt at cross-country skiing and I am not a natural. The ice floor beneath me keeps giving way so that I shoot down alarmingly between the cracks. In the end, I abandon the skis and attempt to walk on the quicksand surface. Every time I seem to be gaining on them, they recede tantalizingly into the distance.

At Resolute I am happy in my familiar role as the outsider. Out on the ice it feels more awkward. Here, I want to forge an alliance, have a pal to confide in. I would quite like to be hugged. I am so used to physical contact – with my boys and my husband – that my arms feel heavy with their empty embrace. The last time I felt like this so strongly was when my father died and I realized that I would never be able to hold him again.

One of the reasons I grow fond of Polar Pen during our time together – which is easy to do, since he is both good-looking and kind – is that he is constantly fussing over me, adjusting my various flaps and straps and peering at my face to check that I haven't got frostnip. It feels like being parented.

It is Pen who points out the parallels between the Arctic desert and the desert of my childhood: the boundless horizon, the oases and mirages, the sculptural quality of the landscape after a storm, the sand and snow whipped up into fantastic, tilting shapes. I hadn't been aware that this journey forward might be a way of stepping back. If I am nostalgic, it is not for a sense of place – since I have no particular yearning to return to Kuwait – but for a state of mind. To see the world through fresh eyes, with a child's unjaded, open-gazed wonderment.

My relationship with the women is not so straightforward. They are an impregnable team. Three of the four were already close friends before the expedition. I am reminded of all the different schools I went to when I was a child on my father's annual leaves in England. I am the new girl once again. One term or less and I'll be gone. In these circumstances, no one makes too much effort to get to know you. One or two of the women are friendlier than others, but I have the sense of being tolerated rather than welcomed. I feel puffy and overweight and a bit hopeless. To compensate, I become the class clown, hamming up my clumsy attempts to behave like an explorer. It's all very well to behave like this when you're a teenager, but perhaps it's a bit sad when you're in early middle age.

My second attempt to be with them is more successful. The trainer has agreed to let me share their tent for a night on the ice. I had been expecting temperatures in the minus-forties but the Arctic weather is considered to be unseasonably warm. When you're sleeping on a carpet of snow, with an icy wind slamming into your tent, minus-seventeen seems quite cold enough to me.

Our campsite is in what is known as a rubbleyard – an uneuphonious name for such a lovely sight. The autumn storms scoop up the snow and hurl it around in a wild dervish dance. Then winter descends and freezes the snow shapes, with their weird, improbable angles, into icy statues for the spring. We are sleeping in an outdoor art gallery, surrounded by objects of a unique and fleeting beauty. By next year they will have disappeared, to be replaced by other hammers and castles and old men's profiles. But they will never be the same again.

The poor Cumbrian has clearly never encountered such a lippy and lewd bunch of women. British expeditions were never meant to be like this. We compare notes on peeing: how best to avoid splash-back when unzipping our ski-suits and parting the vents in our special double-layered crotchless thermal leggings, and the importance of covering our tracks in order to maintain the pristine appearance of the environment. Despite the ingenuity of the customized ski-suit, I have already encountered the woes of my zip jamming in the vicinity of my birth canal.

Like the women at Pine Gap, the women in Team Alpha, regardless of their cycle, all ended up bleeding at the same time on the ice – and this was despite having taken the Pill without the normal break in an effort to suppress menstruation. Some members even attributed their simultaneous periods to polar gravity. Tampons were in such short supply in the first few weeks that they were bartered in exchange for food. Subsequent teams, learning from Alpha's experience, took hormone injections in order to avoid the same fate.

I like the way the women are so earthy. Why be coy about the basics when your entire journey is about stripping away the artifice to confront the elemental? But there is something bloke-ish, and a quintessentially British bloke at that, about distancing your fear through lavatorial banter. Even the one anxiety to which they admit is in the stiff-upper-lip tradition of a Shackleton or a Scott: 'I don't want to let my team members down.' Only one woman, the one I find easiest to talk to, with her sly northern wit, concedes to harbouring a deeper fear. But she cannot find the words to express it.

Resolute Bay began life as a weather station and, in the 1950s, the Canadian government planted the Inuit colony in an untidy sprawl of basic housing in order to protect Canada's rights over the land of the High Arctic. A nomadic people, whose skills had been adapted over centuries to living off the inhospitable tundra, hunting and fishing and building igloos, shedding anyone who threatened to destroy their tribal harmony as they made their way across the Arctic wastes, the Inuit were persuaded to settle into a lifestyle which has effectively left them stranded between two cultures. The suicide rates in the Northwest territories, among young men, are the highest in Canada. I have been told that of the seven Inuit hunters in Resolute, only four remain: one was murdered, one committed suicide and the other is in prison.

Everywhere you look you can see the shifting alliances between the old ways and the new. Inside a classroom in the little school, there are papier-mâché bears and posters in Inuktitoot (the Inuit language), flanked by banks of computers and a fax machine. Every house has a satellite dish for its television. A shed has a spiky roof of tusks and musk-ox ribs. On the snow below, the ivory hide of a polar bear is staked out with sharpened bones to dry in the sun. Attached to the back of a skidoo – a motorbike on skis which has become the favoured mode of transport – is a hand-chiselled harpoon.

In 1999, the land of the High Arctic will be handed back to the Inuit and the Canadian government will begin to withdraw its financial support. The community here will have no economic reason to exist and, with no abundance of wildlife, no reason to stay on at all. How long, I wonder, before this collection of houses – this Portakabin encampment – will be swept away by the high winds, and scattered as so much debris over the white desert, until – like my childish fears for Ahmadi – Resolute might never have existed?

Unless, of course, tourism takes off. The locals are amused by what they call the 'Arctic crazies' who flood in during 'the silly season'. I ask one of the Inuit hunters if he finds it funny that these people who are wealthy enough to get here need the hardship of exploration to make themselves feel alive. The question, at least, makes him smile. The Inuit have never travelled anywhere, he says, simply for the sake of travelling: 'It seems like a kind of waste of time – y'know, "I made it there, all by myself and with no resupply!"'

For the time being, the two Resolutes are curiously interdependent. The Inuits' future may depend on their ability to preserve their past for the tourists, their traditional skills kept alive because of consumer demand – and there are a fair number of these consumers back at my hotel.

Everyone in Resolute is waiting for something. Except me. The old fellow with the trilby is here waiting for some fellow passengers to fill the flight for the Pole, and the man from Minnesota, who spends his days watching crappy game shows on the snowy TV screen, is waiting for his tourists to arrive. Pilots from the different air bases drop in, big men with booming voices, waiting for their planes to refuel. And a couple of millionaire trophy hunters, one dressed in head-to-toe caribou, are waiting for an Inuit guide to show them some wildlife to kill. I must be the only person whose idea of an adventure is the place itself.

Pictures and words have led me here, but it is not often in life that reality exceeds your fantasies. Even now as I write, if I close my eyes and let that great white wash surge over me, my head feels cleansed, my worries purged. The purity of the Arctic landscape is partly to do with the way you look at it. In the late twentieth century, it is difficult to behold anything with fresh eyes. So often when I go to a new place, I feel that I've already been there, which leaves me with a faintly lowering sense of having been cheated. I find myself comparing what I see in front of me to some other person's vision, unable to see it for itself.

But you can't do that in the Arctic, because hardly anyone has been there and it looks like nothing else. There are no signposts, cultural or otherwise. It just is – and even in its essential nothingness, there are shifts and changes and surprises. At first, all your eye can see is a white blanket. But the longer you are out on the ice, the more you take in. And you begin to realize that the camera does lie, because there isn't any white at all, but a shimmering range of pastels and creams which alter according to the time of day and what you guess is the night because of the cold kicking in and the subtle infusion of a different light.

At midnight, the outsize blood-orange sun sits briefly on the horizon and drips its rosy residue over the ice, or heats it from below so that it glows in fairy-tale colours – baby blue or candyfloss pink. A sight so radiant that you feel like a child again.

Still, you seek to get your bearings by comparing it to something that you think you know. It looks like the moon, you say. It looks like the Sahara – because it doesn't, in the end, remind me of the Kuwaiti desert, which is already mapped out in my own memories. And when you hear absolute silence it does not deafen, but seems to contain sounds which do not exist. Is that the shriek of ice splintering? Can you hear that far-off rumble?

It is not the wind or the cold which flays away a layer of your skin, but the terrible feeling of being alone in such a boundless expanse with no human markings. It is overwhelming to step on land which no one else – before or since – has ever seen. This knowledge, far from creating a sense of omnipotence, makes you confront your own profound irrelevance. Out here, where there is nowhere to hide – career, family, friends, all my buffers removed – it hits you hard. Part of the feeling is a naked physicality, somewhere between terror and a sexual swoon. In a cathedral-like ravine, where I am left by myself for what seems to be for ever but also no time at all, my whole life shrinks to this one point and one place, and I find myself weeping – the tears freezing on my cheeks – with a strange kind of joy. It is the closest I have come to a spiritual experience.

When I speak to the polar women, on my last day, one or two of them confess to having had similar experiences. We have hired a plane to fly to Beechey Island, a couple of hours east of Resolute, which has a talismanic significance for all explorers who come to this region. Paddy the pilot – a wild, preposterously whiskered character, who uses his majestic belly to jam the controls – invites me to join him in the cockpit. We search in vain for our polar bear, but the closest we get is a crimson stain, which Paddy claims is the legacy of a seal feast.

We land, after several attempts, in a place which chills the body, without and within. It is a vast flat expanse, hemmed in on three sides by great cliffs, their black pleated ridges emerging from the white. Far in the distance are four tiny bleached-wood crosses bearing the names of the young men who died searching for Sir John Franklin, who disappeared on an expedition to Cornwallis Island in 1845. His body was never found. But he and the British men who came to look for him, and met their own deaths in this lonely desolation, opened up the North-West Passage for the next generation of explorers.

Back in London, everyone was wearing shorts and T-shirts and great, cheesy grins. Labour had got in after eighteen years of Conservative rule and the whole country was abuzz with the idea of a new future. My family wanted to hear about my polar trip, but not quite as much as they wanted to tell me about election night.

Team Echo made it to the North Pole, but were stranded for several days when conditions were too dangerous for the plane to land and airlift them off the ice to safety. It was enough of a delay for the newspapers to lose interest. What coverage they had differed wildly in tone – they were either heralded as Arctic heroines or pilloried as frauds. Women's achievements are invariably viewed as a special category, and if you do not follow the rules which have been laid down by men you run the risk of being accused of cheating.

I wait for the images of my time at Resolute to fade, but my polar infatuation merely deepens. The trip itself seems to have left me satiated, my craving for adventure is abated, so that I no longer continually hanker for something more. My going there, even for such a short time, has released something in me. I have done it once, and not only is it alive in my imagination but I know that I could do it again; mid-life does not have to be a trap. Quite often, in London, sitting in front of my computer, I feel as though I am all head attached to a useless collection of limbs. At Resolute, my body came to life again. As someone who has never learned to drive a car and is frightened by speed, it is hard to convey the adrenalin rush of graduating from my first fearful manoeuvres on a skidoo to riding with confidence and finally accelerating to the point where the landscape flew past me. I crashed twice, injuring my leg in the process, but nothing would have stopped me getting back on. This experience alone taught me something new about myself.

The ice is still very much part of my life. At every turn, portents and signals seem to beckon me. Lost in west London, my taxi driver stops to check his map in North Pole Road. Stuck in a traffic jam off the King's Road, I gaze at the blue plaque on the house next to me and it reads: 'Captain Robert F. Scott lived here'. I spend my spare time looking at maps, plotting to go back – this time to the South Pole. The journey does not end here.

Hard Currency

GHANA

'Hey, everyone, this is ma woman! Meet ma woman!'

It was that lethargic moment when daytime turns to evening. On the terrace of Kin's Hotel on the edge of Accra, a group of men sat arguing and laughing over beers. The light had faded but the heat was still intense, heavy with the smells and sounds of the tropics. Vines swarmed across the trellises; leaves and blossoms made a ceiling. In a corner a light bulb flickered. Mosquitoes circled, while ants scurried across the table. Hi-life – the feverish, rhythmic, body-swaying music of Ghana – pounded from a ghetto blaster. On a dusty patch of ground opposite, some lads were kicking a football around, yelling exuberantly.

I knew two of the men already – Charles, bearded and mellow, and the irrepressible George, crackling with ideas and wit. The others turned expectantly to greet us.

The newcomer grabbed a chair and pushed me forward. 'Meet ma woman!' he cried, his smile huge in the darkness. I was glad to be his 'woman', not his 'wife' or his 'girlfriend'. Calvin Klein T-shirt notwithstanding, he was no soft city dude but a brother, a homeboy, back among his people, rough, tough and manly – or so the word seemed to imply.

I shall call him K, because most men's names in Ghana begin with K: Kofi, which in the Twi language means 'a male born on a Friday';

Kwesi, 'born on a Sunday'; Kwame, 'born on a Saturday'; and Kojo, 'born on a Monday'. Not that the story I have to tell is in Western terms especially shocking. But Ghana is a claustrophobic society and, like the inhabitants of many small countries, Ghanaians are extremely sensitive, particularly when it comes to their country's image. I would not like to endanger his position there in any way.

Fresh off the plane, K was still spangled with the allure of London, where he had lived for a decade and a half. Now he was home and Ghana was soon going to know all about it; he had every intention of making his presence felt. Charming and charismatic, he was bubbling over with plans, ideas and idealism. The others might have had their dreams battered out of them by years of poverty and hardship, but his were still intact. He ordered me a Coke, then threw himself into the discussion.

It was February 1992 and there was plenty to argue about. The country was still dominated by the military. Police and soldiers armed with ancient rifles were highly visible. We had already had a run-in with the police and had been in the country barely twenty-four hours. After twenty years of military rule, Ghana was to go to the polls at the end of the year. Its masters had decided it was time for at least the appearance of democracy.

We had arrived at night, the plane sweeping low across the swaying silhouettes of palm trees. As I stepped out, the sweet febrile air of Ghana, as fierce as a sauna, swept me up in its embrace. It was my first moment in Africa. I felt its intoxication – the passion, the pulse, the red earth beneath my feet. Hoisting his bag on to his shoulder, K walked into the airport. Already soaked with sweat, I followed behind him. Customs officials swarmed around us, 'porters' hustled to carry our bags and arms grabbed at us. K brushed them all off like insects and strode out to where Charles and George, his half-brothers, were waiting.

By the time we had loaded Charles's ancient green Peugeot, it was sinking on its axles. The boot was flapping open with suitcases piled high. K had spent his last weeks in London shopping with the desperation of a man who might never have the chance to cross the portals of Paul Smith or Harvey Nichols again. As for me, I had kept my baggage to a minimum in order to carry his, plus his new state-of-the-art ghetto blaster, which I took as hand luggage.

We had not gone far when a leathery-faced policeman flagged us down. Charles, the quiet, reasonable one, got out to see what the problem was. The excitable George was next. The voices grew louder and louder. 'Stay here!' barked K, flinging open his door. I sat, hardly daring to breathe, while he joined in what was by now an enormous row. Then a younger policeman strutted up, making much play of his rifle. Fresh from the placid streets of London, I was petrified.

Finally, the voices lowered. The three men got back into the car and we drove off, arguing vociferously. What had been the problem? I ventured. The policeman, apparently, had accused Charles of running a taxi service, for which he had, of course, no licence. He was therefore committing an offence. Some 'dash' – a monetary gift to the policeman – would have ensured that it was overlooked, but K, fresh from England and full of Western notions, refused to countenance such shameful Third World practices. Hence the row and the rifles. I never discovered how the argument had been settled.

Down a dark bumpy road lined with tiny stalls, we stopped to buy food. On each stall an oil-soaked wick flickered with a yellow flame. A roly-poly woman wearing a bandanna sold us kenkei, fermented cornmeal wrapped in banana leaves, with a chilli-hot sauce to dip it in and some grilled herrings. The whole lot was rolled up in newspaper, a hot greasy bundle which I held well away from my lap as we headed for Charles's, where we were to spend the night.

I had never planned to come to Africa. It was the last place I had ever expected to find myself. My roots were in Asia, my work in Asia. I had spent a large part of my life between two complex, complicated, rather cold and passionless small islands – Britain and Japan. My father, a China specialist, had always said there was one country in the world which one fell in love with. In his case it was China; in mine, Japan.

But then I met K at a party. At the time, he was going out with an acquaintance of mine. Years later, when they separated, he called me. On our first date he took me to the gym. On our second he showed me a photograph of a formidable African matriarch, stern and frowning, with a bouffant halo of hair. 'This is my mother,' he said. Then he opened an atlas at the map of Africa and pointed out a small oblong country on the hip of the continent, bordering the Atlantic, a little above the equator. 'This is Ghana. This is where I come from.' He always explained matters to do with Africa in simple language, as if talking to a child. It was only after we had been seeing each other for some time that he deemed I was ready to learn his surname.

I had never before met anyone who knew with such clarity what he wanted. K had a life plan: to study at the London School of Economics, get experience in local government in London, then go back to Ghana to set his country in order. Unfortunately, when we met he had already completed the first two stages. He was due to move to Ghana in less than six months, which I assumed would mean the end of our relationship. But there was another part of his plan too, and that involved me. He had decided that I was to go with him, as his woman.

My preparations for visiting Ghana were patchy. From time to time K sketched out fragments of the complicated political situation, the good guys and the bad guys. His hero, Kwame Nkrumah, had won independence for Ghana in 1957, making it the first country in Africa to free itself from colonial rule. In 1966 Nkrumah was overthrown in a military coup. Colonel Acheampong, a pudgy potato-faced character, the Mobutu of his day, salted away millions of dollars in Swiss bank accounts while the country's economy lurched into a hopeless downward spiral. I heard about the terrible hardships that followed when, even if people had money in their pockets, there was nothing in the shops to buy.

Finally, a dashing young flight-lieutenant, Jerry John Rawlings, led yet another military coup, taking a stand against corruption. Larger, fatter, less dashing but immensely popular, he was still in power thirteen years later. He had set the economy on its feet again and was now planning to legitimize his rule with elections.

K also explained that Ghana was a matriarchy; perhaps, I thought, that was why he had shown me the picture of his mother. I didn't know the half of it. Later, when I met her, I began to understand better. She was an extraordinarily powerful woman who, even in old age and illness, dominated the lives of her sons.

And he told me about his grandmother, who had brought him up. Following Ashanti tradition, she had carefully moulded his head, pressing it every night with her hands and giving him a rounded pillow to sleep on. You could tell Africans who had grown up in Britain, he said, because their heads were square, flattened at the back from sleeping on a flat surface. As for him, his shaven head was a smooth and aesthetically perfect egg shape.

But there were many things about Africa which he didn't or couldn't tell me, and which I could not even begin to understand until my feet had touched its red soil and I had breathed the moist scented air.

On my first morning in Ghana I was woken by children's voices. Safo and Selassie, Charles's children, unable to control their curiosity any longer, had pushed open the door a crack, anxious to see their uncle and new auntie. Outside a cock was crowing lustily. I dropped into the kitchen to greet their mother, a tiny, warm and high-cheekboned woman named Julie. Charles had introduced me to her the previous night, pronouncing her name in the African way as 'Jilly'.

While Selassie, who was two, clung to my hand, five-year-old Safo ran ahead to show me his domain. Charles was a farm manager. His house stood all alone at the top of an escarpment. Together, the children and I surveyed the grasslands which spread as far as the hills on the distant horizon. The land was not tamed like the English countryside. There were no fields, no hedgerows; there was no sign of the hand of man. It was simply bush, wild, uncultivated, undeveloped. In the distance herds of skinny cattle roamed, nuzzling under rocks and around thorn bushes for blades of grass. Behind the house was a large shed where chickens lived.

While K had had the good fortune to be out of the country during the bad times, Charles had lived through them. He spoke of hiding under the table while mortars exploded and of how, five years before, his car had been impounded by the military at gunpoint. He told the story almost as a joke. 'Things have improved since then,' he said, smiling.

K was hypercritical of his newly rediscovered country, burning to change things. But Charles was content to watch and comment and joke. He had seen enough of life and death and had an almost preternatural calmness. I thought he seemed one of the wisest people I had ever met.

The latest news was that the leader of the opposition had been imprisoned. His 'crime' was that he had not stood up quickly enough for the national anthem on some major state occasion. The brothers discussed this with a combination of outrage and incredulous humour. I listened in silence, trying to get to grips with what kind of country this was.

Charles turned to me. 'Do you know what the national anthem sounds like?' he asked, teasing me.

'No,' I confessed.

'You'd better find out,' he said with mock sternness. 'And make sure you stand up quick when you hear it.'

Driving into town there were plenty of reminders that this was a country under military control. From time to time we would come to a police barrier set up across the road and a soldier with a rifle (always ancient and usually rusty) would peer into the back seat and order us to open the boot to ensure that there were no hidden arms caches. My presence as a white female, however, rendered it less than likely that we were on our way to perpetrate a military coup, so quite often they would just wave us through.

Accra was the greenest, poorest, most laid-back city I had ever seen. I kept expecting to reach the bustling commercial hub of the place or at least to pass the odd skyscraper or an enticing shop or two; every city I had ever been to, even ones as poor as Manila or Canton, had enticing shops. But there were none. With Charles's ancient car sputtering along, spewing out smoke, we drove through street after dusty street of low flat-roofed houses with mud walls painted pink and blue, surrounded by palms and banana, plantain and papaya trees. It was like a city sprouting in a jungle which threatened to swallow it up at any minute. The only shops we saw were strictly functional, selling fabric, watches or electric fans, or cavernous buildings like warehouses with fridges and cookers piled outside.

We passed the military camp and the firing range where the potato-faced Acheampong and two of his predecessors had stood a few years back, lonely and blindfolded, to face their nemesis. Perhaps, then, they regretted the ruin they had caused. The eight numbered boards stood side by side in a row on a bleak escarpment beside the road where the Atlantic waves lashed the shore, a grim reminder to anyone passing by. I wondered what had become of the millions of dollars they had stashed away in Swiss bank accounts.

While I looked around with the magpie eye of a journalist, snatching up shiny nuggets of information, K's experience of the country was very different. For him it was a homecoming, in some ways a tortured one. But this was his country. He needed to rediscover himself there. The quirks, the inefficiencies, the ramshackle banana-republic nature of the place which I found endearing, to him were infuriating. How could his country, for which he had given up his Notting Hill flat, his VW Golf and his managerial position in the civil service, be such a mess?

For me all the allure of this seductive new country, this breathtaking new continent, focused on him. I would run my fingers across his velvety skin, admire his neat bottom, his expressive hands, his huge liquid eyes set wide apart. In the morning, if I woke up before him, I would lie in bed just looking at him, incredulous that such beauty could be mine. But already I knew that I was losing him. He was moving into a different world. I could see him changing.

A couple of weeks later we were on a bus, rattling and bumping our way upcountry along a broken red road, pitted with ruts and potholes. In Nkrumah's time, it had been a splendid highway. Then for twenty years, while the country's economy crumbled, so did the road. Under Rawlings's rule, parts of it had now been resurfaced. In others, the bus slowed to a crawl, cautiously manoeuvring around yawning furrows as deep as ditches.

We passed villages of mud houses with straw roofs, out of which the occasional TV aerial poked, and a small town of decaying plaster houses with balconies and shutters, zigzagging up a hillside. Mainly we were in rain forest, 'semi-deciduous', as K insisted. It seemed to go on for ever, mammoth trees caressed by sinewy vines, familiar plants – Swiss cheese plants, rubber plants – sprouting to monstrous proportions in the clammy greenhouse air. Little villages huddled in clearings, but there was almost no cultivation. It was pure virgin forest.

The bus driver put on a tape of gospel music. Ghana, I was discovering, was passionately Christian. Taxis and trucks were emblazoned with ornate stickers proclaiming 'Trust in God' or, rather alarmingly, 'I am covered by the blood of Christ.' It was just as well that God was their insurance; they had no other.

The tape came to an end and a voice crackled from the recorder, urging us to repent, to go to the Lord, before we suffered eternal damnation. For a while we endured it, then the passengers became restive. 'We want more songs,' bellowed a deep female voice from the back. The other passengers took up the complaint. 'More songs,' they chanted, 'more songs. Stop the preaching!' But the driver had control of the tape recorder and the preaching continued.

Our first stop was Kumasi. In the nineteenth century, before the British took over, Kumasi was a splendid city, the capital of the Ashanti people and the home of the Asantehene, the Ashanti king, who was wealthy and powerful enough to employ Europeans as military trainers and economic advisers. In the colonial wars it was razed to the ground, but it had risen from the ashes. It was a charming place, far more of a city than Accra, a jigsaw of shuttered buildings three or four storeys tall, painted in creams, pinks and beiges, which spread up the hill around the central market. It even had appealing little shops stacked with rolls of colourful fabric, clothes and shoes. There was a prosperous feel to the place. For a moment, as we pushed through the throngs of people beneath the rusty corrugated-iron roofs of the market stalls, I lost sight of K's shaven pate among the myriad black heads and wondered how I would ever find him again. In London he had been the exotic one. Here it was me who stood out from the crowd.

We climbed a hill, past a football ground, to the Asantehene's palace. It was hidden behind a high wall and we could see no more of it than a forest of coconut palms swaying behind. A peacock stalked past the gate, spreading its tail feathers. An elderly woman, very dignified, in a colourful cloth draped like a toga, was standing on the road outside, bidding farewell to some guests. She waved in our direction. 'It's the queen mother,' hissed K. 'Go and speak to her.' But I was too bashful.

Later he told me the tale of the greatest queen mother of all, Nana Yaa Asantewaa, who in 1900, at the age of sixty-one, led the Ashanti troops in their last desperate attempt to drive the invaders out. The British were holed up in Kumasi Fort, a rather ugly red-brick building which is now a military museum. The battle raged for days, but in the end the Ashanti lost and the lands which now make up Ghana became the British colony of the Gold Coast. Outside the palace some lads were kicking a football about in a swirl of red dust. Inside, I suspected, life continued with as much splendour as ever before.

On our way down the hill we visited one of K's friends, who had lived in London and played in a band. Now he was home, in a mud-walled house with a central courtyard open to the sky. While the two reminisced about clubs, concerts and friends, a woman was pounding fufu, dropping a pestle the size of a small tree trunk into a barrel of cassava dough. The rhythmic thud punctuated their words.

The next day we were up at six. At the bus station we boarded a minibus and waited for it to fill up. 'Full' meant at least four, if not five, people squeezed along a seat made for three, petrol cans hanging off the back and sacks of rice and a trussed, squawking chicken under the seats. Barefooted hawkers gathered around the bus, balancing tin basins on their heads piled with Chinese toothpaste, shoe polish, batteries, tooth-cleaning sticks and nail clippers. One skinny lad in a ragged jersey peered through the window as I sat scribbling notes. 'Your handwriting is very good,' he observed. I stopped, thinking the bus was about to move off. 'It's OK,' he said urgently, as if his life depended on watching me write. 'You can write. Write it! Write it!' He did not care what I wrote, it was the act of writing that fascinated him. Perhaps he was illiterate; yet he could speak English, even if not perfectly.

Half a day later, sweaty, sticky, dirty and battered, we straightened our cramped limbs and stepped into the stillness of the noon heat. The huge trees with their thick foliage and the hummocky red track which led away from the road were bleached of colour in the fiery sunshine like an overexposed photograph. We were in Abofo, where K had spent the first fifteen years of his life. As we picked our way along the earthen track, goats and chickens zigzagged back and forth in front of us. I had never felt the gulf between us so strongly. For all his designer T-shirts, expensive trainers and Armani body lotion, for K this village with no electricity, no running water and no sewerage system was home. As he strode purposefully in front of me, I tried to imagine the schoolboy growing up in the bush. How had it been, arriving for the first time in the crowded metropolis of Accra? Even more unimaginable, how had it felt to travel to the grey streets of London at the age of sixteen or seventeen? But K had without a doubt been at least as cocksure and confident then as he was now. He had probably just strutted into these new worlds, certain he was the coolest guy on the block and that whatever he got was the very least he deserved.

But he was also sweet. Sometimes he seemed a bit like a child. He was completely lacking in self-doubt or irony, always brimming over with joyous enthusiasm for one project or another. At that moment he was searching for his avocado tree. He had planted it almost two decades before and still remembered where it had been. But there was no trace of it.

Grateful to find some shade, we sat under the eaves of the house where he had grown up and waited for his cousin, who now lived there.

The house was two small earthen rooms with an open-air kitchen between, set on a raised terrace. Here K had lived with his grandmother and a dozen small cousins. It was a perfectly normal arrangement for

Ghana. His mother had had an important position in Nkrumah's government and later worked for the Ghanaian foreign service in London. From time to time she visited. Once she turned up after eight years' absence, stayed for half an hour and gave him some money. In his mind that was what she was: someone who came and gave him money. It was his grandmother whom he loved, and he thought of his cousins as his brothers and sisters.

Before we left London, K had tried to fill me in as much as possible on his country and his culture; it was his way of telling me about himself. Ghana, he had already explained, was a matriarchy. As far as I understood, that meant inheritance was through the mother's line. Fathers were fairly irrelevant. Your maternal uncles, not your father, took care of you and passed on their goods not to their children but to their nephews. You belonged, in other words, not to your father's family but to your mother's. The present Ashanti king was a nephew of the previous one and would be succeeded in turn by one of his nephews, not his sons.

K's mother, in fact, had had a succession of children by different fathers. Charles and George were the sons of her first husband. K also had a younger half-brother from another father. As for K's own father, K once let it be known that he might have been Nigerian. He certainly did not stay around for long. While the other sons bore their fathers' surnames, K had his mother's name.

Sadly, by the time I met her she was ill, but I was still terrified of her. She lay in bed receiving a succession of government ministers and powerbrokers. I saw photographs of her as she had been, hosting state functions, a large imposing woman in formal floor-length gowns, very upright, flashing a regal smile. There was also a picture of her as a young woman, in a white dress, looking rather lovely. She was already an official in Nkrumah's government at the time. Of all her sons, K was the closest to her. He had inherited her imperious personality, which meant that they frequently fell out.

Now he sat like the young lord returned to his domain, waiting to receive homage. First came the cousin who lived in the house, with her baby. Then came an uncle, then Joe, the next-door neighbour, a boyhood friend of K's. Little by little, more and more neighbours arrived to greet the wanderer returned. Joe turned on his radio and hi-life boomed out across the yard.

'Hey, man!' cried K with a huge smile, greeting the newcomers with the Ghanaian handshake, which ends with a snap of the fingers. 'How're you doing?'

I sat swinging my legs on the veranda, chatting to the people who could speak English, while he held court, arguing and laughing in Twi. The cousin brought out plates of sweet fried plantain and a rich green sauce swimming in palm oil. A few people started to dance.

Before we left, K wanted to visit his farm. It had belonged to his grandmother and now it was his. Led by a lad with a machete, we trekked off into the bush. The red road became a red track, then a dried-up stream, then disappeared into a cocoa plantation. We cut our way through groves of cocoa trees like small silver birches with pods which changed colour as they ripened, some green, some yellow, some brown. The cocoa fruit was white inside and rather sweet, with a large pip. Pushing through bushes and scrub and climbing across fallen branches, we shook down papayas, standing under the tree to catch them, and cut bunches of plantains, like large bananas. After an hour and a half I was wondering when we were going to arrive at the 'farm', until I realized that this was it. K was brimming over with plans. Last time he visited he had given an old man in the village 2,000 *cedis* and look, now there were groves of plantain trees. Next he would plant oranges, avocados and tangerines. He would use his grandmother's land and the area and the village would become prosperous again.

In the bus on the way back I asked him tentatively about his father.

'Africans don't talk about that kind of thing,' he snapped. 'Just listen! Don't ask questions!'

A few weeks later our car was ready. It was a Frankenstein's monster of a car, made up of bits of at least two wrecked Peugeot 106s stapled and welded together, with one normal headlight and one laboriously created with a blowtorch out of a piece of transparent plastic. I suspected that K thought he deserved better, but I was fond of it.

By now K had started work. He had a post in a government department, but was finding it more and more frustrating to be living at Charles's farm, half an hour out of town, with an unreliable vehicle to get around in. As for me, I was becoming bored hanging round the farm. Sometimes I went with K into town and sat reading in his office library; it was one of the few places in the city, it seemed, that had air-conditioning.

Every day without fail the car broke down. The exhaust blew, the lights failed, something went wrong with the engine or a piece fell off. I made sure I always carried a book. I would stay in the car to discourage scavengers, who otherwise would have stripped the car bare in no time, while K hitched off in the first transport that came along. Sometimes I had to wait for hours before he reappeared with a mechanic with a spanner. After some grappling or a few twists of wire, we would set off, only to break down again some time later.

One weekend we decided to put the car through its paces. It was May, the rainy season, and everything was sprouting and intensely green; you could almost see the plants and trees and bugs getting bigger and bigger. We headed off down the coast through coconut and palm forests, where great trees jutted into the sky. The car, of course, had no air-conditioning. The air, unbearably hot and heavy with moisture, swirled through the open windows while we rattled along sticky with sweat.

Ghana's Atlantic coast is where every European power that ever invaded this part of the world built castles to keep slaves. We stopped at Fort Amsterdam, a crumbling ruin on a headland overlooking the white breakers. On the shore fishermen sat beside their boats mending their nets, seemingly oblivious to the dark history that had been enacted on the cliffs above them. A few miles further on, Cape Coast Castle gleamed white against the blue ocean. We saw the dungeons where hundreds of slaves were left to fester in pitch darkness for months until a ship arrived from Liverpool. Those who survived were sent to the United States or Britain; slavery was not abolished here until 1833. We saw adverts in old British newspapers for 'black girl, handy with needle, speaks English' and '3 black men in fine condition'.

Heading west along the coast, the vegetation grew lusher. We started to see gigantic billboards with a picture of a great eagle with outspread wings and the apocalyptic words: 'Behold. The Eagle has landed.' We saw signs for the Eagle Club too – Eagle Club Cape Coast, Eagle Club Elmina. These turned out to be part of Rawlings's overblown election campaign. The election was coming up fast and for some people, including Rawlings, it might be a matter of life or death. If his enemies came to power, would he find himself on the same bleak hillside where the potato-faced Acheampong had met his end? There was no harm making things difficult for the opposition, which he did by putting limitations on campaign fund-raising. The only loophole was private clubs, which the opposition parties started feverishly forming. So Rawlings's supporters had formed Eagle Clubs. But from time to time we still saw tattered little posters pasted up by the Heritage Club, pitifully pleading for 'Freedom Ever!'

At Cape Coast the car had refused to start. K left me reading and went to find an electrician, who fiddled about under the bonnet to get it going again. As we spluttered along, it was obvious there was something badly wrong with the exhaust. When we got to Takoradi, where we were to stay, we drove straight to the breakers' yard. K stayed with the car and I went off by myself to look around.

In its time, Takoradi must have been beautiful. It was a port city and it still had that indefinable glamour about it. Down at the docks, ships and tankers steamed in and out, sounding their sirens. There were containers piled high and great drums filled, I assumed, with oil. I strolled past streets lined with shuttered buildings which had been grand, now ruined and thick with dust. The pavements were crammed with stalls selling food, tea, biscuits, matches, cigarettes. People squatted in the crumbling doorways of once splendid mansions or dozed beside the stone lions which still brooded outside. The open drains were strewn with rubbish.

The main street was a kind of decaying Champs-Elysées, a wide boulevard of stone buildings with balconies and parapets, charmingly painted in pinks, blues and yellows. Walking towards me, keeping to the shade, were three women in identical pink frocks with red cummerbunds and red scarves knotted into turbans round their heads. It was the perfect picture. I walked a little closer, focused my camera and took a couple of shots. I was angling up another shot when a man appeared out of nowhere and blocked my way.

Perhaps he was wearing a black T-shirt or a jacket with the letters CDR, which I knew stood for Committee for the Defence of the Revolution. At the time I didn't notice, but I remembered later.

'Your permit! Where is your permit?' he barked. 'Show me your permit!'

'What permit?' I asked nervously. 'I didn't know . . .'

'Your tourist permit. You have no tourist permit?'

'I have a tourist visa. I wasn't told . . .'

'You're a tourist and you have no tourist permit?'

'No,' I stuttered, horrified. Had I unknowingly broken some law? 'I . . . I'm terribly sorry. I didn't realize . . .'

'It's all right,' he said less sternly. 'You can get one at the police station. They will issue one.' He grabbed my arm. 'Come along with me.'

It was only as he shepherded me off down an alley that my brain began working again. Who was this man anyway? He had no uniform. What right had he to make me go anywhere? And how could I be sure we were going to the police station? Perhaps he was a robber or a kidnapper or a serial killer. I had only been off the leash for a couple of minutes and already I was in trouble. K, I thought gloomily, would be cross.

We skirted a rubbish-filled ditch in a forest of palm trees and walked across a building site strewn with rubble. I was getting more and more nervous when, to my huge relief, we arrived at a police station. Two young uniformed officers were standing behind a wooden counter in the dingy room with a pile of rifles stacked beside them. There was a brief exchange in Fanti, the language of the area. The policemen looked at me gravely. It was time to take control.

'I've come to get a tourist permit,' I said. 'Can you give me the forms, please?'

They looked at each other and laughed scornfully.

'You can't get a permit here,' they jeered. 'You have to get it when you enter the country. You've been taking photographs without a permit! You're under arrest!'

The man in the CDR shirt was grinning triumphantly.

The first thing they did was take my camera. 'We have been trained in the English system,' they said proudly. 'Your system. We have to uphold the law. This man says you've been photographing our streets. Why were you photographing our streets?'

K and I had had long arguments about how to comport oneself in Ghana. My theory was that the best way was to be nice to people in any situation. This infuriated K. In this obdurate country, he said, the only way to get anything done was to throw your weight around.

'I'm a tourist,' I said, trying to mollify them. 'I love this city, it's beautiful. I was photographing your streets because they're beautiful.'

This only enraged them further.

'You are adding insult to injury,' shouted the policeman. 'Our streets? Beautiful? Look out there!' He pointed through the door to the building site outside. 'You call that beautiful? Is that beautiful? Are our gutters beautiful? Our dirty gutters? This is my country. You can't go around photographing just anything you want. You can't just walk around England taking photographs, can you?'

'Yes,' I said defiantly. 'You can.'

'You expect me to believe that? Of course you can't!'

'I'm a journalist,' I said. 'I've applied for a permit.' I realized too late I had made a mistake.

'You were photographing our gutters! You are going to show the world that Ghana has dirty gutters! You want to shame us!'

I was getting deeper and deeper into trouble.

'Are you alone?'

'No. I'm with my husband.' We always said we were married in Ghana, to keep things simple.

'Is he English?'

'No, Ghanaian.' Saying that my husband was Ghanaian always gave me honorary Ghanaian status. Perhaps that would do the trick.

'Bring him here! Go and fetch your husband!'

This was disastrous. I knew they couldn't shoot me because I was white and British, which gave me a degree of immunity, but K had none. They could do anything they liked to their own people.

Scared and depressed, I left my camera as security and went off to find the hotel where I had arranged to meet K, desperately hoping that the car was fixed by now and he was back from the breakers' yard.

As I had expected, he was outraged by my tale. It was supreme evidence that I had no idea how to behave in Ghana. Why had I allowed this man to hustle me off to the police station? What right had he to push me around? Why didn't I just tell him he was talking nonsense? There was no such thing as a tourist permit! It was perfectly obvious that what they were all after was dash. They had seen a white face and thought I would be an easy touch.

Back at the station the policemen made me sit on a bench behind the counter, next to the cells. K was shouting and thumping the counter with his fist, while the policemen and the CDR man yelled back. I hadn't noticed the prisoners before. They appeared from the depths of the cells, crowding behind the iron bars of the door, cheering K on as he grabbed a policeman by the collar and offering advice to both sides. It was the best entertainment they had had for months. The policemen appealed to me. 'Tell him to calm down,' they begged. One picked up his rifle and started loading it. I watched with horror.

In a back room I was shown the CDR man's statement. I had been taking pictures of gutters, he wrote. I was a spy. A spy! An image of the eight numbered boards on the bleak hillside, lashed by Atlantic waves, swam in front of my face.

While K was preoccupied arguing with the police, I dealt with things in my own way. I wrote a grovelling statement. I had not realized, I wrote, that I needed a tourist permit. I was very sorry if I had offended in any way. And I was certainly not a spy. My concluding sentence was 'I am very, very sorry.'

I was freed on bail. We had to leave behind my camera and 20,000 *cedis* – about thirty pounds; not a vast amount, I thought, for such a dangerous spy.

The journey back to Accra was uneventful except for a flat tyre, though we drove very slowly as both the exhaust and the radiator were on the point of giving out. K was lambasting me because once again I hadn't stood up for myself. I confessed that I had written an apology, but he brushed over that and launched into a tirade against the corrupt practices of his countrymen.

A few days later we went to police headquarters to search out Detective Inspector X of the CID Flying Squad. He was from Abofo, the same village as K. I didn't see what good this would do, but it became clear when he picked up the phone to call the far-lower-ranking staff sergeant at Takoradi.

I couldn't understand what he was saying but the purport was clear. 'How dare you offend someone from my village, you little runt? How dare you confiscate his wife's camera?' With satisfaction I imagined the policemen in Takoradi squirming in their seats.

As we left K dashed him 1,000 *cedis*. 'Buy yourself a beer,' he said. By now I was able to see the funny side of it. This struck me as the most absurd of all, that even a top-ranking detective inspector in the Flying Squad had to be dashed.

I got my camera back and my name was cleared. Shortly afterwards I left Ghana. 'You have to be in England, earning hard currency,' was K's attitude. In the elections that November, Rawlings won more than 90 per cent of the vote and became president, as he still is.

From time to time since then I have been back to Ghana, and K comes to visit me here in London, though the visits have grown less and less frequent. Every time I meet him, he is more African and the gulf between us grows deeper and deeper. But to this day, when I step out of the plane and my foot touches the red earth of Africa, I feel the old surge of exhilaration and joy. The palm trees sway and the throbbing heat, permeated with the earthy smell of the tropics, engulfs me in its clammy embrace. It's easy to imagine that one could fall in love in such a place.

SHENA MACKAY

Tinsel and Kalashnikovs

PAKISTAN

In the perpetual battle between dust and glitter that is Pakistan, brown mud, clouds of sand and black exhaust fumes were winnning the day. We had set out to drive to the Old City of Peshawar, but the road ahead was blocked. Men and boys throwing stones were converging on a hijacked bus, windows were smashed and a lorry had been tipped into the canal. 'It isn't really like this,' my daughter and son-in-law kept reassuring me. And it was, and it wasn't.

This was my first visit to Pakistan, and I was staying for just over two weeks with my eldest daughter, Sarah, and her husband, Bruce. They had been living in Peshawar for eighteen months, working with Afghan refugees for one of the relief agencies known as NGOs or Non-Governmental Organizations which operate there and in neighbouring Afghanistan. Although I was overjoyed to see them, and delighted to find them not wasted by dysentery, the rioting reinforced my fears for their safety in this volatile part of the world, particularly in view of their possible relocation to Kabul, over the border in Afghanistan, where General Massud's forces are still fighting a rearguard action against the fundamentalist Taliban. When Sarah and Bruce last visited Kabul, they got out just before the airport was bombed. On my arrival in Islamabad, a day or two earlier, my anxieties had not been allayed by the sight of men casually toting Kalashnikovs as they shopped or by the heart-stopping, bone-crunching drive to Peshawar on the Grand Trunk Road, which has more potholes than surface.

But it was strange: although I was scared by the riot, news bulletins from around the world had made violent demonstrations seem almost familiar, and while being caught up in one was rather different from watching it at home, the car windows had something of the distancing effect of the television screen. I shielded my face with my borrowed *chuddar*, the long silky scarf that kept slipping off my head to reveal my foreign hair. Sarah, who had an Indian grandmother, was less conspicuous, but Bruce's colouring is undeniably Scottish, and even in his *shalwar kameez*, the loose long shirt and trousers worn by Muslims, he can't pass for one of those Pakistanis who henna their hair and skin. I felt that we were vulnerable, but if we did attract some attention, the men's anger was never directed at us. The people were hungry, protesting at the continuing nationwide *atta*, or wheat, crisis, which was depriving them of naan, a staple of their diet. Corruption of various sorts had caused shortages and sent the price rocketing, and the government lorries delivering flour were guarded by tanks and armed troops.

Bruce managed to turn the car back, into the hooting, honking mêlée of lorries, rickshaws, buses, goats, sheep, buffaloes, battered Toyotas, bicycles laden with whole families, and tongas, the small carts pulled by horses, all ribs and scabs, that look too frail to stand, let alone haul a dozen or so people. The lorries are masterpieces of swirling colour, intricately decorated in an Islamic approximation to Western fairground or canal art, as are the motorized rickshaws, like three-wheeled milk floats driven by barefooted men. Passengers cling to the ladders at the backs of the painted buses and hang off the sides and roofs, with their *shalwar kameezes* billowing in the wind. Male passengers. In some of the places we visited we could have played a game called 'Spot the Woman', for you might have supposed that there was only one sex, and very monotonous it became. Black rags flapping from the backs of vehicles look as sinister as the Evil Eye which they are meant to ward off, and some lorries have circles of blades on their wheels, useful for slashing the tyres of fellow drivers on roads that are free-for-all combat zones where the rules of the Highway Code include overtaking at any cost, undertaking, and swerving into opposing traffic with your hand permanently on the horn. But at least you can assume the drivers won't be drunk, as this is a dry country even in the rainy season.

We headed for the peaceful gardens of Islamia College. Mynah birds and white-clothed students carrying books were walking beneath the flame trees, among the fallen blossoms like scarlet parrots' crests that scattered the grass, and parakeets flew, as if in a different world from the guns and politics and hunger. One of the students, egged on by his companions, sidled up to us. After the standard greeting, 'I love your country, Where are you from?', he presented us with his English homework and asked our advice on a point of grammar. Luckily we could do it, because we suspected they had known the answer all along.

Behind high walls and locked gates the gardens of the wealthy bloomed, while droves of poor relations squatted in the dust outside, waiting for alms. It was March and familiar cornflowers, roses, delphiniums, larkspur, hollyhocks and wallflowers flourished among bougainvillaea, bottlebrush trees, hibiscus and the last of the orange blossom. Armed guards called *chowkidars* sat outside the gates night and day, and I wondered if they longed for some ambush or attack to relieve the tedium. Many of the animals on the roads had but a short time to live, because with the full moon would come the religious festival Eid-ul-Azha, when they would be sacrificed. That ram caught in a thicket who saved Ishmael from death at his father's hand was bad news for succeeding generations of flocks. The fleeces of doomed sheep and goats were daubed with magenta, buffaloes wore garlands round their necks and ornaments on the tips of their horns, bicycle handlebars were similarly adorned, and the bazaars glittered with streamers of coloured foil, tinsel, lametta and excelsior. The exhortations of the mullahs crackled from loudspeakers, men unrolled their prayer mats in the streets and the concrete slopes of the canal bank were draped with carpets and rugs that were being washed, for Eid, in water the colour of milky tea.

There is a Christian church, All Saints, in Peshawar which is built like a mosque and topped with a little cross that looks as if it was sneaked on when nobody was looking. Inside are memorial tablets to soldiers and missionaries, and they died so young, from fevers or as martyrs. The names of incumbents' infant children are there too, inscribed as if they had had no mothers to mourn them. The church was beautiful, cool in its little island of wild flowers, but it was a melancholy place to me. I was glad to leave it for the stinking street outside and contemplate the heaps of second-hand plastic sandals and Birkenstocks stained by aid workers' feet that were on sale on the road outside.

Sarah and Bruce live in the part of the city called University Town. A gravel road leads to a gate set in a galvanized-tin fence which gives privacy to the tiled courtyard in front of their single-storey house. They have planted flowers and shrubs in terracotta pots and trailing climbers against the walls. By mid-morning, even in March, the tiles are too hot to walk on without shoes. Inside, the rooms open off a marble-floored hall which runs the length of the building, and shutters and grilles over the windows protect from heat and mosquitoes. Wooden fans whirl on the high ceilings, and an air-conditioner augments their breeze as the temperature climbs. From time to time, a wizened snake-charmer, playing on a swollen-bellied pipe that looks as if it has just swallowed some prey, wanders down the gravel road, carrying his partner coiled in a cloth bag.

On my first day, I noticed wisps of grass in the shower of the bathroom adjoining my bedroom. I removed them, but the next day there were more. Then one morning I looked straight into the bright eyes of a little bird and saw that she was cramming the narrow space between the window and the mosquito grid with dry foliage. By the time I left, the window was completely obscured, with seemingly no room for eggs or nestlings, but I guess she knew what she was doing. People start their day early because of the heat, and I would wake to voices and the clashing of utensils and spicy smells as the neighbours cooked breakfast in the adjoining yard. A background tapestry of sounds was woven unceasingly from the chirping of cicadas, the calls to prayer, birdsong, the barking of dogs, gunshots and the cries of the ubiquitous crows. When we had walked out of Islamabad airport, I remarked on the black birds swooping against the deep blue evening sky. They looked magical, like birds in an illustration to a fairy-tale. 'They are crows,' Sarah said. 'You'll come to hate them.'

When people I met there asked me about my impressions of Pakistan, I found it impossible to say. Image followed image in scenes and tableaux, all in a rush of colours, sounds, sensations and emotions. I had come, albeit as a recent computer illiterate myself, from the world of the Web and the Internet to a place where a large percentage of the population cannot read. I was a vegetarian, like Sarah, in a culture of slaughter, but here the eating of animals was less obscene than at home, where the newspapers are bloated with recipes for all creatures great and small, from farmed exotic species to roadkill. I had brought along memories of stories of Victorian travellers in good thick skirts beating astonished natives with their umbrellas for ill-treating donkeys, and I was relieved that I never saw anybody striking a beast. The few cats I glimpsed were skinny and feral, and dogs are generally despised except as guard dogs. They are also used in the 'sport' of bear-baiting, where they, like the bear, sustain hideous injuries. We seemed to see the same two dogs wherever we went, the yellowish skulker limping on three legs and his mate who, dragged down by successive litters, slunk about as if she knew she was doubly despised for being female.

As a woman in an Islamic society, I was regarded as a second-class person by people whose thoughts and lives I could not presume to imagine, in a country situated simultaneously at several points on the human and historical spectrum. So, overwhelmed by impressions, I could only gesture to convey the hopelessness of trying to describe them, say that Pakistan was beautiful, and fall back on the travelogue cliché 'Pakistan, land of contrasts.' One abiding memory I have is of the blind woman who was deposited every morning on a street corner, where she would stand begging in the same spot until she was taken away at night.

Before I left London, I felt some resistance to the thought of wearing the *shalwar kameez*. I had hated the limp garments that had been lent to Sarah for her own arrival in Pakistan the previous year. Seeing her in a drab mustard-coloured affair that hung off her, I had experienced in a diluted form the emotions of a mother watching a beloved daughter prepare to enter a convent. I had always known that I would support my children in any circumstances and that nothing they could do would affect my love for them, but it can be hard when a child's choice of career turns out to be something laudable that takes her far away. My resentment at society dictating what she should wear was compounded by my feelings of loss at her departure and anxiety for her happiness.

When one has been in Pakistan for a short time, Western dress starts to look odd. I had travelled out in a big shirt over baggy trousers,

nervous of attracting the disapproval of my fellow passengers, and
when I arrived we went clothes shopping in Islamabad for something
for me to wear in Peshawar. Peshawar is not like the parts of
Afghanistan under Taliban rule where a woman can be arrested or
have stones thrown at her in the street for showing an ankle. (The
disruption, distress, probable death and social and economic havoc
caused by the Taliban's barring of women from working outside the
home, particularly in hospitals and schools, are well documented;
their most recent edict orders women to walk quietly, lest their shoes
make a noise.) However, it is politic and polite to wear the *shalwar
kameez* and *chuddar* in Peshawar. You might think that all tunics over
trousers are pretty much the same, but there are styles and fashions,
and Sarah wanted to check out the new season's patterns and choose
some material to have made up. She told me that foreigners often
make the sartorial error of buying the pretty gypsy dresses hanging
in the bazaars, unaware that they can cause offence and provoke scorn
on some social occasions. Later, I bought a more formal outfit in
peacock blue with elaborate embroidery, and another with trousers
which turned out to have been made for the forelegs of a very thin
giraffe. My involuntary *chuddar* always remained a problem, and I had
to resort to a brooch to keep it on my head and shoulders. Women
are supposed to cover the upper part of their bodies with the *chuddar*,
but I did notice that even women born to centuries of this awkward
shawl were constantly hitching and twitching it. However, once I had
got over feeling slightly silly in a dress on top of trousers, I found the
shalwar kameez as easy to wear as I had been told it would be. The
men's clothes come in practical shades of sand and mud, and in the
soft spice colours, cinnamon, saffron, turmeric and sage green, of
the conical piles of granules that lie by the roadsides.

We ate dhal from metal plates at roadside stalls, and had breakfast
and coffee in bland, grand hotels of gilt and crystal and bevelled glass

which, some idiosyncrasies apart, could have been anywhere in the world. Moghul art and architecture and marble mosques testified to man's ingenuity and grace, while houses of mud huddled around open drains that bred malaria-carrying mosquitoes. I saw camel markets and the meeting of the Indus and Kabul rivers, where the green waters mingle with the brown, and advertisement hoardings for Hush Puppies and Wall's Ice Cream, the latest imports to hit town. There were girls like butterflies in orange, crimson, pink, jade, emerald and yellow silk, and women who looked out through the narrow lattices of black all-enveloping *burkas*, gliding along like shuttlecocks in this garment that falls in pleats from the crown of the head to the ground. Although most *burkas* are black, tangerine and turquoise occasionally prevail. Infants picked over the garbage in the communal rubbish bunkers, and little entrepreneurs collected cans and bottles and old newspapers, and hustled chewing gum, cigarettes, matches and polythene bags of sugar cane. Marvellous machines like hurdy-gurdies extract the juice and cut the cane into short lengths, which are splintery and take for ever to chew. We walked along a road draped with long skeins of kite strings which men were sugaring with powdered glass in preparation for a festival during which they would slash their rivals' kites out of the sky.

Boys flying orange kites on the flat roof of the building opposite waved to us as we stood on the balcony of the Garnet Room at the Khan Klub, where each room is named after a gemstone. We had gone to drink cooling tea in this glamorous refuge from the din and squalor of the Old City, where the heat was intensified by the fires of the kebab sellers and all sorts of braziers and ovens. Across the street from the Klub, ancient rickety buildings with makeshift extensions and toppling superstructures held each other up above the cavernous shops, and in front of this warren of homes and godowns soldiers were supervising the latest consignment of flour.

*

The NGO personnel come from many countries. I enjoyed meeting Sarah and Bruce's colleagues and visiting their Dutch and Afghan friends. The Afghans were refugees and the men had been professional people in their own country. The handsome grown-up son of a former headmaster had been badly beaten by the Taliban on a recent trip to Kabul. He had not yet recovered from his injuries. Although our Afghan hosts kept purdah, their wives joined us, and despite their shyness and my Pashto being limited to the greeting *salaam aleikum* and *merabani* (thank you), we made some contact through the children, and smiled a lot. Nevertheless, I felt awkward in talking to their husbands in English and having conversations from which the other women were excluded because they couldn't understand what we were saying. The children were dressed in their festive clothes and some had their heads shaved in honour of Eid. One baby was wearing the minutest *shalwar kameez* imaginable, and as the babies don't have nappies he had to change his tiny trousers during the afternoon. We were seated in the place for special guests on cushions ranged round the walls, and green tea was carried in and set on the floor, with cakes and biscuits that had been saved for Eid, which is a time of hospitality and reconciliation. We had brought flowers and sweets.

The Blind Project forms an important department of Sarah and Bruce's organization's work among the Afghan refugees. I have to admit that it was with more than a little apprehension that I embarked on a guided tour of some of their schemes. I wanted to see the practical side of the organization and learn more about it, and about Sarah and Bruce's work in particular, but I did not want to be a tourist of other people's suffering, or cherish any delusion of myself as a 'roving ambassador of hearts'. Sarah was unwell, so it was just Bruce and I who set out early, calling first at the offices, where I was shown a Braille printer and a Taylor's frame, which is a device with steel pegs for mathematical calculation, and I came to the conclusion that a sighted person would have to be a genius to operate them.

Three black-bearded men, wearing the black Afghan waistcoats and circular hats, and I, with Bruce conferring on me the respectable status of mother-in-law, drove in a jeep to meet some of the Blind Project's Afghan refugee clients. We parked and picked our way through labyrinthine alleys to the house of a man who had been blinded by a mortar shell. This gazelle-like, scholarly man now made bags and plant-pot holders to sell for a few rupees. He played us a tune on the harmonium which dominated the bare room. His delicate fingers twisted coloured plastic wires and beads into rosettes and knots and braids while his young nephew served us tea. I told him, through our guide, that his bags would be very fashionable in London. Bruce and I bought bright red and blue shopping bags; mine is very useful, but I really coveted one of the samples, the pink one with pearl beads. I couldn't say so, because I was sure he would have insisted on giving it to me.

We were received with some ceremony in the apartment of a man who had once been been an actor and musician and now dreamt of making a record in the country of his exile. His elderly father greeted us and tea was set down outside the door by an invisible woman and served by a boy. The rugs, which had been removed for cleaning, were replaced on the floor. The musician put in his teeth and we watched in silent alarm as he risked electrocution groping among loose wires to plug a keyboard into the hazardous light socket. When he had got it working, he sang in our honour. Bruce's song came with the refrain 'O Tazagul, Tazagul . . .' – the Pashto name given to him by his language teacher which means Fresh Flower. Sarah's is Gulalay, Flower Bud. My song was the English hymn 'Lead us, Heavenly Father, lead us . . .'

We drove to one of the refugee camps, a sprawling city built of mud and interspersed with slender green trees. Its inhabitants have fled successive waves of persecution and some of them have lived here since the Russian occupation sixteen years ago. These people have set up shops and enterprises, while the latest arrivals, driven out by the Taliban, are in pitched tents. The temperature was in the mid-eighties, and as we got out of the jeep we were surrounded by a crowd of men and children in gaudy, ragged clothes. Some were pale-skinned with turquoise-coloured eyes. Two young men, victims of congenital blindness (the result of incestuous marriages, we were told), demon-strated their 'cane work', tapping their way across the ruts of dried mud with long sticks. Although I felt uneasy at first, wondering what they were feeling as they performed for the visitors they could not see, the young men seemed pleased by our interest in their achievement.

I was on the verge of tears all morning, and I had to blink and look away for a moment when two blind boys were brought out of a tent and pushed through the onlookers to show us their skills in reading and counting. Each boy clutched a treasured photograph of himself which he thrust in our direction. Their movements were uncoordinated and their teacher had to guide their hesitant bodies. I asked him to thank them and tell them that they were very clever boys, and one of them, sight unseen, said that I was a beautiful flower. I had nothing left to give them, having already slipped the packets of chewing gum from my pocket into the hands of other children. When I asked if blind girls were taught to read too, I was assured that they were, and our guide offered to take me to visit a woman who was learning to do housework. While we were saying goodbye, a little girl got under my feet as the children pressed all round us. Turning, the beautiful flower concerned about women's rights saw her wince and disappear into the crowd.

Although I came away very impressed by the relief agency's efforts, if daunted by the vast scale of need, this was perhaps not the best day to go on to the American Club, where the children of foreign aid workers sported in an aquamarine pool while their mothers watched from loungers on the astroturf. It was not that these children shouldn't have had the pool, and a childhood, but that all the other children we had seen should have had them too. By the age of three, the average Western child has accumulated more pieces of primary-coloured plastic than it knows what to do with, while children in Pakistan carry younger siblings, buckets of water and bundles of firewood. I did not see a toy in any of the Afghan houses we visited.

The train trip from Peshawar to Lahore takes ten and a half hours. I was excited by the prospect of making the journey, not only because it was a chance to see more of the country but because I had read about train journeys in the subcontinent in so many novels and seen them in dozens of films. Would there be chaos and drama in the heat and dust, shouting and steam, and *chai* wallahs and food-sellers running up and down the platforms? It was difficult enough to believe that I was actually there (from time to time I had to say, 'I'm in Pakistan!'), and here we were about to travel through places imbued with the romance of history, leaving the North-West Frontier for the Punjab and stopping on the way at Rawalpindi. Sarah told me that in their early days there, she and Bruce would say to each other, 'We live in Pakistan!'

In fact, the embarkment was fairly orderly. The track runs level with the road (there are no pavements) through the Old City, the train rubbing shoulders with stalls of bananas, guavas, oranges and strawberries, silks and aluminium hardware, while flocks and herds shift nonchalantly to let it pass. We were travelling second-class and we had our brown-panelled compartment to ourselves, except when we were joined by a haughty mother and her giggling twin daughters, all with much gold jewellery. Was it my workaday *shalwar kameez* that amused them, or that we were foreigners, or was it simply that they were teenagers? Whatever, it came as a relief when they flounced out after an altercation with the ticket inspector. We passed graveyards where the mounds glitter with tinsel and the headstones point towards Mecca. I believe, although I may have got this wrong, that stones commemorating women have to face the opposite direction. People were hunkered down working in the fields or making bricks from clay and mud, white egrets rose from the reeds, colours flashed from the clothes of the women, and bulbuls watched from the telephone wires. When the train drew into Rawalpindi and we sat like fictional characters, drinking tea sweetened with coarse sugar and served in china cups and saucers, everything seemed exactly as it should be.

We were staying at a girls' college in Lahore which has a guest house supervised by a nun of a not immediately recognizable Order. Sarah could not understand our frosty reception, until Sister Violet revealed that on their previous visit 'one of your party' had tipped a 'servant', causing trouble in the ranks. Our cause was not furthered when 'one of our party' inadvertently helped herself to Sister Violet's personal apple jam at breakfast and another accidentally said grace, not noticing that Sister Violet's head was already bowed to ask, or demand, a blessing on the meal. Once we had to sneak into her private bathroom while she was out, and our regression to naughty novices was complete. The college is a large red-brick collection of buildings with stone galleries and balconies, all set in gardens where tiny striped squirrels run up and down the tree trunks and parakeets fly. It was such a joy to watch a pair of hoopoes, Liquorice-Allsort orange, black-and-white striped, flirting their crests and strutting and pecking.

Inside the guest house the unmistakably institutional air was redolent of homesick girls. Meal times brought stilted multicultural conversations punctuated by the nervous laughter of young women en route for foreign service, looking ill at ease in their new Pakistani dress, perhaps wondering why God had sent them there. Surrounded by heavy dark brown furniture and antimacassars stitched by vanished hands, I had a sad recollection of those young missionaries and teachers on the memorial tablets in All Saints Church: how had they coped with the heat in their heavy clothes, dealt with their laundry and the problems of perspiration, the miseries of upset stomachs and bad complexions? Had they suffered the torment of religious doubts and the pangs of unrequited love? They must have been so lonely at times. My thoughts went to the plight of governesses growing sallow in exile and poor relations at the mercy of demanding families, women without status who, tolerated for their usefulness and despised by the servants, must always hide their own emotions and difficulties. I had to shake off my gloom and tell myself that the person in the room next to mine who played loud tapes of sacred music through the small hours was doubtless as happy as a hoopoe in clover. There was possibly no need for me to have placed a chair against the door that separated our bedrooms, although I did worry that she might report me to Sister Violet for smoking, and I kept my ceiling fan going at a rate of knots. From my window I could see a vultures' nest in a tree and watch the parent birds feeding their chick. I was thrilled, but relieved that I was not close enough to see *what* they were feeding it. Large bats flew by day.

Strawberries were in season. One of the guests brought a votive basketful to the breakfast table, before putting in a request to Sister Violet for clean sheets. Restaurant windows in the city were plastered with signs that said 'Berry Berry Strawberry', and in the Holiday Inn where we had lunch 'Merry Strawberry' menus decorated the tables and paper strawberry garlands were hung round the ceiling. As we enjoyed our strawberry delicacies, there was a sudden fracas between the waiters and the bodyguard of one of the Mafia-like men at a neighbouring table. The heavy strode down the restaurant waving his gun. Somebody shouted in English, 'Get him out of here!' There was a furious argument and an armed policeman appeared at the front desk. The bodyguard was ejected, with no shots fired, and it was all over. People resumed eating and the mafiosi carried on their discussion over platters of crustaceans, but the incident left me with a bad taste. There had been a split second in which I had almost pushed Sarah under the table, but I didn't. What if my daughter and son-in-law had been killed because I was too slow or embarrassed to react in time? But they were alive. None of us had moved, and there had been no need for heroics. Thus hindsight eases the conscience and allows one to continue eating strawberries.

Lahore, in the Punjab, is the second-largest city in Pakistan and its historical, cultural and artistic centre. It is the site of the triple-terraced Persian-style Shalimar Gardens, with their marble pavilions, ornamental pools, waterfalls and fountains. 'Shalimar' means 'a place of love and happiness'. I got that information from the leaflet we were given by our excellent Tourism Development Corporation of Punjab guide, because we took the morning excursion, just the four of us in a minibus, which did not visit the Gardens. On their previous visit Sarah and Bruce had found them rather run-down and they did not want me to be disappointed. We did go to Badshahi Mosque, which was built in 1674 and is said to be the world's largest living historical mosque. The poet and philosopher Iqbal is buried there. The red sandstone of the vast courtyard was hot under our bare feet as we squinted up at the white marble edifice. There was nothing to say; one could only gaze, feeling as insignificant as an ant, with less right to be there than one of the parrots flying in and out of the arches.

Lahore Fort is a Moghul architectural masterpiece which was constructed between 1566 and 1673. There Pakistan's only surviving elephant steps, with wide shallow treads to accommodate their great feet, curve up to the elephants' inner courtyard. It was curiously moving to imagine those long-dead elephants trundling upstairs to bed after a long day's battle or ceremony. The Moti Masjid or Pearl Mosque glimmers nacreously and in the Hall of Mirrors, the Shish Mahal, one of the guards lit a flare to show how the firelight once sparkled and reflected off the million facets of the ceiling and transformed the chamber into a glittering mosaic. The Fort was a palace designed for intrigue, with hollow niches where spies could hide, secret passages and circular rooms cooled by fretted stonework and the fountains where assassins could whisper without fear of being overheard. A lurker made a grab for Sarah and melted into the shadows when she hit out at him.

I felt a bathetic happiness under the palm trees in the gardens of Nur Jehan's tomb, because I had often eaten at the Nur Jehan restaurant in London without understanding its name. Nur Jehan, whose name means the Light of the World, had this mausoleum built during her lifetime and was buried there in 1645. She was the beloved wife of Jehangir, the fourth Mogul emperor, whose own tomb, when it was erected in 1637, had a wonderful display of mosaics inlaid with precious and semiprecious stones. Now it is pocked with holes where stones have been gouged out, looted by the Sikhs, we were told, for their Golden Temple in Amritsar. As our guide escorted us through that morning of splendour, he conjured up the ghosts of the dancing girls who had once undulated in the perfumed night air for the emperor's entertainment, on a moonlit stage set among the fountains of a lake. If imagining those dancing girls long since crumbled to dust gave the sunshine a wistful edge, it was not as eerie as looking into the deserted harem. An almost tangible silence rose with the heat from the paving stones of the courtyard and yet the voices of the favoured wives, odalisques, slaves and eunuchs who once inhabited it seemed trapped for ever in that walled hierarchy of love, rivalries and injustices.

It was on the drive to the museum that we saw the hanged horse. It looked like a public execution, the animal dangling from a harness in the air as if on a gibbet, belly exposed, hoofs flopping. Then we realized that the weight of his cart of leafy fodder had tipped it backwards, suspending him. The horse was alive, bewilderedly chewing a green stalk while men gathered round to lessen the load and see-saw him back to the ground.

The most popular exhibit in the Lahore museum is the statue of the Fasting Buddha. Our time was very limited and we joined the other tourists who bypassed the art and antiquities to cluster in front of him. As an inveterate buyer of postcards, I had already purchased a lurid green reproduction of the saint in the throes of ascetic anorexia and I wanted to see the original. In the flesh, as it were, the Buddha is all bronze ribs and bones. A blasphemous voice in the crowd remarked that he could do with a McDonald's.

This was our last day in Lahore and we all felt the need of a quiet interlude away from the traffic. The racecourse was turned into a park a few years ago, when betting was declared un-Islamic, and the track is now a path paved with a design of rabbits where people promenade in the cool of the evening. As we strolled along we saw a family who had brought their parrot for a walk, swinging his cage from hand to hand through the air above the grass. Two black-robed, black-bearded men stood by the side of the path watching through black glasses. 'Taliban,' Sarah whispered. They seemed surrounded by dark shadow and even at a distance I felt a jolt of fear.

We flew back to Peshawar. The airport at Lahore was snowed under by crowds of people dressed all in white. They were pilgrims, making the Hadj to Mecca. Special flights had been laid on to get them there because it was essential that they should arrive by a certain date and time was running out. A day or so after we got back to Peshawar the tragic news began to break. A terrible fire had swept through an encampment in Mecca and many of the pilgrims would never return home.

*

The drive to Swat reminded me forcibly of those tiny news items in the papers at home reporting huge wedding parties killed when their buses plunge into ravines. As the road climbed through rocks striated with waterfalls and glaciers, our car was full of the sweet decaying scent of the garland of white flowers we had bought from children along the way. However high in the mountains you are, however hazardous the way, you always see somebody. In the most desolate landscape and torrential rain there will be a man walking with a sodden blanket over his head and shoulders. Orange-sellers huddling under umbrellas on the hairpin bends are sprayed with gravel by passing lorries.

A sign directs the eye up to the relic of the Raj known as Churchill's Piquet, the outpost on a jutting escarpment where he served as a young soldier. We had a cup of tea at the top of the Malakand Pass and later stopped to eat at a café, a cooking stall and benches in the grass, on the bank of the Swat River. The plates were slapped down by a snarling man who made it clear that he was profoundly insulted by being asked to serve women, and foreigners to boot, but the food was good. I just hope he didn't spit in it. We drove on, up through Miandam, to the Pakistan Tourism Development Corporation hotel.

Steps cut in the grass led from the road to the hotel that stands in a circular garden, as if in a high green oasis. The surrounding mountains, now clear, now hazy, still had wreaths of snow and far below us an apple tree in blossom clung to a ridge. A mullah's badly amplified voice ricocheted off the hillsides. There were commemorative plaques on many of the trees in the hotel garden. One of them read: 'This Tree was Planted by the Senior Staff of the Domestic Energy Saving Proj. and PakGerman Fuel Efficient Cooking Technology Project on the Occasion of Their Teamwork Seminar 20 the Sep. 1990.' While we sat outside on the terrace choosing from the dinner menu, silent bearded men built fires in our rooms from pyramids of resinous sticks that burned fragrantly and spat showers of sparks when we opened the doors of the grates.

Why are the British dismayed to encounter their compatriots abroad? (Perhaps other nationalities feel the same way; after all, they have as much to be ashamed of as we do.) Does our fear stem from the danger of hearing about somebody's diarrhoea or their child's gap year? Do we avoid our fellow countrymen because they break our spell and recognize *us* for who we are and appropriate *our* experience, or is it that travel narrows the mind, making voices which would be unremarkable at home an embarrassment? Anyway, among the guests in the dining room for the evening meal were two elderly men from Woking who wore matching shorts and had upset stomachs. There was also a French family and a group of four French women. They would have been absolutely OK in France, but in Pakistan they brought Europe a bit too close. We were united during dinner as we got involved in the melodrama of the all-singing, all-dancing Indian soap that was playing on the television. A spontaneous groan went up when a power cut plunged us into darkness and there was applause when somebody got the generator going. The staff were obviously hooked, and I couldn't help wondering what these austere mountain-dwelling Muslims were thinking as they watched the Bollywood scandals interspersed with advertisements for consumer goods they would probably never see, let alone possess. Pudding came. It was a large bowl of custard, and it was the same every night. On each table was the cutest little chalet with a roof that lifted off to reveal a bunch of toothpicks. Who had designed it and where had the idea come from? Did the chalets' patina indicate that they were treasured heirlooms, or was there even now a factory where people were expending their lives on a production line of miniature plastic chalets?

*

The following morning the three of us went for a walk. Rounding a steep slope, we would suddenly almost bump into somebody carrying a huge pile of wood, or find ourselves in someone's backyard among their children and chickens, outside a house with smoke gusting through a hole in the roof. The mountainsides are farmed in terraces of wheat, vegetables and fruit trees, and sheep and goats graze vertiginously. Women filled metal pots from the river. We met a goat with its black kid and Bruce picked up the kid and gave it to me. It lay in my arms calmly, with its forelegs folded at the knees and muddy little hoofs, looking up at me through rectangular pupils and breathing its kid breath on my face, a soft baby creature that I could hardly bear to put down because I was so touched by its trust and generosity.

Arriving at a roaring torrent, Sarah and I said we would turn back. Bruce was braver, unlacing his boots in macho style while we dithered feebly. From nowhere, slithering down the rocks, three small girls in bright bedraggled dresses appeared and offered to take us across. For a fee. We were shamed into taking off our boots and wading into water that was so cold it felt as if it were cutting off our feet. The girls skipped nimbly from sharp rock to rock in their jelly shoes, pulling Sarah and me along with their tiny hands, while we squealed like cowardly elephants, and they laughed. I have never felt so big and stupid. On dry land, they raised their price. Then they tried to take our earrings, bracelets and rings. The two older girls had gold nose jewellery and the youngest, a frail child in an orange *shalwar kameez*, had a thread through her nose, a kind of sleeper, in preparation for an ornament. I wanted to photograph them, and they insisted on rearranging the combs in their long hair before posing like little Loreleis on a rock. Suddenly they spotted their father and some other men approaching and tore off to meet them, waving their handfuls of rupees as they crossed the river. The youngest slipped midstream and fell in. Her orange dress clung to her thin body as she ran, howling, her threaded nose streaming, to her father, who, laughing, picked her up tenderly and carried her home like a shepherd with a kid.

Later that afternoon we drove through nearby Bahrain, which we had heard was known for its bad vibes, sullen air, hostility to visitors and misogyny. It looked like any other town, with a main muddy thoroughfare bisecting the jumbled stalls and buildings, but the atmosphere was certainly oppressive and there was not one woman in the street or the bazaar. Then we spotted with alarm the French women from our hotel. In shorts. Snapping away with their cameras. We did not see them again.

Although the mullah's voice crackled regularly around the sky like forked lightning, that night it was outdone by a natural pyrotechnical display with explosive thunder and rain so torrential that it seemed the mountains, let alone the mud houses on their slopes, would be washed away. I lay awake by candlelight when the generator gave up, worrying about the people and animals we had seen and imagining the road turned to a river and the car floating away. The rain slackened somewhat by morning and the road, although eroded, was still there. The Toyota's engine was flooded but the car started after the hotel manager helped to push it downhill. Very wet people were trudging along with and without umbrellas. Shale flew from the tyres of buses and lorries screeching past with black rags flying. It was business as usual at the orange stalls.

'Bruce! Bruce!' We all thought we heard it, but as it was impossible that anybody in this waterlogged town where we had stopped could be calling Bruce through the pouring rain, none of us said anything. 'Bruce!' came the voice again, and we saw a man behind the counter of a tea place. It transpired that he had been the cook in a hotel where Bruce had stayed the previous year. Of all the *chai* joints in all the world . . . We sat at a table under the leaking roof, but the men who had been sitting in a dry room at the side of the yard insisted on moving out for us, and we were brought tea and a packet of savoury biscuits several years past their sell-by date which had been preserved for just such an occasion. Almost everything in Pakistan goes through several reincarnations and the tablecloth had been wrapping paper in a previous existence. Magazine pictures were glued to the walls and plastic flowers bloomed in wicker-covered salt and pepper shakers. These decorative touches and the assorted patterns of paper and fabric had turned a damp lean-to into a bright and pretty room. The reunion made our host's day and ours.

'Next left for China,' Bruce said as we approached a crossroads. I don't know why we should be affected by a glimpse of a place we have read about, but I felt awe, even at this distance from the old Silk Road, and moved by the blurred colours of half-remembered history and the glamour of the ancient name. Hoardings along the way advertise hotels so many miles before you actually reach them that anticipation mounts and you would be hard put to decide on the Heaven Rose or the Nice, and the Bobby Soxer Hotel sounds irresistible. When we reached the town of Kalam, it proved to consist entirely of hotels in various stages of development and abandonment, all girded with bamboo scaffolding. Kalam is a popular resort for rich Pakistanis, and a few foreign tourists, but apparently some failed scam has delayed the provision of running water. The hippies who used to swarm over Swat when the fields were heavy with opium poppies are long gone. I've fancied trying opium just once myself, ever since I first read about Sherlock Holmes puffing away, but my fantasy remained a pipe dream in Swat.

Back home in Peshawar we found the amaryllis in flower on the terrace. We could lounge in seclusion here without worrying about exposing our arms and legs, or lie reading on the *charpoy*, which is a rattan base stretched over a wooden frame on legs. In the indigo evenings yellow geckos run around the walls and lie in wait for insects attracted by the lights. From time to time one of them drops with a sickening splat to the ground, lies stunned for a moment, then picks himself up to start all over again.

Zora, whose husband abandoned her with three children, came in to clean and do the ironing. She did not use the ironing board, preferring to crouch down on the floor. (Everywhere you go in Pakistan, men are squatting on their haunches sweeping the dust from one place to another with little whisk brooms.) Sarah can practise her Pashto with Zora and they get on well. Rather different is the story told by some of Sarah and Bruce's friends, a married couple, about the woman they employ. She approached the husband one day and asked him to drive her and her delinquent son to the middle of a bridge, so that she could push the boy into the river. He had to turn her down.

Men in Peshawar can have their hair cut by roadside barbers; we visited the Blue Heaven Chinese Beauty Parlour when Sarah wanted hers done. A wealthy-looking woman, having had her hair baked into a sort of piecrust while her two bored children watched her in the mirror, decided to have her eyebrows plucked. I think she did it out of ennui, because it looked like a form of torture. The stylist, holding the end of a double thread in her teeth, wrapped it round each unwanted hair and wrenched it out. These Chinese beauticians were sadly deficient in salon protocol, obviously ignorant of either the Pashto or the English for 'Booked your holiday yet? Going anywhere nice this year?' or even, 'Where did you have your hair cut last time?' They talked among themselves over their clients' heads, snipping and tweaking with sublime scorn.

When we went on to the women's sewing cooperative, where Sarah has made some Afghan and Pakistani friends, I enjoyed hearing her speaking Pashto with them while I drank tea and chose souvenirs. Sarah, being a woman, has fewer opportunities to practise the language than Bruce has. Pashto is rich in proverbs ('a woman in the kitchen or in the grave' is perhaps the most memorable) and Bruce can supply one for almost any contingency. It is a guttural language, so being Scottish is a help with the pronunciation. If ye can say it's a braw bricht moonlicht nicht, ye're all richt, ye ken. One of the ladies at the cooperative (women are always referred to as ladies by the foreign community) presented me with a beautifully embroidered bag. Her gesture was characteristic of the generosity I met with on so many occasions. I riffled through the racks of handmade dresses, shirts and waistcoats, noting that they would cost a small fortune in some chic ethnic shop at home.

In the relaxed, friendly cooperative there was none of the angst or aggression of the bazaar, where I had been happy to let Bruce negotiate for me. I have always loathed haggling and hate tourists who boast of getting the better of, so they think, shopkeepers in poor countries. One of my groundless worries before I went to Pakistan was that by a process of osmosis Sarah and Bruce might come to suspect that women *should* be subservient. No chance, either at home or at work, but Sarah did tell me that she felt guilty sometimes because it was so much easier to do the acceptable thing and just let Bruce take charge when they were out. She added that if a woman were to brave, for example, the tourist office for airline tickets, she would automatically be allowed to go to the head of the queue, but as the counters there are surrounded by shouting, gesticulating men, and there is no queue, I was glad I did not have to put this information to the test.

I had been dreading the drive back to Islamabad, not only because it meant parting but also because now I would be able to imagine my loved ones driving back on the Grand Trunk Road. Perhaps I had become acclimatized, for although our heads did hit the car roof regularly, it didn't seem quite so bad as I remembered. The same old donkeys, turned loose when their working life was over, stood and stared vacantly from the verges as if turned to stone or wandered, dazed and confused, into the traffic. We checked in at the Sun Guest House, where Sarah and Bruce had stayed the night before they met me at the airport. Then, they had kept the room on so that I could have a shower and some coffee before we had breakfast at the Marriott Hotel. I had made the mistake of touching the shower curtain and the whole aluminium superstructure came crashing down. Now, after just over a fortnight, my perceptions had changed and I could appreciate the comparative luxury of the Sun Guest House, with its courteous, efficient reception, clean sheets and running water. Usually it is better not to go to the loo unless you are really determined. We turned on the television in my room and lay back to enjoy an ancient episode of *Are You Being Served?*.

People say that Islamabad is 'fifteen minutes from Pakistan' and not representative of the country and that it is a city without a centre. We planned to visit its most famous building in the evening, the Faisal Mosque, which was a gift from King Faisal of Iraq. The afternoon was for shopping. Sunshine streaming through a display of Herat glass lit up all the deep and delicate blues and greens of goblets, candlesticks and vases in the shop that was our first stop before going on to Threadlines in search of wedding and birthday presents. Threadlines is a government-owned chain of fixed-price shops selling textiles, ceramics, brass, silver, onyx and jewellery. There are sequined toy camels and tin models of buses and rickshaws (my grandson has one that Sarah sent which he used to call his 'looking-at bus' because it is too sharp to play with). The salesmen pulled out tablecloth after cloth, flourishing the heavy cotton so that it cracked like a sail in a brisk wind, and giving the origin of each piece before spreading it on the ever-rising pile on the floor, until we were confused by names and dazzled by patterns and had to say, 'Enough. No more.' We had cups of tea while we made our choices, and when the manager heard that I was going home the following day he gave me an appliquéd fan as a leaving present. The plot for a thriller came to me later when I packed it, a story featuring an innocent tourist who is used to smuggle something out of the country in a fan and then pursued by someone who will stop at nothing to retrieve it . . . So far the fan is still hanging peacefully on my wall and as yet I have had no visits from any mysterious bearded strangers.

In an evening scented with white flowers we looked up at the triangular façades and lighted dome of the Faisal Mosque, with its four slender minarets soaring against black mountains and the rising moon. We followed the moon's reflection across polished marble courtyards, terraces and steps lit by clusters of globes on golden stalks, and saw it shimmering in the blue water of geometrically shaped pools. The operatic tenor of a mullah rose and fell. Bruce was allowed to enter the dome, while Sarah and I had to look through the glass doors from what we termed the infidels' court to see the men praying inside and the spectacular chandelier at the centre of the rotunda. Like the ancient mosques in Lahore, this modern edifice had created space for thousands of men to worship simultaneously. Three or four women were kneeling in prayer on a ledge outside the dome.

Islamabad at night came as a culture shock after Swat and Peshawar. We felt like bumpkins in the big city, with its neon lights, restaurants with flaming braziers and flambeaux, and fairy-lights in the trees. There was a cosmopolitan, holiday, eve-of-Eid atmosphere. Young trendies in sharp clothes were hanging out among the children, carrying balloons and eating candyfloss. Men and women never touched in public, though men strolled hand in hand. It was in the glitzy shop in Islamabad where Bruce was choosing sunglasses that I saw my one and only overtly gay person in Pakistan, a style queen wasting his sweetness on the desert air.

*

As we drove through the dawn to Islamabad airport, garlanded animals were taking their last mouthfuls of grass from the verges. We tried not to look at them, but it was impossible not to see those soft throats without thinking of knives and the bloodbath to come. The prospect of saying goodbye without knowing when we would see each other again was bad enough. I was about to fly thousands of miles away leaving my child in a strange land.

Islamabad airport was a hell of confusion and anxiety that made horrible Heathrow seem like paradise. Once aboard the plane, and during the long delay in taking off, I buried my sorrow at parting in the pages of Dick Francis's *Come to Grief*. It turned out to have a very unpleasant plot about the mutilation of horses, but it served as an aid to re-entering my own culture and a defence against the American woman in the next seat. After bashing everybody's ears with complaints about the porter who had ripped her off, she settled down to convert the Muslim man on her other side to the *Baha'i* faith.

When I flew out to Pakistan I thought it was a really big deal and so I was surprised, not to say piqued, to discover that it was the season for parents of foreign personnel to visit. The skies were black with mothers converging on Peshawar from the four corners of the globe, aircraft laden with sensible food were stacked up on the flight paths into Pakistan. Some parents were regular visitors. How could they afford it, I wondered, and how could they be so sanguine about their children living in dangerous societies where they would always be looked on as strangers, and their grandchildren being born in hospitals that the local papers described as scandalous? The answer was usually God. Talking to Sarah and Bruce's colleagues made me aware of the worldwide network of folk, volunteers and staff of relief agencies, teachers and medics, who were the latter-day successors of those early missionaries and philanthropists. One teacher from an inner-city school in England had made the trip to Pakistan to see for himself the village from which many of his pupils' families originated.

Naturally there are those who need the relief agencies more than the agencies need them – I heard one American boy say, flexing his muscles after a hearty meal, 'Yup, I'm really gonna do some prayer up in the mountains.' Almost without exception the people I met out there were extremely nice and energetic, and they made me feel unworthy in my suspicions that there are some parents a little too eager to push their chicks as far from the nest as possible, into the world's remotest trouble spots, and that there are churches who would welcome the reflected glory of a martyr's crown. The tales told by veterans who had spent their lives in service made me feel wimpish to have thought my visit from London was anything special; they laughed as they recalled sleeping in a house in Jalalabad which had been half-demolished by the unexploded rocket still embedded in the floor, or facing bandits and surviving earthquakes and mortar fire.

What a rich country we live in, I thought on the drive back from Gatwick through hawthorn blossom and cow parsley, passing cars that weren't beat-up Toyotas and smug-looking corporate buildings and unremarkable solid brick houses and shops with windows and doors. In Pakistan I had been nagged by these thoughts: what is life like for women who in other circumstances would be writers and artists? How do women born with the same sensibilities as mine but condemned to illiteracy endure their days? How does any artist exist in a regime which dictates what may be depicted? We visited one small exhibition of paintings but the only picture I can remember was a still life of a vase of flowers beside a closed book titled *Great American Paintings*. At home we make the assumption that ours is the real world and other cultures are deviations from the norm. My holiday was in the spring of the year of the fiftieth anniversary of Partition, but the celebrations, recriminations and post-mortems that would mark Pakistan's golden divorce from India had not yet begun. As we drove through the hinterland of Surrey we overtook a middle-aged woman stumping along the pavement on pale sausage legs under a short black skirt; she was a walking argument for the dignified *shalwar kameez*.

Miami Vice

USA

He leaned over and said, 'Damn, I love your accent. I just love to hear a lady talk like that. Just say something. Anything.'

'How about fuck off?' she answered, her eyes never leaving the money for a minute. Did he really have a cowboy hat on? She couldn't make it out – the drugs were starting to haze her up.

She could see only the money.

He looked hurt. In a single movement she put her bag over the money on the bar and scooped it all up in one go. God bless America and all the dumb American men who lived inside her.

Out in the truck she and Sherry counted up the money, popped another Quaalude and drove off into the night.

It was just like being in a movie, except that even I realized we were in fact driving dangerously slowly.

I had chosen Miami over New York because I thought New York was too scary. New York was where you got mugged, shot at. It was full of 'Saturday night specials' and murders that were not called murders but 'homicides'. Miami, though, was where tourists went. That's why the flights were so cheap. To be honest, I wasn't exactly sure where it was.

I was twenty and the exchange rate was good and America was calling. Or something was that could be America. Perhaps it was in my blood. My father had been American, or was American. I didn't even know whether he was dead or alive. I didn't know him. I didn't know anyone there at all.

Still, it was something I had to do. 'I might even live there,' I announced breezily at goodbye parties. This was not mere travelling; it could be actual *living*. This bravado evaporated as I got on to the plane and could smell my own sweat. I was terrified, but it was too late now. You must never lose face.

Gusts of hot air were blowing in my face from some kind of fan; that's what it had to be, this unreal heat. Real air couldn't have been this hot. I was feeling slightly shaky and guilt-ridden and thought it was something to do with being surrounded by people in uniforms telling me to 'Have a nice day' in the middle of the night.

Everywhere there were signs: instructions on washing your hands and being pleasant and smiling and being happy and not taking drugs and not dropping litter and getting in the right line.

I got in the right line. I got let into the country. Vacation or business? Definitely business. I would hate anyone to think this was some kind of holiday.

'Well, lady, you wanna hotel? You have to pay for it.' The taxi driver looked me up and down.

'I can pay for it. Just not that much.'

'You know Miami Beach? You know a motel? Hey, you know what you are doing?'

It was already taking too long to get to wherever it was that I was going. I felt sick, like I had swallowed too much of this hot air, that it had wriggled inside my stomach. My savings, a few hundred pounds, were ticking away on the meter. I would spend it all in one cab ride while Miami unravelled itself in front of me.

We stopped somewhere with cardboard walls and the promise of air-conditioning. Everything in the room was brown, with a fridge that whirred all night long. I fell asleep to the wailing of sirens and noises that sounded like gunshot. I guess I must have been dreaming.

The first thing I did when I woke up was put on the TV. The TV would look after me. The TV would mean that I didn't have to do anything. It made me feel safe. It must have been the afternoon, because the soaps were on. Soaps to steady me up. One was particularly soothing, about a couple, a modern-day Romeo and Juliet who had run away and broken into a department store. They were living there in secret. I was jealous. They had everything, it was a heaven on earth. I never wanted it to end, because if it ended that might mean I had to go outside. Yet if I didn't go outside, how was I going to get a job? How was I going to live in America?

I had always wanted to travel and meet people. The careers officer told me to join the army or become an air hostess. I was appalled. 'No, travel. Like in *On the Road*.' Having experiences, moving around, never being tied down, being wild and free. My ambitions stretched way out past the dull flatlands of Suffolk in which I grew up.

But then I was a girl and I knew things weren't always the same for girls. I had hitched up and down the country and round Europe a few times and sometimes it had been good and sometimes it had been bloody awful, and no book had been written about that. No books about all the charming men with their stubby little dicks in their oily hands, wanking away while we – me and my friend Janine – ate our sandwiches and did our best to ignore them. 'Anyway,' I'd say if anyone ever asked me, 'being a girl is good. You always get lifts. Sometimes they buy you things too.' That was our trip, getting as much as you could. A drink was good, a meal was better, even if you weren't hungry. It was the principle of the thing; they owed you one.

*

In some ways, I must have already known America. I had lived there when I was little and my mum used to show me pictures of snowdrifts and talk about soda fountains and the neat little gun that my father bought her to carry in her purse. My mother had, in fact, married two Americans, with an Englishman in between. Her attraction to Americans had always been part of a desire to escape to something bigger and brighter than the confines of small-town life. It was also due to her interest in consumer durables. If love could be measured out in things, then how much better if those things were not readily available in Britain.

So I had grown up surrounded by air bases, little prefabricated versions of America in which we would eat onion rings and hamburgers, considered exotic at the time. We would visit the PX air-base store and buy petrol for nothing. The phone boxes took dimes and sometimes the base would go 'on alert'. The planes would be made ready to fly off and start a war wherever a war might be needed. My mum would moan about her third husband being late for his dinner again, unimpressed by his excuses concerning world politics.

The town was full of GIs with virulent strains of the clap freshly cultured from Vietnam. This was gonorrhoea that didn't respond to antibiotics, or so they said. One of my best friends lost her virginity to a black GI who was named after the president who never told a lie. She got the clap. She took her little pills, telling other people they were for 'radiation', but I knew she had to sit in the clap clinic week after week in her bottle-green grammar school uniform. For we were women of the world. Oh, yes.

I finally turned the TV off and left the brown room. In daylight I was surprised to find that the motel had a swimming pool. There was no one in it. I had no idea where I was, or where Miami Beach was in relation to anywhere else. The beach itself was a strip of sand – nothing great, but full of women wearing bikinis cut high up the inside thigh. They were sunbathing even though it wasn't sunny, just humid and hazy.

Perhaps the thing to do would be to plan my next trip. That's what travelling is like, isn't it? You get to a place and immediately start thinking about where you're going next.

Wandering off the beach, I found a travel agent with posters of Cuba in the window. Cuba, yes, that would be good. It was beginning to dawn on me that Miami was already too huge. It would be easier to get to Cuba than negotiate this place. I picked up a leaflet about Cuba and went back to the pool with it.

'Cuba? Forget it,' announced a woman in high heels and a sarong who came tottering up. She was much older than me, blonde, and drinking some primary-coloured cocktail. 'Cuba. There's nothing there. Believe me. I know.'

Marnie was her name. She was pretty enough, but a bit bloated-looking.

'I used to go everywhere. Everywhere. I was an air hostess for American Airlines. The best, I tell you, the best. We had a ball until the jerks grounded me.'

'What for?'

'Oh, I put on a little weight, just a little. They gave me several warnings, but, you know, I couldn't shift it, honey. It's glandular.'

After several warnings and no weight loss, Marnie had never flown again. She didn't want to be ground staff, she told me; she was insulted by the very idea. Perhaps her flesh would have brought the plane to the ground all by itself. She had been fired for being too fat, but fat was a word that she scrupulously avoided.

Once she had had it all. Now she lived in a car. 'Couldn't pay my rent on the room last week. They let me stay in the lot though.'

All she wanted to do, all she had ever wanted to do, was be a flight attendant. Now she was crying.

'Perhaps, honey, I could just keep my things in your room? Use your shower?'

I don't think she even had a car.

After two days I found a job in a diner. I lied and said I had been a waitress before. This diner looked like every diner I've been in since, like the diners my mother described to me when I was little, like every diner on every screen. Retro, repro, an imitation of an imitation. It was, for me, absolutely the real thing. It was run-down, right by the beach, still done up in 1950s style, with a counter at the front and red shiny seats in the booths. You could eat every kind of meal there for not too much money and it didn't shut until three in the morning.

Every waitress was given her own tables, though it was always better to be on the counter: more single men, more tips. We were paid way below any minimum wage.

The kitchen itself was tiny. Three or four guys sweated it out, frying away to heavy-metal music. It was unbearably hot, though you only went into the kitchen for a row or a spliff.

My waitress uniform was disgusting: a white nylon zip-up dress, red-and-white-striped apron and, worst of all, we had to wear white sneakers with those little socks with poms-poms at the back. Nightmare.

Suddenly I was serving grits and eggs-over-easy and all sorts of stuff I had never heard of. Vivian, one of the older waitresses, was also English – a shrivelled-up little woman who had lived in the States since the 1950s. Like Marnie, she also claimed that she had had it all; in fact, she lived in a trailer park. She never helped me at all, and used to accuse me of stealing her toast when I was in a hurry. The cooks made most things, but there were some things you had to make yourself, like toast, waffles, malted milkshakes and massive ice creams with names like Suicide, which you served with sparklers in. Anyway, I think Vivian was jealous of the tips I got. As she found it virtually impossible to be nice to anyone, her tips weren't great.

In the heat it was hard work and the tips didn't start coming in till you got your own regulars. Hookers I always found were the biggest tippers and the sweetest to serve. English people were the pits. Old men coming in for breakfast were not too bad.

The bus boys were all Cuban. Most of them hadn't been working there long either. Castro had chucked out a load of undesirables and I appeared to be working with most of them. The white guys I worked with wore T-shirts that said 'Nuke Iran' on them. Word soon had it that I was a communist and one smartarse short-order cook would never get my orders up on time as a result. So I would chat to the bus boys and try and help them with their English. 'This is a fork . . . a fork,' I would say very slowly when I wanted the tables cleared, and they'd nod. Then one day, a bus boy looked me in the eye and said, 'I know it's a fucking fork, lady.'

My God, we worked hard. Americans don't have tea-breaks or even allow you to be late in the mornings. No excuse is good enough. I was already in trouble for not saying 'Have a nice day' when I put the bill on the table.

'It just doesn't come naturally to me,' I attempted to explain.

'It's company policy. I suggest it does come naturally to you,' said the manager.

I tried, I really did, but I was soon in the manager's office again. A family had apparently complained that I had said 'Have a nice day' in a threatening manner.

At night I used to go back to my motel room and Marnie would be asleep on the bed. I realized that I would have to get rid of her somehow. She always said the weight was dropping off and soon she would be flying again, but I knew she ate potato chips all day and anything else that I could smuggle home from the diner.

Sometimes, after work, I would sit outside drinking beer with Kevin, one of the cooks. Kevin was from Carolina and the person I liked the best since I had been in Miami. His accent was gentle, his face soft. He was a gentleman and would ask me about England, talking until late. He never once made a move, though I kind of hoped he would, but just knowing him made me feel more secure. There was something innately trustworthy and decent about him, which was why he didn't really fit in with the other guys in the kitchen.

One day at work, a couple of men in suits came in. They sat down and I got their coffee.

'Is there someone working here called Kevin?' one of them asked.

'Oh, yeah, he's out the back, in the kitchen.'

They ordered donuts, drank their coffee, got up and made their way through to the kitchen. They came out with Kevin, still in his apron but in handcuffs. They took him away.

'Oh, my God, Kevin, what's happening?'

He looked up shyly. 'Don't worry, sugar, don't worry at all,' he said, and they were gone.

They were the FBI and Kevin was wanted in Carolina for killing several people. 'Shot them up,' as they say. He had held up a bank or something, on some kind of spree that went wrong. He never meant to kill anyone.

I went back to the motel. There was a note from Marnie: 'Got a good offer in St Louis.' I knew she came from St Louis; I knew, too, that she had probably stolen some of my clothes, even though she would never get into them, but I couldn't be bothered to look. I switched on the TV and wondered about myself. I had been living in America more than a month and my best friends were a murderer and a grounded air hostess. And even they weren't around any more.

I sat down and wrote a letter to my mother telling her not to worry about me. Everything was fine.

*

The *Miami Herald* was so thick you could hardly carry it. Pages and pages of crime stories, killings, gangsters, prostitution, torture, extortion, heists, smugglings, shootings, muggings, race murders. Every crime was violent crime. At the end of each story a line appeared informing us that the police suspected the particular crime in question was 'drug-related'. Soon I realized that everything in Miami was drug-related. I started taking a lot of drugs myself.

My life turned around when I switched to the night shift. The night shift was much more like it. The waiters were hipper. We would turn up the jukebox and play Frank very loudly. 'New York, New York' is a great song to wait tables to, strutting up and down to.

Alain and Mikey worked the night shift. Alain was French, a hippie-ish beach boy, good-looking as hell. Mikey was an Irish chancer who had lived everywhere. They always had loads of 'ludes. It wasn't that they were into downers, it was just a way of making sure you got drunk quicker.

The trick was to pop the 'lude half an hour or so before we finished work, so that it would be kicking in by the time we got to the Space Invaders machine in the bar. It was a question of timing; it didn't always work. On several occasions Mikey would flounce up to a table, take an order and immediately collapse on the floor. The customers seemed to matter less and less. They were always complaining about roaches in the food. I would rush out into the kitchen, pour on some more spaghetti sauce and take it back to them. Well, what did they expect?

It was through Alain that I met Sherry. She claimed to be his girlfriend, but he never saw it that way. Sherry was an all American girl: big arse, bad skin, permanently erect nipples and the neatest strip of pubic hair you ever saw. She was very attractive to men. We would all meet in one of the various motel rooms we ended up in. Alain and Mikey liked to shoot coke because they couldn't wait long enough for the rush. Alain had a load of James Bond-type devices for drug-smuggling: aerosol cans that came apart, that sort of thing. I thought it was daft. Sherry tried to pretend he was big time.

We had to switch motel rooms because they made a fuss about the needles in the toilet. I could just about afford to stay. What I earned covered the rent, but I wasn't saving anything and Cuba, once only a few hundred miles away, seemed to be getting further. Sherry came from Miami but she wanted to get a room together with me.

Soon I was kind of in love with her. I had wanted to experience America and she was the most American person I had ever met. Everything she did or thought was the opposite of what I did or thought. At first I snobbily regarded her as some sort of anthropological specimen. Soon, though, I found myself thinking the things she thought. If she told me that a certain man was worth having, I believed her. She fixed me up with someone who was important. Important in that he owned a lot of things – clubs, restaurants; important because of his connection to Miami's mafia. He liked me, apparently, because he thought I was 'a lady'. We went on a double date. Mr Important, Sherry and Mr Important's henchman. I took a 'lude, felt nothing, had another and started to drink what Sherry told me to drink – White Russians.

'That's a nice drink for a lady,' said my date.

White Russians. Milk and alcohol. I dropped another 'lude. I woke up at the table. It was so dark I could hardly see anything except a carcass of ribs in front of me. I must pull myself together and get to work. I sensed that I was in some kind of restaurant and therefore must get to work.

'I'll be over in a minute,' I slurred to some horrified people at the next table before nodding off again.

'I'll take your order in a minute,' I shouted across to Mr Important, who was sitting opposite me but seemed a very long way away.

His car was the biggest car I had ever been in. 'Is there a bathroom in here?' I asked in my ladylike way.

'No,' he growled.

'Oh dear,' I said, as I threw up all over myself.

'Let's go to a club.'

We arrived somewhere in Fort Lauderdale and I found a real bathroom, took off all my clothes, rinsed them, put them back on again sopping wet and reapplied some deep purple lipstick. I felt ready for the night to begin. I asked him for another drink and hit the dance floor. I never saw him again.

Work was becoming boring now that I could actually do the job. Filling up Heinz ketchup bottles from vats of slop that clearly wasn't Heinz ketchup, I would find myself thinking about the middle-aged guys who sat in silence while I 'refreshed' their cups. One of them could be my father and I wouldn't even know it. One of them could take me to a hotel room and then afterwards I could tell him . . .

One of the bus boys was called Freud. He dealt the best grass around.

'Quite honestly, it's not what we thought it would be. Sit down Simon. *Now*, Simon.' An English dad with his pink children was explaining to me that Miami didn't live up to his expectations. 'I mean, Disney is one thing, but you can't go there every day now, can you, love?'

'No.' I imagined that there might be other things to do in Miami, but none that I could recommend to him off the top of my head.

'Don't you ever get frightened? You know, round here. It's a bit dodgy, isn't it?'

'No, I don't get frightened. It's fine.'

'What time do you finish? We can make sure you get home all right.'

'I only live over the road. Really, it's fine. Thanks.'

I didn't think I needed anyone to walk me home, though it's true that everyone thought I was peculiar for walking at all. I liked it, especially when it was raining that hot sticky rain and out at sea you could see a tornado. Cars stopped all the time offering me lifts, because they thought if I was walking either something was terribly wrong or I was a prostitute. Telling people I couldn't drive was more shocking than telling people I was a communist.

When my shift finished, I was too tired to even change out of my uniform. I was crossing the road when a car stopped and a man said, 'Get in the car.'

'I don't want to.'

'Get in the car, now.' He had a gun. Did he *really* have a gun? 'Get in the car or I'll shoot.'

'Shoot me, then,' I said, because I didn't know what else to say and whatever I did I knew I wasn't going to get in the car. And then I ran. It was not until I got back to my room that I started shaking, still not believing that he would have really shot me. I couldn't gauge my own fear because it was too close to the kind of fear you felt when you were watching a scary movie.

'You did the right thing,' my friends assured me.

'Did I?'

'Oh, yes. He was just trying to frighten you. You showed him.'

'Did I?'

'You showed him that you weren't scared of him. That's good.'

The police arrived. They did not seem the least interested in the man with the gun in his car. 'Why were you walking? Do you make a habit of this?' they kept asking me. 'We could take you in,' one of them snarled.

Now I was afraid.

Miami had been up in flames only recently. Some black guys had cut the tongue out of a white policeman. Annette, a Jamaican waitress I worked with, whispered in my ear, 'It's justice. You know what I'm saying? I'm only telling you that because I know you are white but you ain't one of these. It's justice. I would have held him down myself.' She glided over to the counter. 'How do you like coffee, sir? Black or white?'

A vote was soon to be taken over whether Florida should be bilingual. Guys like Sherry's dad were tooling up for the inevitable.

Sherry's parents had an unhappy marriage and a pool that badly needed cleaning. It stank, but her mother was half-cut most of the time and somehow they just all lived with the smell. All the children in the family had names beginning with Sh – Sherry, Shaun and Shane. The kitchen was full of tiny little holes where one of Sherry's cousins had accidentally shot himself with one of her dad's guns. Her dad was a huge John Wayne-ish man and he was, as he kept on telling me, a good Christian, a Baptist, a proud father and a loving husband.

'Do you want to see my guns, Suzie?' he asked the minute I arrived. 'Been shooting stags last fall. Got a swamp rat the other day. Never know when you might need them for the niggers.'

Sherry's mother just sat there snarling and snorting while he told me these things, pouring out the bourbon. We had only come to the house to ask if we could borrow the pick-up truck. We desperately needed some transport as Sherry had been offered a job as a barmaid, mainly on the strength of her nipples.

When I got back to my room I started to cry and I couldn't stop. I really had thought of myself as a pacifist. Violence was always wrong, but I believed, too, in revolution. And, come the revolution, someone, maybe even me, would have to shoot Sherry's dad, who had after all lent us his truck. I cried, too, for all the other people who would also have to be put up against the wall, lots of the people I worked with in fact, and just about everybody I had met since I had been here. It would be a massacre. And my mum, working-class Tory that she was, would also have to be executed. Was this the revelation that I had come looking for? Was this the point of having 'experiences'? This extreme gut reaction to America made me realize that violence was necessary. Things could never be the same again. No one would have called me innocent, but something was lost.

There was a letter from my mum. She had been, she wrote, considering computer dating, but it was a little too pricey.

By now I was seeing Joe, a Seminole Indian who rolled the tightest little joints. He lived on a reservation, which seemed kind of glamorous. Besides, he always had lots of money because of the casinos set up on Indian land. Seminoles didn't have to pay tax and, because Joe was an expert in land rights, he would explain to me how huge tracts of America would be handed back to the Natives at any moment. At first I lapped up this land-rights stuff, then I got bored. I guess I liked the idea of Joe more than the reality. Still, at least he had all his fingers, so I had made the right choice. Most of his friends didn't, because they earned their living wrestling alligators for the tourists and had hands full of stumps.

Joe always carried a gun. 'Put this in your bag,' he said to me the first night we went out.

'Sure,' I replied coolly.

I spent the whole evening terrified that I was going to accidentally kill someone when I tried to find my lipstick. I went to the toilet and dropped my bag on the floor. Christ, there is a gun in there. Stay calm.

Maybe I was getting back to my roots – my father had been part Cherokee – but Joe disappointed me. He was just so . . . American. He even bought me a ghastly see-through nylon nightie that he seriously expected me to wear.

*

'I'm in love. This is real,' announced Sherry. 'Look at this.' She showed me a glittering bracelet. 'He bought me this. He brought it right into the bar and gave it to me in front of everyone.'

Sherry's new love was Roger. Roger, according to Sherry, was a real gentleman; he was also a proper drug dealer. Little bowls of coke sat on every surface in his house. He had a light aircraft and an endless supply of revolting jewellery that kept Sherry happy. Every time he had a nose bleed, which he did frequently, she would gaze at him in admiration.

But none of Roger's attractions stopped her hankering after one of her old boyfriends. 'We made love on rubber sheets. Have you ever done that? It is the greatest,' she would say, fingering the glitzy necklace she was wearing.

Nor did it stop us getting out together. When Roger was away on business, which he was frequently, we'd go and hang out in the tranny bars and strip joints where Sherry had worked. Middle-aged women wiggled suspendered thighs over men who wiggled their tongues in return. This ritual dance only emphasized the distance between them. I tried not to stare, as Sherry chatted up the bar staff in the hope of getting another job.

'I haven't felt like this for a long time, chile,' a tall black woman said, caressing my hair.

'Did you used to be a man?' I asked.

'Baby, you don't never get used to nothing.'

I needed another job myself. The diner was going downhill fast. No one gave a shit. There was a job going in a Jewish restaurant in the mall near where Sherry's parents lived.

'Are you Jewish?' they asked me.

'Sure,' I said, not realizing that the customers ordered in Yiddish. Besides which, what the hell was gefilte fish? I was a disaster, but a source of amusement. I had chutzpah, they said, whatever that was.

I wanted to leave anyway. No one had ever been so rude to me, talked to me this way. 'Wipe this table,' they yelled. 'Get me some water.' Then one day I yelled back, and everything was hunky-dory and I got massive tips. Unlike the diner, these people expected good service and they paid you for it. Most of the customers were New York Jews retired to Miami. Soon they were bringing in their ugly dentist sons to meet me, and I played along as these poor guys stuffed their faces while their mothers relayed their career prospects to me.

At the table I would patiently write down the order. Then the wife would say, 'He's not eating that. No dairy.' Everything was sweet and lo, but with extra cream on the blintzes and sour cream on anything resembling a vegetable.

Adele was the best waitress there. She was dark and quivery, gorgeous, in her early thirties, already with four husbands behind her. She was very emotional especially when she didn't get big enough tips. She would follow old couples out into the car park and throw their tips back at them through the car window. 'Why don't you just go home and suck his cock?' she would scream at astonished octogenarians. She was always being fired and rehired the next day, because Adele knew how to get anything she wanted. The day John Lennon was murdered, she came to work and burst into tears at every table she served. She went home that night with hundreds of dollars in her pockets. She taught me how to tip apple sauce over difficult customers, sometimes whole plates of food. 'Oh, I am *so* sorry.'

I learned from her that to be a good waitress you need a good story. Looking for my father she reckoned was a particularly good one. Waitressing was a performance and soon I was acting my heart out. Telling them about my mum, the GI bride – which was never true – telling them that I was saving up in order to see my daddy, telling them that I wanted to go to college, telling them whatever they wanted to hear. 'My name is Suzanne and I'm your waitress for the evening,' was just the beginning.

The money started piling up. I began to think I could go to Cuba if I really wanted, but I didn't want to leave Sherry.

Some English guys I knew wrote telling me that you could get a flight from New Orleans to the Yucatan for seventy-five dollars and all the tequila you could drink on the plane. I walked around Miami Beach, the hotels, the juice bars, the rows of diners, the malls, the dives. Had I seen anything of this place? Maybe not, but I knew what it was like. We drank margaritas in the airport and Sherry told me that she loved me. I persuaded her to get on the plane with me to New Orleans. Roger gave her the money for the ticket. She lasted a couple of days and went back home. I went to Mexico.

Years later I read in magazines that Miami is fashionable, that it is full of art-deco hotels, that Madonna has a house there. The very streets I walked down are now considered stylish. Can it be the same place? Perhaps I didn't see Miami at all. Perhaps it was just a movie playing in my head. How do you ever tell the truth about another time, another place, when you have seen too many movies, when you have got too old to let mere events write the script for you?

So, I was young in Miami. You could say young enough not to know what I was doing, but that would be wrong. For I was young enough to know exactly what I was doing and still do it. I miss that, the certainty that youth gives you.

Nothing is as clear to me now as it was then, for everything is overlaid with other versions of America, none of them mine. And even my version doesn't really belong to me. I still don't know my father. I never bothered to find him. The only thing I am certain of is that all the cocaine I have had ever since pales in comparison.

And this. Many years later Sherry wrote to me with news of her marriage. She had been through some hard times but had finally found the right man. She had married him, as Americans do, in the front yard of her parents' house. She sent me a picture. How respectable it all looked.

'PS,' she wrote. 'Did I ever tell you that I went to the doctor's and he told me that there is something really quite wrong with my brain, something chemical, some sort of imbalance?'

No, she never did tell me that. It would have made too much sense.

KATE PULLINGER

The Good Ferry

BRITISH COLUMBIA

I've been an expatriate Canadian for fifteen years. The two words go together to describe me now, 'expatriate' and 'Canadian'; they are virtually inseparable and should, perhaps, be hyphenated – Expatriate-Canadian, like Chinese-Canadian or Korean-American. In my case it means not quite Canadian any longer, not quite the real McCoy, but not anything else either. Certainly not British, despite the fact that I've lived in Britain all this time. Sometimes I imagine there's another self out there somewhere, another Kate Pullinger, one who did not leave Canada but stayed on in British Columbia. When I was nineteen a friend and I went to see a psychic. It was just a couple of weeks before we were leaving Canada to travel for a year, and I had a secret plan to stay away for much longer. The psychic did not pick up on any of that, she did not 'see' my passport in my pocket. She told me I was going to live in Vancouver and be an academic, marry an academic, have three kids and drive an estate car. At the time this seemed a terrible fate, the very fate from which I was running away, hoping to avoid. So perhaps there is another Kate Pullinger, the one who stayed in BC, the one who drives a Volvo station wagon to pick up her kids on her way home from the university. Now, when I think on it, it seems a great life.

I've always travelled to escape. I've always travelled in an effort to be someone other than who I am – someone who knows the world, someone who stays in hotels, someone who travels very light, with the smallest of carry-on bags. The irony is that so much of the travelling I've done over the past fifteen years has involved going home. Flying back to BC. Taking the ferry from the mainland to Vancouver Island, to Sidney, the retirement community outside Victoria where my parents live.

After making the journey dozens – hundreds? – of times using all the available methods of transport, I can say that the best way to travel from Vancouver to Vancouver Island is by ferry. Other people might disagree. These people would all be people who live there, on the island, or people who have to travel there frequently. They would say it's a bloody drag; they would say it's a waste of time; they would say it's boring.

To take this ferry you need to drive out of Vancouver along the highway to Tsawwassen, through the fertile delta deposited there by the Fraser River. Pass the ruin of Fantasy Gardens, built by Bill Van der Zalm, once-upon-a-time Premier of the province. Van der Zalm – a tulip magnate in his spare time – bypassed agricultural zoning laws to build his theme park. Neither Van der Zalm nor Fantasy Gardens are mourned by many; he ran a government composed of used-car salesmen. Swing by the sharp escarpment on which the town of Tsawwassen itself rises. Then drive out on to the long man-made spit to the ferry terminal. To the right lies Roberts Bank Coal Port, also man-made, with its large heap of coal at the sea-going end of the pier. Look behind and on a clear day – these days are rare enough that the view is startling, extraordinary – you can see the mountains that abut sharply above the city of Vancouver, navy blue against the sky. Look south towards Seattle and there is Mount Baker, standing on its own, always snow-capped, like a peak in a child's drawing. Look forward, and there's the ferry terminal, all streamlined multilayered precision, able to shift thousands of cars and foot passengers smoothly on and off again, on the hour, every hour. Boats depart from here to

Vancouver Island and to the smaller Gulf Islands – Maine, Saltspring, Galiano and several others – that lie between the big island and the mainland.

I too used to find the ferry awesomely boring. I too used to dread that journey. We lived on Vancouver Island and the drive from home to the ferry terminal used to take almost an hour. Then the wait, the dead, boring wait. Even if we got up before dawn and drove out early, there always seemed to be a wait, seagulls circling overhead like vultures. Back then they used to run smaller, and fewer, ferries and in summer we always ended up queuing on the causeway, sometimes for as long as half a day. We'd park and go down on to the rocky beach to watch the birds, not straying too far because every so often Dad would have to move the car forward. Then we'd park again. If I was lucky, Mum would have brought a picnic and I'd drink so much apple juice that once the car got going again on the other side I'd have to puke; if I was even luckier, I'd get to walk forward along the line of cars all the way to the terminal, where there was a little cafeteria. Eventually the car would get up as far as the paybooths and this time when we parked we'd get out of the car and count the number of vehicles ahead and try to figure out if we'd make the next boat, or have to wait for another.

Then the drive on to the ferry itself, the alarming clunk as the car tyres left the asphalt and hit the metal ramp – I'd always think of James Bond gunning his car into the air as the stretch of water between tarmac and boat grew wider, but my father wasn't that kind of a driver and the ferry wasn't that kind of boat. The car deck stinking of exhaust fumes and the oily sea, we'd lock the old red Ford Mercury and begin the slow climb up the steep stairs to the passenger deck. The boat journey itself was an hour and three-quarters, longer in bad weather. I'd wander up and down the ship, inside the front passenger lounge where it was too warm, too crowded, the big windows always steamed up, outside on the deck where it was too windy, too wet. I'd spend my allowance in the news-stand on girls' magazines and candy, and sometimes we'd have lunch on the ferry – clam chowder and French fries. Then the docking, and the giant muted thuds as the huge boat nudged into its pier. And the long drive from the ferry to wherever we were going – to get anywhere in British Columbia requires a long drive, everywhere is hundreds of miles from everywhere else. Interminable. The ferry interminable.

That was before I left that island for another slightly larger island – only slightly, mind you: Britain, that crowded little chunk of rock composed of three countries – England, Scotland, Wales – glued together by geology, their backs turned to each other like Greek and Turkish Cyprus, not quite as bad, but it almost feels that way sometimes, with Northern Ireland overseeing it all from across the Irish Sea. Now when I return to British Columbia that ferry ride is a high point. That ferry ride makes everything else worthwhile; the stately progress from mainland to island is the journey home for me. I take that boat and a curtain falls between me and the rest of the world.

When I was a child I used to watch a lot of television. I used to lie on the floor in the basement, in the rumpus room as we called it, the room where we could create a rumpus, although by the time I was born, a late child, there was no one left to rumpus with me, the TV on, no other light, the blue light flickering over my head. I watched everything, but my favourites were *I Love Lucy, The Jetsons, Gilligan's Island* (yet another island, seven castaways stranded in the tropics, forever doomed to entertain each other) and *Dark Shadows*, a soap opera about a vampire that I found terrifying. I remember watching a lot of movies, black and white movies from the previous decade; there's that scene in *The Incredible Shrinking Man* when the man who later shrinks and his wife are out on their motorboat, a dinky pleasure craft. They are wearing their bathing suits and taking in the sun. The wife goes below deck to do something – mix cocktails, spear olives

with toothpicks – and just at that moment the boat passes through a
fog, a kind of dense little cloud that's just sitting there on the water,
despite the brilliant sunshine. It's this fog, poisoned with 1950s
radiation or some such thing, that makes the man begin to shrink.
He shrinks and shrinks until he's so small that he has to fight an epic
battle with a spider on the cellar staircase. Anyway, because of that
movie I've always been vaguely fearful of fog, and there's a lot of fog
between Vancouver and Vancouver Island, especially in the winter, a
lot of large, heavy, sodden, dark fog that makes the foghorns blow
up and down the coast, blow and blow, ominously and continuously,
night and day. And then the journey really is like passing through a
curtain, a black velvet curtain that cuts out all the light and I can feel
myself starting to shrink.

And on the other side is sunny Victoria. But don't bother going
there.

I was twenty in 1982 when I came to live in London. I arrived during
the Falklands War. Demonstrators beat their loud drums in Trafalgar
Square, 'Maggie, Maggie, Maggie. Out, out, out.' I had been to London
twice before, once with my parents when I was sixteen, and on a
school trip the year before. A school trip – that sounds very posh; I
went to a small state school on Vancouver Island, Dunsmuir High,
named after an evil Scottish tycoon who made his money out of coal-
mining. The school was in Metchosin, outside Victoria, near the sea,
semi-rural, almost suburbia. We always said Metchosin was an Indian
word meaning 'stinking fish', but I have no idea if that is true – which
Indians, which language, which fish? The school had a long sparkling
green playing field out back that I loved, although I despised sport – I
was no good at it. In March 1977 I came to Britain on a trip organized
by our French teacher, an Englishman known to us for some reason
I can no longer recall as Danny Boy, after the song, whose shirt collar
was always spotted with blood from where he had nicked himself

shaving. 'Oh, Danny Boy,' we used to sing behind his back. There were twenty of us and we travelled around Britain in a coach with a couple of other school groups, stopping at York and Gretna Green on the way up to Edinburgh, Chester and Stonehenge on the way back down. For me the trip was redolent of Opium; my friend Pam spilt her perfume all over her suitcase and she stank accordingly. Another friend, Nancy, cried throughout the entire journey; I think she missed her boyfriend – she was the only one of us to actually have one of these things – and didn't really like being away from home.

Music featured heavily during this trip; we all loved English music. I was a secret punk – secret because, to the outside world, in no way did I resemble an English punk. I had long thick curly hair parted in the middle, was a little overweight, didn't know how to put on make-up (still don't, although I try) and my wardrobe ran to corduroy trousers and shapeless V-necked sweaters that had a tendency to ride up my back. (I love clothes, although I've never been able to wear them.) We came to Britain for the music and even though we didn't go to any gigs – would we have known what a 'gig' was? – we had a soundtrack that continually played in our heads – a bit of the Beatles, the Rolling Stones, the Jam and the Sex Pistols. In the photographs I have of that trip, my friends and I posed as though we were a band trying to find the right image for an album sleeve. An all-girl Roxy Music beside Hadrian's Wall; T-Rex at the foot of Arthur's Seat.

In London we stayed in the hotel on Sloane Square, which, back then, was a bit of a shabby dive. There was a bellboy with a crooked jaw who looked like a young Donovan and we were in love with him. A girl from one of the other schools actually managed to get off with him; I saw them kissing in the hotel phone kiosk. We were amazed at her luck because, although this girl was pretty, she wore glasses, large glasses with plastic frames. In our experience – my experience – boys were not interested in girls who wore glasses. I wore glasses. But instead of feeling cheered by this development, we were jealous.

London smelt of diesel and garbage, and I loved it. It was always dark and windy. The yellow lights of the taxis at Sloane Square swept by me and I could have swooned. I could have lain on the steps of the British Museum and wept. I don't know why I was such a teenage Anglophile, I can't remember, I can't fathom it from where I sit now, why I wrote in my diary when I was sixteen that the thing I most wanted to do in life, the thing that would fulfil me more than any other, would be to live in London. I had other ambitions, of course: I wanted to write, I wanted to travel, I wanted a boyfriend. But I knew, I just knew, that I wouldn't be able to do those other things unless I did this one first. Everything in my life was predicated on coming to live in London.

And that is what I did, eventually. I took detours along the way – a year and a bit in Montreal, where I found out just how little French Danny Boy had taught me, and the better part of a year in the Yukon, northern Canada, where I learned that minus forty degrees Celsius is the same as degrees Fahrenheit, and, because in winter the sun does not rise, around lunch time a kind of translucent twilight opens up the perpetual night. But then I arrived. By the time I was twenty I had made it to London. City of my dreams.

And here I sit fifteen years later. I'm thirty-five years old and married to an Englishman. But even after all these years in London, after voting in three general elections, paying poll tax, income tax and water rates, and labouring in an NHS maternity ward – after all that, I'm still a tourist here. When I get on the Underground I'm a traveller setting out on a new journey. And when I fly home to British Columbia, I'm a tourist there too, with a foreigner's sense of the uncanny. I take that ferry through the grey fog and I get off the boat in sunny Victoria. It looks just like the place where I grew up, and yet it isn't.

My advice: don't bother going there.

*

Two train journeys: London, King's Cross, to Market Harborough, Leicestershire; London, King's Cross, to Cambridge.

Though I love to travel, I do less of it now, with less of a spirit of adventure than before. I travel a fair bit for work. This often amounts to taking a train to Manchester or some other city, taking a taxi to a hotel, taking a taxi to a bookshop, getting up in front of an audience of anywhere from two (including the publicist who has travelled with me) to 200 people, reading a passage from a book I have written, answering questions, perhaps taking a taxi to a restaurant for dinner with the publicist and the people who run the bookshop, getting back to the hotel, sleeping, then taking a taxi to the train station the following morning to travel back to London or on to a further city, where that routine will be acted out, lived through, once again. It's not a bad way to see the country. You learn a lot about what people in bookshops think about Manchester or wherever, and somebody else pays for everything.

But occasionally I do more protracted types of tourism, residential tourism perhaps, part-time journeys that last six months or a couple of years. In 1992–3 I spent a year travelling by train to Market Harborough, where I was working as writer-in-residence at HMP Gartree, a prison for men serving life or long-term sentences. Market Harborough is an affluent town in that part of middle England where people argue about whether they live in the north or the south; you can tell a lot about someone who takes the time to explain to you that Harboro' is actually part of the north. I'd travel up to the prison first thing Wednesday morning, spend the night in town at a friend's place, travel back to London late Thursday evening. Market Harborough – birthplace of Thomas Cook and ye olde traveller's cheques – is an old town. In the centre there's a sixteenth-century grammar school, one tiny room on a set of stilts. Behind that, the old corset factory. There's a posh hotel and nice pubs and the women wear green Barbour coats and scarves on their heads, unless, of course, they think they live in the north, in which case they wear old and weathered black leather biker's jackets.

The prison is a couple of miles out in the country. When the weather was fine I'd cycle up the hill on the back lane, through the little hamlets with their cottages covered in rambling roses. On Gallow Field Road, HMP Gartree sits like a great dark walled-in council estate that's been exiled from the town. To get inside I passed through an iron door into a small room where I was checked over by the security men on the other side of the glass. Once I was given my keys, I was allowed through another iron door, and then a whole series of locked and barred gates. Inside I'd find the men, the prisoners, and those other men, the officers, and it was like passing into another world, an elaborately hierarchical, coded, masculine world where things looked normal but once I scratched the surface, or looked again, I would discover that no, this was not a world I recognized, this was an echo world, a netherworld, to which I'd been given privileged, temporary, access. Prison is hell, believe you me; prison is not a holiday camp. Politicians may tell you how comfortable and soft it is (and it isn't), but in prison they take one important thing away from you, the one thing that makes life worth living: your liberty. It may seem silly to mention it, but the thing about prisoners is that they are not free.

Every day I'd meet inmates and talk to them about their writing. Conversation would inevitably meander and we'd get on to other topics – their lives, their crimes, their families, my life – but I'd always bring us back around to the subject at hand: writing. For the most part, I'd see them one to one, and once a week I'd meet with the writing group. At lunch I'd go to the staff canteen and have toasted sandwiches or baked potatoes or omelettes and chips, watch the officers play pool, turn the pages of the staff copy of the *Sun*. I'd have supper there, and sometimes breakfast as well, white toast dripping with margarine. Prisoners would be banged up for two hours at lunch, two hours over dinner, then twelve hours after eight p.m. Sometimes in winter, when it got dark by the four p.m. dinner break, the prison would fall very silent and I would stand and peer through the bars across the fields at the cars going by on the main road, and I would think about the men locked up all around me – they were murderers for the most part – and I would swear to myself that I would never do anything wrong, never commit a crime ever again (I had a colourful youth of shoplifting and smoking dope) – anything to avoid prison, anything to avoid becoming one of the shufflers, one of the slow-paced, sad-eyed or demented and manic men I was getting to know.

On the train home I would look out at the flat English countryside – Kettering, Peterborough, Luton – at the towns and steeples and creeks, and I would marvel that I – me, a foreigner, a Canadian, not a Brit – was being allowed into this place, this most intimate of institutions. It was like I was being allowed to look at the entire country's dirty laundry. I was being shown the British, the British people, the British system, at its lowest, at its very worst, at its most dreadful and ugly and painful. I was being allowed inside. Not only that, but I'd *been given keys*.

I'm the kind of tourist who always wants to live wherever I'm visiting. I always set myself up in a nice little fantasy about how wonderful life would be if I could live in that place, where I'd have my flat, who my friends would be, where I'd go for dinner, where I'd do my shopping. In Gartree, in Market Harborough, I bypassed all that. I was doing it, I was living it; the prison was, in a way, my place. OK, it was a job, I was not on holiday, but my time there shared an essential ingredient with any other kind of travelling, particularly travel in the Third, or Developing, World: voyeurism. I was looking in on my murderers, trying to come to grips with their fascinating culture, and at the end of the day I went away, went home, went back to my own life, my own things. At the end of the day they stayed put, they weren't going anywhere, they were stuck in their world, unlike me.

And there were some very bad moments. The day before I started a prisoner who had worked as a cleaner in the Education Department offices tried to hang himself in the staff ladies' toilet. When I went in to use the loo for the first time, his footprints were still there on the toilet seat. A sex offender I'd come to know quite well got into some kind of trouble over debt and, in an effort to get himself moved off the segregated wing and away from those threatening him, he took a sharpened chair leg and disembowelled himself, letting his guts slide out of his body and on to the bed where he lay. He was duly moved to hospital, and then to another prison. Apparently, or so I was told, he had done the same thing several times before. Not long after that a burly young prisoner stopped me in the corridor and, in the hard-edged banter I'd yet to accustom myself to, asked me – in front of a group of other prisoners – why I wore such weird clothes all the time. This comment upset me and I told him he was horrible, that it was a horrible thing to say, and I used my keys to open the door and slip away. That afternoon I got a call from an officer, asking me to come down to the wing. I went along and when I saw the young prisoner he was red-faced and shaking. He said he was sorry, he said he'd been in prison since he was nineteen and he no longer knew how to talk to women, he no longer knew what was the right thing to say, would I forgive him, he liked the way I dressed, he thought it unusual. He almost cried, and I almost cried with him.

And things were good as well. We had a laugh. Prisoners know how to have a long, bleak laugh.

And then, a couple of years later, I found myself with a similar kind of commute, another kind of part-time tourist commitment, another stint as an unqualified anthropologist abroad. This time I was the Judith E. Wilson Visiting Fellow at a college in Cambridge. Judith E. Wilson was a wealthy woman about whom little seems to be known except that she was a great friend of the actress Dame Edith Evans. There is a lovely photograph of the two women side by side, wearing very large hats. Together they cooked up the idea of establishing a visiting fellowship at Cambridge – every year one or two writers or theatre directors are awarded a couple of terms at the university. The fellowships float between the colleges; the year I was chosen I was given two terms at Jesus College. The college gave me a set of rooms and the fellowship paid me a good wage and in return I was expected to . . . well, to be there. No academic duties, no obligation to write anything in particular. So I began the shuttle between London and Cambridge, train up on Monday, train down on Friday, the journey from my real life to this other life, the autumn and winter months spent ensconced in my rooms overlooking the green cloister, watching the students and the academics and their comings and goings.

Cambridge is a strange place and Cambridge academics are, it has been said before, cold fish. Monumentally so. As well as my set of rooms and my bedder (cleaner, in college parlance), I was given dining rights, which meant that I could take meals at High Table, which was actually two tables set on a dais at the top end of the college dining room. Lunch was a casual affair, sort of self-service from the buffet (different – better – food than the students' buffet at the other end of the room). Protocol, and a Cambridge college is nothing if not a place of great unexplained protocol, required that when you came in you filled the tables in an orderly manner, sitting next to whoever had sat down last, no heading off to the far end of the table to eat your tomato soup, scampi, chips and bread and butter pudding in solitary peace. So you could end up next to a physicist, or an historian, or a mathematician, which could have been wonderful, except too many of them seemed to think that being a novelist, a lady novelist in fact, was just about as frivolous as you could get. Not all of them, of course, but you get the general drift, or rather I did, quite quickly.

All of which is fine. I got a lot of work done, unlike my year in prison, during which I found it impossible to work, too caught up with the trauma of the place and the prisoners and their terrible stories. In Cambridge there was little to do but work. And there were sparks of light for me. I enjoyed the students a lot – they were much like students anywhere, young and excited by words and books and drugs and parties. I took pleasure in the fabric of the small city, bicycling along the medieval walls, walking through the colleges that back on to the River Cam. The bookshops are glorious. At night the town is very dark, the greens and commons largely unlit (for the sake of the astronomers, who like it dark, is one theory; for historical veracity – it's dark simply because it has always been dark – another) and I enjoyed being slightly frightened in the black evening.

My dining rights extended to the evening meal, but that is an affair beyond the pale and I did not attend often. At Jesus College formal dress is required, which means academic gowns; I was loaned a 'dead man's gown' from the porter's lodge, so called because that's exactly what it is. Fellows – college academics are all known as Fellows, regardless of sex – gather before dinner for sherry in the Combination Room (a place to mingle, or combine). At the appropriate time a bell is rung and the Fellows file into the dining hall, places in strict adherence to a certain unwritten hierarchy with which I never came to grips. A Latin grace is read off an ancient hand-held board and everyone sits down. Dinner is served to those at High Table by the butler, a terrifying ex-policeman, and his flunkies. At the end of four courses – starter, main, pudding, savoury; everyone eats quickly because nothing can happen before the last person is finished, and heaven save the unwary visitor nervously playing with her food – the Master of the College, or whoever is in his place, stands, as does everyone else, pushing back their chairs and stepping right away from the table so that the Master can then begin the process of 'peeling off', which basically means he leaves first and the others follow in rotation. The opportunities for fucking up are legion.

There was one Fellow who refused to speak to me throughout my six-month sojourn. Whether he had decided he loathed me before meeting me, or he disapproved of my appointment, or had some quarrel with those within the college who had approved me, I'll never know. I decided I wasn't just being paranoid and he really was going out of his way to pretend I didn't exist when at a college reception he went round the room with a bottle, filling everyone's glass except mine. He even went so far as to break ranks at High Table and move away when I unwittingly ended up next to him as we filed in one evening. One minute he was there staring studiously over my shoulder, the next he was gone, leaving me standing next to an empty seat, disrupting glorious tradition.

To be fair, I had my own set of difficulties to overcome in Cambridge. I'm a university drop-out, a fact to which I don't, ordinarily, give much thought. However, in the university environment I find myself overcome with doubt – there are too many important books I have not read, too many critical texts I have not studied. In the academy I'm easily intimidated, so I end up hating academics at the same time as looking at their lives – teaching, reading, writing, all marvellous activities – with envy. After all, it's what that psychic told me I should be doing, way back when I was still a fully fledged, non-expat Canadian.

So perhaps I was never going to be really happy as a Visiting Fellow in Cambridge. And yet the thing I could not get over, throughout my stay, apart from the fact that when I invited people around to my rooms I could say, 'Come to Jesus', was how similar a Cambridge college is to HMP Gartree. First off, there is the overwhelming masculinity of both places. I expected a men's prison to be full of men, but a coed college? Of the sixty-odd Fellows, there were seven women. Overall, the university student body is only one-third female. And then there's the mysterious rituals, the secret clubs, the inexplicably rigid hierarchies, the unwritten rules. The cliques, the malicious gossip and rumour-mongering, the continuous jostling for power. The emphasis on sport. The casual racism. An ability to accept behaviour that in the outside world would be seen as completely mad. Both places have a wall around them, both places are locked up tight at night and, luckily, in both places I had keys. The similarities were most disconcerting. Except, of course, in the end the prison was a lot more friendly.

One of the best journeys I've ever made in British Columbia involved taking four ferries. The ferry from Vancouver Island to the mainland, there's no getting away from that one. We'd borrowed a car from an old friend of mine and a tent and some camping equipment. I grew up camping in the short, hot summers that grace the mountainous interior of BC, but it was a new experience for Simon, my Englishman. We drove through the Fraser Valley on the Trans-Canada Highway, the thin rope of road that runs from BC to Newfoundland; sometimes it feels like this road is the only thing that holds the enormous blurry entity called 'Canada' together, that and the CBC, the Canadian Broadcasting Corporation. We stopped at Harrison Hot Springs at the south end of Harrison Lake. The water there is a remarkable azure turquoise blue common to glacial lakes; the colour is caused by the refraction of light off particles of glacial silt suspended in the water. After lunch we drove on to set up our tent at Emory Creek, a campsite just the other side of the Fraser River from Hope. The site had been an encampment for Chinese indentured labourers brought over to help build the railway in the 1880s; you could argue that the Chinese, not the British, built BC. Nothing remained of what had once been a thriving community.

Provincial campsites, administered by the Province of BC, are wonderful places. Each site has a fire pit, a picnic table, room for a big car and a tent, and enough trees around so that it's hard to see your neighbours. We put up the tent and discovered that it was a pup-tent, the perfect size for a child and, therefore, a little cosy for the two of us, but that didn't matter. We cooked veggie burgers over the campfire, swatted the mosquitoes and went for a hike. Our sleep was punctuated by the rumble of freight trains as they moved down the narrow valley and, in the morning, when we woke up, the air was fresh and cool and smelt of pine and brewing coffee.

Our destination on this trip was the Queen Charlotte Islands, an archipelago just south of the Alaskan panhandle, off the northern coast of BC. We camped our way up the highway, past countless lakes, through gold-rush ghost towns, following the course of the mighty Fraser as it churns through the land for 500 miles before we turned off at Prince George and headed out to the coast. Up here the province flattens out for a while, and becomes a land of ranching and horses, the winters too long and harsh for agriculture. Towards Prince Rupert, the northern port, the towns become more closely identified with the aboriginal people who live there. In Kitwanga we saw teenagers spearing salmon as the fish headed up the river; Indians are the only people still allowed to fish this way. In BC salmon travel great distances in search of their spawning grounds, as much as 800 miles inland from the Pacific.

The interior of the province is hot and dry in the summer, while the coast remains cool and damp, much of it covered with temperate rain forest. In Prince Rupert it is always raining. It feels as though it might rain there every day. An old and rotting town of lumber yards and fish canneries, Prince Rupert has a slightly dandified port; you can get a great meal of halibut and chips while you sit and watch the otters play down below where fresh water spills into the sea. It was drizzling when we arrived and it was drizzling at seven the next morning when we drove out to catch the ferry to the Charlottes. This ferry takes seven hours to get to its destination, across the shallow and rough-watered Hecate Strait.

The Queen Charlotte Islands, or Haida Gwaii, as the area is now known in more politically astute circles, is composed of two big islands, Graham and Moresby, and a whole lot of smaller islands that cling to their sides. The southern half of Moresby, accessible by boat only, is now a World Heritage Site: abandoned Haida villages disintegrate in the mist, cedar totem poles and longhouses are reclaimed by the rain forest. We stayed on the more northerly Graham Island, where there is a road; we had decided not to camp, given the climate and the likelihood that the little tent would be unable to keep out the rain.

Without a boat it is difficult to see much of the Charlottes. On Graham Island there are three towns. Queen Charlotte City is tiny and charming, with wooden houses strung out along the driftwood beach and great blue herons tiptoeing along the log-booms in the bay. This is where the white people live. Its neighbour, Skidegate, a Haida town with a beautiful museum of Haida artefacts and totem poles that run down to the sea, is just a couple of miles along the road, beyond where the ferries dock. At the top end of the island is Masset, an altogether more depressing place, with a naval base and a wide open, rather drunken, small-town atmosphere. From Masset you can drive out to one end of the longest and emptiest beaches I have ever seen, Agate Beach. When the tide goes out, it exposes half a mile of grey sand, riddled with clam holes. The water teems with crab, and to catch them all you need is a pair of wellies, a net and a tape measure for making sure they are big enough to keep. In law-abiding BC, keeping undersized shellfish and salmon is seen as an immoral act, tantamount to adultery, child abuse and dropping litter in the street.

We stayed in a little green motel on the road out to the beach. The owner invited us into his office, which was actually his kitchen, for a cup of coffee. It turned out the other units were all filled with American soldiers up from Washington State on some kind of recce. They'd been out to the beach and caught hundreds of enormous crab and were having a cook-out on the motel lawn. They asked if we would like to join them, so we did for a while, helping them drink their American beer while we wondered, but did not ask, where they kept their weapons.

The next day, through the drizzle we saw an eagle grab a flounder at the mouth of the river. As we tramped through the forest we came across a ruined cottage with a gone-wild kitchen garden out back, rhododendrons twenty feet high. The dense undergrowth of the island is peppered with the remains of boilerhouses and steam engines and buildings long since collapsed, abandoned by settlers who fled these too distant islands at the beginning of the century; although the climate is relatively mild and certain crops thrive, the cost of shipping to and from the mainland has always proved too high for any industry to survive, making the cost of living very steep.

I'd never been to the Charlottes before, but I know I'll go back. To me it feels like what the coast around Vancouver must have been like before a million people moved in, ultra-natural. There is a lot of mist, and a lot of scary fog, and a lot of muffled quiet. It truly feels like the land that time forgot, except for the fact that it's the one part of BC where the aboriginal people have met with real success when it comes to securing self-government. They control the lucrative tourist fishing and hunting trade, as well as having won other concessions from the government. In BC, language politics parallel that of the US, where 'Negro' became 'Black' became 'African-American'; 'Indian', in BC, became 'Native Indian' became 'First Nations', and the Queen Charlotte Islands will officially become Haida Gwaii in due course. It is not a coincidence that the Haida have been so successful with land claims in a part of the province that has no real economic growth potential, a place so remote to the people down south that it doesn't really matter who controls it. But still, victories are important, however small, especially to the beleaguered aboriginal people of North America.

The one disappointment we had on this trip was that we didn't see any major wildlife. We saw the minor players in abundance – eagles, otters, seals – but I had promised Simon the animals of my childhood: from the ferry, whales and dolphin; inland, elk, moose, bear, perhaps even a grizzly. They failed to appear, even in the campsites on the mainland, where bear warnings were posted and we were told to make sure to lock all our food into the boot of the car at night.

At the end of the week we took the ferry back to the mainland and spent another sodden night in Prince Rupert. The following day we took yet another ferry, this time from Prince Rupert all the way down the coast to the northern tip of Vancouver Island. Journey time is around fifteen hours and the boat travels through the Inside Passage, a narrow waterway between islands and mainland; on either side mountains roar upward, slashed by glaciers and fjords. The ferry was full of German tourists and we found this a little odd. We were used to European holiday destinations – the south of France, Spain – being full of Germans, but hadn't expected to find them on a ferry in northern BC. In Port Hardy we stayed in a bed and breakfast where the owners plied us with home-made red wine and showed us their scuba-diving photos until the small hours. They were a strange pair, he seemed especially shifty, and we thought they might abduct us into a weird sex cult. Then we drove down the island in one great sweep, speeding past barren mountainsides where there had been clear-cut logging and where forest fires had done untold damage, crawling through the endless small towns with their strip malls and gas stations, closing our eyes and dreaming of Haida Gwaii, our foot on the gas pedal all the way to sunny Victoria.

Sunny Victoria. Why do I hate this place? Yes, it is full of dreadful cod

Britishness – red double-decker buses, high tea, Madame Tussaud's, tweed – but it is also very beautifully situated on the south end of the mellow island with views of the Olympic Mountains across the sea. The UN recently published a report claiming that Canada is the best place in the world to live – highest incomes, longest life-expectancy, least pollution, best state education, etc. – and Victoria epitomizes all that. People walk to work; strangers speak to one another in the street. Spring comes earlier than anywhere else in Canada and life is good for most people.

I used to think that everyone hated where they grew up, everyone burned to move away, but I've since learned that this is not the case. I know a number of Londoners who are Londoners still and wouldn't, couldn't, live anywhere else. I know Jamaicans who've gone back to Jamaica, South Africans who've returned to post-apartheid Cape Town, Australians who've gone home; I even have one friend I've known since primary school who's gone back to Victoria. But not me. Why? On the journey home I take the ferry and pass through a fog, that incredible shrinking fog, but instead of getting physically smaller, I diminish mentally, relapsing into my former, childhood self, in particular my perpetually unhappy, tortured, pompous teenage self. When I was sixteen I used to write terrible poetry – who didn't? – and it makes me cringe – shrink – even now: 'I push a pen like Sisyphus pushes a rock/uphill/straining', the emphasis on that loud and lonely 'I'. And yet it still has a grip on me, the country of my childhood, and as I get older I find my thoughts returning there with increasing frequency.

I have two fantasies about going back to live in BC. One involves gracious high-rise living in Vancouver; I'd live downtown in English Bay in a tall, narrow apartment building with a swimming pool on the ground floor and a glorious ocean view out of the twentieth. I'd do my shopping in the posh organic supermarkets, I'd eat out in the fabulous restaurants, I'd cycle around the sea-wall in Stanley Park every day. On the weekends I'd go sailing in summer and skiing in winter and in spring I'd do both activities in the same day. I'd be calm, relaxed, slightly tanned and healthy.

The other fantasy involves going Back to Nature. I'd live on a small island, a barely inhabited island that the ferry reaches only once a week. I'd dwell in a house built of cedar wood with large windows and a wide veranda overlooking a small rocky bay. On sunny days I'd potter about in a canoe and when the mist came in, when the creepy fog rolled down, I'd stay wrapped up warm inside my house, in front of the fire, making cups of tea and writing.

But here I am in London, city of my dreams. And here I am in Britain, a country that has made me welcome, however much I've resisted its charms. I've always said I live in London, not England, that the two can be separated, and in many ways they can. But the fact of the matter is that London is a solid part – the heart perhaps, or at the very least the cirrhotic liver – of the UK. Perpetual tourist status is an illusion that suits me; it helps me feel creative, free. And at night when I'm in bed asleep the ferry comes to reclaim me – the good ferry, the BC ferry – and I'm off through the fog once again.

Mirror Images

BOSNIA

Back home to a city of screaming police sirens. To newspaper reports of paedophile clerics, of politicians taking backhanders, of syringe attacks on taxi drivers. Where pavements are stained with chewing gum and urine and where – last week – two women lay all afternoon on the footpath outside my house, red-faced and purple-legged, their minds wiped out by alcohol. To a city where the body of a murdered woman was found, discarded, by a rubbish skip . . .

Here, in my own city – Dublin – I pin photographs of Bosnia on the wall of my study to remind me of the benign and fruitful countryside I travelled through last October. And as I stare at them, a road sweeper passes my window, diligently sweeping the gutter. A man cycles up the street whistling, both feet shrouded in white plastic bags against the rain. A horse and cart clatters down in the other direction, the driver enthroned on an old car seat, behind him on the cart a doorless fridge, a television, a battered armchair. Chattering children skip along the footpath on their way to school and six loaves of bread, delivered at seven a.m., will sit on the steps of the pub opposite, untouched, until the bar staff arrive. At my local shop, beggars regularly ask for – and are given – a bun, a cabbage, a few oranges. This is boom-town Dublin, a thriving European capital. Places, like people, have more than one face . . .

And so it was in Bosnia, after four years of war and a peace less than a year old. I have no television so never saw the pleading faces, the shuffling lines of refugees, the burning houses. *My* image leads me back to an autumn that flames through wooded hills, to orchards bright with incandescent plums. To yellowing corn, green meadow grass, cabbages large as footballs: the year is being gathered in, the land and its people at peace. Some households have even permitted themselves the flighty luxury of a small garden, bright now with the yellow of evening primroses. In the fields, whole families – the women in long skirts, heads wound round with scarves – rake over the hay, leaving it in piles for the men to pitch up on to the top of tall haycocks moulded round narrow branches stuck upright into the ground. They cut the hay three times a year and disbelief crosses their faces when I tell them that in damp, soggy Ireland the farmers save it once – if they're lucky.

Luck plays a part in the game here too, though the stakes are higher. Death is only one footstep away for, though the densely wooded hills may appear beautiful, lying along the climbing goat paths that lace their slopes, hidden deep in the grassy fields or tucked away behind the door of a bombed-out hillside farmhouse, lethal mines have been placed with seeming carelessness. Anti-personnel mines nowadays are made to maim, blinding or crippling their victims rather than killing them: wounded survivors, needing to be fed and cared for, give more grief to the enemy. So, though the war is over, homes will remain empty and land uncultivated for many years to come.

But in fields where cattle graze and people work, you know it's safe – or as safe as anything can be in Bosnia. The late-afternoon sun shines down on men sharpening their scythes, on women tossing the hay, on small children put to sleep in the shadow of a tall haycock. It's a rural idyll, as peaceful a scene as you might get anywhere in this country until you learn that, the other day, two farmers walking across a field a few miles further north trod on a piece of metal and were blown to bits.

This news takes the warmth out of the sun and leaves me feeling uneasy. It's not normal for violence and death to walk hand in hand in the sunshine. Sunny days are for picnics, for lying in the long grass, for taking a bottle of water and setting out to walk across a bog. But then this is not a normal world. It's one turned upside-down; one in which, from the leading car of an exuberant wedding cavalcade, a triumphal hand extends, holding aloft a grenade; where the presence of foreign soldiers and their clanking armoury is not threatening but reassuring and where home-going horse-drawn carts, trundling along on rubber tyres, share the potholed roads with tanks, armoured personnel carriers and army trucks. Long accustomed to encountering the blackened faces of heavily armed British army soldiers manning checkpoints along the border between Northern Ireland and the Republic, I recoiled at first when I saw a jaunty cockaded beret on top of a menacing tank stationed outside a shop or a mosque. To local people, of course, armoured cars and tanks and guns are simply the furnishings of post-war Bosnia and most people are glad they're there.

The road is marked, every so often, by Muslim burial grounds where the old carved and turbaned stones of Islam lean haphazardly towards each other for comfort and support. On some stones a ragged piece of green cloth flutters, showing that it is a young person who lies beneath the soil.

Mevlida tells me this – this and lots of other things. She wears the international uniform of the young: a baggy blue sweater, blue jeans, hands lost in the sleeves of her khaki coat. Her black hair is thick and long, her face devoid of make-up. Before the war disrupted her life, she used to sing in a local band. Next year, she will go to Sarajevo University to read philosophy. Mevlida is twenty-three, young for her age but old and hardened as well: some of her schoolfriends did not survive the war. Like many young people in Bosnia, she's been learning English from an early age, her knowledge of it expanded by watching English-language films and listening to pop songs. We first met when, with a group of Irish people, I joined a team of international supervisors sent to Bosnia for the 1996 elections. Mevlida had been assigned to me as an interpreter. On Sundays, when we weren't working, she took me to meet her parents, her friends, and to the places where she'd played as a child. Most days Mevlida was bright and chirpy, but sometimes she settled into silence, her pale face drawn and tired-looking, and I thought of the rogue card fate had dealt her.

This part of Bosnia – in the extreme north-west corner of the Bihac enclave, close to the Croatian border – suffered a war within a war when Fikret Abdić, a local, charismatic businessman (or crook, or maverick Bosniak* leader, depending on the teller of the tale) tried to broker his own peace with both Serbs and Croats. In so doing, he precipitated a deadly power struggle within not only his own town of Velika Kladusa but the whole of the Bihac region. The rotten fruits of this local war – in which Bosniak neighbours killed each other – still show on the walls of houses, where the marks of a mortar radiate like the blossoming of a flower. On other walls the gaping wounds of more lethal hits have been boarded over.

Mevlida hates the businessman – now in hiding somewhere in Croatia – because his war meant she was sent away from home, for safety, for nine months. *Her* hero is a young commander of the 5th Corps of the Bosnian Army 505 Brigade who, forming an alliance with the Croats and backed by the US, fought against the businessman and his Serb-backed army during the latter part of the war and who died at the age of thirty, ambushed and shot in the neck while trying to liaise with a Croatian platoon.

We drive out to visit his grave on the hillside overlooking the small

* Bosniak is a secular term used to describe all Bosnians of Muslim origin, some of whom are Muslim in name only.

town of Buzim. It's a peaceful spot, with only four or five graves, all sited on a sloping field a few feet away from a gathering of houses. The gravestone, neat and upright, reads: 'Izet Nanić 1965–1995'. His brother, who died three years earlier, is buried close by.

Standing on another hill at the edge of Buzim is a large mosque, its tall, narrow minaret aimed heavenwards, rigid as a streamlined rocket.

The young soldier who takes our money at the one-roomed war museum in Buzim leans his crutch against the table and struggles to his feet to point out bits of twisted metal, old hunting rifles, maps, a scattering of photographs – and a packet of Colombian cigarettes, date-marked 1974. 'We liberated them from Abdić's store. He had whole cases of them, to sell to people,' he said and then smiled. 'They tasted dreadful – but they were better than nothing.'

The photos of Nanić show a strong-faced young man, battledress collar turned up against the snows of winter. I can see why Mevlida fancied him. But he went to war at the age of twenty-six and died four years later. Did he have time, I wonder, to feel the solace of a woman's hands on his soldier's body?

You won't find Buzim in the index of any of the many books written about Bosnia although the town took the brunt of this local war. 'The world looked at Buzim with closed eyes,' said the young soldier. 'We would have been like Srebrenica except that we fought back. And we won, but so many people have been killed – fathers and brothers – that it means a bad tomorrow for our children.'

Mevlida's former primary-school teacher in Velika Kladusa fought as well. Not from the beginning of the war, though. At first, he continued working in his school as best he could. Then he began travelling out, under fire, to teach children trapped in outlying villages. Eventually, he took to the hills and joined the 5th Corps. His metal crutch, propped against his desk, is painted a cheerful blue. 'Before the war,' he says, 'I'd been a teacher for ten years.' The light in his eyes is soft, his smile is gentle and his hands gesture outwards, pleading for understanding. I can't imagine those same hands cupping a grenade, cradling a rifle, focusing on a target, finger curling into the trigger . . . pulling it. His face, finely sculpted, is not that of a killer. Then he turns away to light a cigarette and in profile I see a different face, the jawline hardened, the nose lumpy, the lower lip full and slack: a coarse face. This is a person I hadn't known was there. Perhaps he hadn't known either, until he picked up a gun. Two people in one man. War brings out what's already there – the best and the worst in us.

Once, hearing about a revolutionary desert society that had dispensed with money, I loaded a tent and sleeping bag on the back of my bike, cycled down through France to Marseilles and crossed over to Algiers. I wanted to see this fiscal phenomenon for myself. It also provided me with the excuse most travel writers need when asked the impossible question: why did you go there? The Saharawi soldiers – members of the guerrilla Polisario army – took me out into the desert and, one empty afternoon, passed the time lying on the sand taking pot shots at a Coca-Cola can with their rifles. But when Ahmed handed me his and they all looked with interest to see how good a shot I might be, a wave of nausea overcame me and I couldn't touch it. The soldiers laughed and returned to their game: it was as they had expected. Later, marching through the night, we had to throw ourselves to the ground as a Moroccan flare went up. Lying closest to where the flare had come from, and envisaging my legs raked by gunfire, I dispensed with loyalty to my desert guides and made a mental note that next time I would make sure that, when hitting the ground, there was a soldier between me and any gunfire. Treachery and survival can go hand in hand.

We go to visit Mevlida's beloved grandmother, who still lives on a sloping hillside in the old family homestead. Mevlida and her friends often walk out of town and up the hill to spend the night there. Today, however, there's no one in so Mevlida wanders off down the slope of the garden. When I follow, I find her checking three sturdy cannabis plants thriving undetected among her grandmother's respectable corn. I stand watching her, sniffing the spicy smoke that rises from a bonfire of corn husks and papery maize leaves and drifts over from a neighbouring farmyard. In the distance, the round thud of axe against wood springs from house to house: winters are cold here, the electricity supply at best unreliable, at worst non-existent. Already, the distant mountain tops are tipped with snow and September is not yet over.

There's a farewell party in the dimly lit hotel in Velika Kladusa. Mevlida sings a song about a young man of twenty, a schoolfriend, gunned down not far from the town. I had expected a soulful lament but her voice is confident and strong, making me realize how little I really know her. Later, the waiter strums a guitar and sings a song as sad and as mournful as his dark eyes. He is courteous, bows when he serves a drink, wears a white shirt rakishly open at the neck and a jacket black as his thick hair. When someone else takes over the guitar, he starts to dance, raising his arms above his head, a white hankie like a flag of surrender in one hand. He is a Serb, living alone among the people *his* people sought to destroy. But everyone dances with him, weaving a circle that dips and rises with his rhythm, turning their bodies in time to his, hips and shoulders moving to his music.

Outside in the darkness there are gunshots as people still celebrate the election results. It's been an edgy time. Voters couldn't understand why the portrait of President Alija Izetbegović – standing again for the presidency – had to be removed from the walls of classrooms doubling as polling stations when he had played such an important role in the Dayton peace negotiations. Nor could they understand how Fikret Abdić was allowed to stand as a candidate when he was perceived by so many as a war criminal. The explanation – that anyone had a right to stand who had not been indicted by the Court of Human Rights at The Hague – left them shaking their heads in disbelief at the strange workings of democracy. When tempers rose, shots were fired from deep within neighbouring woods or from somewhere among the blocks of high-rise flats. It was a way of letting off steam. As election day drew near and tension reached simmering point, huge armoured tanks rumbled into town, growling round the square until everything had quietened down again.

On 14 September, however, all tanks and military vehicles were confined to barracks while school playgrounds filled up with tractors, carts and beribboned horses as electors came to cast their votes, the majority in favour of Alija Izetbegović. Now, a week later, although no one is supposed to have a gun, there are still celebratory shots being fired.

'We did a sweep last week,' said a British army peace-keeper, 'and rounded up 365 weapons.' Some they missed.

Four forty-five a.m. in the square of Velika Kladusa. An autumn chill in the air. People huddle in thin coats. I pull the sleeves of my cotton jacket down over my hands. With the elections over, I'm free to travel round Bosnia on my own and my first journey is the long bus ride southwards to Sarajevo. I'd been told that independent travel round Bosnia was impossible because nothing worked. Further, it was said to be risky: the British Foreign Office had the country on its list of dangerous places, advising people to travel only if their journey was absolutely necessary. Mine was, I decided. I wanted not only to see Sarajevo but to stay there. Its citizens' will to survive was inspiring, its bombed landscape an icon to survival. It had always been an international city and now its continuing existence was proof that even against the ugliest of nationalist wars, people with a broader vision of the world could hold out.

I'd made inquiries among local people and discovered that there was, in fact, a perfectly viable, if slow-moving, network of coaches back in place – a legacy of communism, when public transport and public housing were priority services. Now I was off . . .

A coach pulls in and picks up a few passengers. Warmth pours from the open door. Its streamlined comfort and smart appearance tell their own story: Croatian-owned, it's heading home across the border down the road to Zagreb. *My* bus – going the other way – is a local one with worn seats and cold metal armrests. It's run by the company formerly owned by Fikret Abdić – until he left town with a trailer-load of Deutschmarks. The driver smokes, the radio blares, condensation streams down the windows. But it's a bus and it leaves for Sarajevo promptly at five a.m. In nine hours' time, we'll be there.

The bus interior is cold and the only thing I have for extra warmth is a slippery electric-blue plastic raincoat I bought in Dublin for three pounds for the occasional rainy day. I had expected an Adriatic climate but most of the time got Irish weather – chilly, damp and muddy underfoot, with only the odd sunny autumnal day. My fine leather walking boots, bought in Cape Town, are not waterproof and I'd been forced to line them with plastic bags. After a month of rain and of replacing the bags – which are not easy to come by – I've given up caring about the tattered bits of plastic which flap over the tops of my socks.

The windows are steamed up, concealing the dripping countryside through which we're passing. Our first stop is the bus station at Cazim, where Mr Tahirović works as a waiter. It's too early for the café to be open and, in any case, I'm glad. Mr Tahirović is a hospitable man who farms his bit of land as best he can under these difficult conditions. We met many times during the election as he was an election officer with responsibility for his committee, his polling station, and for liaising with me. He and his handsome wife have a large family, one child born every year for eight years. The waitering job is a financial necessity, but I couldn't bear to see him trapped behind a counter, dispensing cups of bus-station coffee. He often invited me into his house for a glass of his own slivovitz and when he took a great fancy to my Antiguan baseball hat I gave it to him. In return, he took down from a high shelf a well-worn, black-tasselled maroon fez and presented it to me. One of my photographs shows us both standing in the farmyard, proud in our respective headgear.

There aren't many people on the bus: a lad in a black, mock-leather bomber jacket, a young woman huddled miserably into her coat, an old countrywoman in a long skirt and wearing two scarves – a flowered outdoor one on top of her white indoor one. She puffs and sighs and shakes her head and says something to me which I don't understand, but I nod anyway.

The road climbs, then switchbacks down into Bihac. When I was last here, an aid worker gave me directions to the bridge across the Una: 'You turn into the road that runs alongside the river, just by the bomb crater. Where the three little girls were killed.'

In this mountainous region the towns and villages, nestling in small, saucer-shaped plains, were vulnerable to mortar attacks and sniper fire from the surrounding hills. Bihac, a UN 'safe area', was overlooked on three sides by hostile hills. The crater, marking the spot where the children had died, was shallow, little more than a scooping out of the road surface. I stared down at the puddle of muddy water in it, imagining the little girls skipping home happily from school. Three dead and it was such a small hole. Somehow, I had expected something more.

The devastation continues: houses stand blasted and burnt, roof timbers methodically removed to prevent the former owners returning to them. Sometimes, among the devastation, we pass a small pile of blackened rubble which at first seems like the charred remains of a cupboard or a shed but which I finally realize is the compacted remains of a home, reduced by war to the irreducible. Occasionally, a kilometre of ruined buildings is interrupted by a few houses intact and occupied. Who, I wondered, lived in the surviving ones? Being on the right side was a matter of life and death but how did you know which was the right side when you might not always know which direction the enemy was coming from? It reminded me of the story of a stranger visiting Belfast for the first time. A gun is suddenly put to his back as he walks along a dark street. Are you for or against? asks the man behind him.

Some houses show defiant signs of life: the green and white crescent flag of the ruling party fluttering from a shattered roof top or a profusion of red geraniums cascading from a window ledge. The fighting in this area was fierce, with Croats and Serbs at times allied against the Bosniaks, at other times fighting each other. Towns were fought over, won and then either annihilated or isolated from outside help.

War can highlight not only the vulnerability of different peoples but also the accidental geography of their dwellings. Historically, a ford was always an important place where, sooner or later, a market stall or an inn appeared as people saw the opportunity to capitalize on passing trade. From these small beginnings grew great cities served by gracious and magnificent bridges. But in Bosnia the *worst* place to live was near a bridge, and in this mountainous country there are many rivers. Time and time again, we passed houses on each side of a river-crossing pockmarked with mortars. Yet only half a kilometre back from the river, the houses would be intact. Those very qualities which in peacetime make such places attractive to live in in war render them deadly.

The young woman across the aisle shakes herself out of her coat, rummages in her plastic bag for a couple of bananas, hands one across to the old countrywoman and starts eating one herself. Taking a cue from this, I pass a piece of bread and cheese over the seat to the old woman. She takes them as her due.

Our journey south continues through a dismal cloud of rain. At one point, we join a long queue and everyone cranes sideways to see what the hold-up is. As the bus inches forward, I see that we have to negotiate a strip of bomb-damaged road leading to what was once a bridge. An army Bailey bridge now straddles the gap but the constant rain has worried away at the foundations in which the bridge is set and the clay is slipping down a steep incline towards the river. Sitting over the wheels of the bus, I monitor the distance between them and the drop. Six inches between life and death.

As we edge along the margin of yellow shifting mud, horns blare, lorries push forward into spaces not big enough to contain them, drivers lean out of their cab windows shouting and, not for the first time on my many travels, I long for a spot of English discipline, a dash of sang-froid. To stay calm, I set myself a task: to memorize a four-figure code for my new bike combination lock. As an *aide-mémoire* for these things, I always choose dates significant in the history of Ireland and England, which means I have a wide choice: 1014, 1066, 1381, 1649, 1798, 1914, 1916, 1918. So why do I find in my Bosnia notebook the numbers 6214? Even now I rack my brains to think what they might refer to, though the mark in the book, heavily scored, should be enough to remind me that they mean nothing and that the whole exercise was merely a frenzied displacement activity. When fear takes over, any number will do.

We edge along mountain roads, close to Banja Luka in Republika Srpska, moving from one military checkpoint to another. Near the town of Kluc, I suddenly glimpse, painted on the wall of an army hut, the words 'The Minstrel Boy'. Had I been on my own, I would have investigated further, but trapped in the bus I can merely stare and ponder. 'The Minstrel Boy' is a popular traditional Irish marching tune, played at parades, at the start of sporting competitions and on any occasion where the spirit needs lifting. The tune is rousing indeed but the words are fearful:

> The minstrel boy to the war has gone
> In the ranks of death you will find him.
> His father's sword he has girded on
> And his wild harp slung behind him.

I wondered how the words came to be there and later discovered that 'The Minstrel Boy' is a slow march often used by the Royal Irish Regiment, a company of which had served in the Kluc area.

I rarely carry guidebooks with me. For one thing, they're too heavy. For another, I've usually got the skeleton of my own itinerary already planned out. Today, however, I have with me a guidebook of sorts. Called *The Death of Yugoslavia* and based on a BBC TV series about the war, it chronicles not the best places to stay or the sights to see or the tastiest dish of the region but the battles, the front lines, the bargaining, the horse trading, the jockeying for position by powers big and small. As we pass through each town, I search for its name in the index. Jajce I already know as the place where, in 1943, Tito was appointed leader of the new Yugoslavia. Some fifty years later, surrounded by the Serb army, some 40,000 of Jajce's fearful citizens – both Bosniak and Croat – abandoned their town to the advancing Serbs and set out along the road my bus is now travelling. The route to Travnik – the next town – was a dangerous one, for the fleeing refugees were hampered by the October weather and by what they were carrying with them. From their vantage point high up in the wooded hills which overlook the road, the Serbs bombarded them with mortars and machine-gun fire. As the wheels of the bus thud along, I think of the tired, panic-stricken feet that trudged this route: old feet, small feet, wounded feet. My map shows that it's about seventy kilometres to Travnik and I wonder why they didn't take the shorter route. Until I realize it's a rocky mountain road and was probably mined.

My heart sinks as we get nearer to Sarajevo. I'll have to leave the safety of the bus and I'm not certain yet where I'm going to stay or indeed what the city will be like after four years of war. Will it be full of sad, stricken people? Will I feel uncomfortable to be among them yet surreptitiously looking at them, searching for signs of suffering? Will my idea of a people triumphing over war prove to be nothing more than a wished-for ideal, sanitized and unreal?

I was last in Sarajevo in the 1970s on a family holiday and have held, in my mind's eye, the image a city of cobbled streets clustering round its old, domed mosques. Tito was still alive, people had the basic necessities for living and – oh, wondrous memory – there were no hoardings advertising soap powder or jeans. Driving down through Slovenia, into Banja Luka, picking up the strange music of Bosnia on the car radio, ending up on a campsite in Slano, near Dubrovnik, we were told, time and time again, that Yugoslavia was made up of different peoples, different languages, different religions. Aware – but not enough – of the complex features that both united and divided the country, we failed to appreciate the miracle Tito had brought about in holding together these many, disparate strands.

Now, approaching a city that had endured a siege of 1,375 days – longer than that of Leningrad – a siege during which 10,615 people died, 1,601 of them children, I was apprehensive . . .

I needn't have worried. Sarajevo has grabbed me by the throat and threatened me with hope. Bright yellow trams trundle up and down the main streets of the city. *Pride and Prejudice* is showing at the nearby cinema. The film festival has just ended, an art exhibition has just opened. Music beats out from the crowded cafés and smart young

women tap along the pavements in their sling-backs. Sadness is
evident, of course, for everyone is grieving, but the time of peace has
finally arrived. The people smile, play chess, sit in the sun and watch
their children and grandchildren playing. This is a city that has risen
from the ashes of a war not of its own making.

My room has a thick wool carpet. White, lacy, full-length curtains
hang along two sides of its walls. In the street below my window, a
huge lorry sways past like a desert caravan, Turkish music weaving
round the green, white and crescented flags that fly triumphantly
from all four corners. My bed, a red plush divan, is piled high with
big snow-white, lace-edged pillows. I feel as if I am in a Turkish
boudoir.

Sarajevo is a resourceful city. Just as they did before the war, many
women now rent out rooms in their apartments as a means of making
a little money. Bedra is one of them. Her front room is now my room,
while she herself sleeps on a settee in the sitting room. This is a house
of women. Apart from Bedra and her sister – both widows – there
is Bedra's daughter, Aida, who lives nearby, and *her* sixteen-year-old
daughter, Suzanne, who often stays the night. There is also Bedra's
niece, Zetra, who was offered a place as a refugee in Sweden but has
returned to Sarajevo and hopes to get a job as an interpreter with one
of the many aid agencies. And finally, there is Amira, Bedra's young
cousin from Tuzla, who works as a receptionist at the Holiday Inn.
And me. The little bathroom is always festooned with dripping tights
and bras, blouses and pants. The water is turned on for only a few
hours each morning, when we all have to do our washing.

Most evenings I eat, furtively and silently, in the privacy of my Turkish
boudoir – yoghurt, bread, cheese, plums – then spend a good five
minutes on my hands and knees picking up the crumbs from the
thick red carpet, fearful Bedra will discover my sin. *Her* eating takes
place, properly and tidily, in the cramped kitchen, but I don't like to

intrude. Later, as quietly as I can, I unscrew the top of the plastic bottle given to me by Mr Tahirović. Slivovitz seduces you with smoothness – then gives you a kick in the stomach . . .

There's not a lot to do on a Sunday afternoon for the bored young British soldiers, part of the NATO force, who, pony- and pig-tailed, wander up and down the narrow, cobbled streets of the old Turkish market – Bascarsija – guns slung over their shoulders.

'Sarajevo's a dump,' one of them tells me, and her comrades-in-arms agree. They can't wait to get back home. I wander round too, and by the old clock tower, close to the Street of the Saracens, discover, through a gateway, a bakery where you can buy fresh, warm bread. A journalist I met who worked for *Oslobodenje*, the newspaper that continued to appear all through the war, told me his sole job throughout the siege was to locate and publish places in the city where bread was available. Queues, however, were what the Serb army liked most and on the first day of May in 1992 a mortar dropped out of the sky on top of a bread queue, killing seventeen people.

Beside the clock tower is the Gazi Husrev Bey Mosque, the height of its dome exactly the sum of the length and width of the building. I stand, innumerate and humble, looking up at it, reminding myself that it was the star-gazing Arabs who gave us our mathematics.

There are people I want to meet while I'm in Sarajevo, but making contact takes time. Messages left on machines go unanswered. Calls are not returned. People are out of their offices. After four years of war, they have more important things to do than answer the intrusive questionings of a foreign writer. In any case, no one wants to hurry. I adjust to the rhythm and take a walk along the embankment, crossing and recrossing bridges. The one on which the Archduke was shot is no longer of interest. I sit in cafés drinking coffee, hang about in the Cybernet Café talking to other customers – a student from Sarajevo University, an aid worker from Ghana, a man with a laptop who keeps looking at me over the top of his month-old *Guardian*. (I suspect he's a journalist who doesn't want to let on.) I even go to the daily news conference held by I-FOR, the international peace-keeping force used as a front by NATO. From the platform, military and civilian spokespersons run through a menu of press statements: '. . . common desire to defuse the situation . . . defusing of the situation continues . . . we continue to be deeply concerned . . . a helpful and constructive meeting took place . . . 100 bodies exhumed'.

I-FOR troops have completed another swoop and the collection of arms they have confiscated is on display: ugly pieces of metal – lethal and foreshortened – which serve as rough and ready weapons, a variety of handguns and one personalized AK47 covered in football club emblems, Smiley stickers and pretty flower transfers.

I-FOR's big problem at the moment is that people keep going back to the homes from which they had been driven by their neighbours-turned-enemy, without first waiting for them to be declared clear of mines. But worse, they have been reclaiming their homes without presenting the official bit of paper that shows they really did live there once. The former inhabitants can't see the point of this. Why should they bother with a bit of paper when everyone knows it's their home? They've got to get back to get the hay in, harvest the maize, chop the wood, repair the roof before the winter sets in. Anyway, deeds and documents were all lost in the war. The UNHCR people, however, are adamant: no one returns to their home without the bit of paper. If it can't be be found, then there are proper channels to go through to obtain a piece of paper.

Still intent on getting in touch with people – Ibrahim Spahic, well-known artistic entrepreneur who wants to bring a Joyce exhibition to the city for next year's Sarajevo Spring Festival, a woman who organizes tours of the city, the mayor of Tuzla – I've forgotten that I've also come to look again at Sarajevo and so decide to spend an afternoon wandering in and out of mosques. For nearly 300 years Sarajevo was ruled by the Turkish grand vizier – *saraj* means palace – and at one time there were seventy-three mosques in the old city. Although many of the minarets have been damaged, a surprising number still stand tall and unharmed. How was that, I asked an old man clearing up debris around a courtyard, and he indicated a zigzag flight path with his hand: Allah had guided the bombs and mortars *between* the minarets.

My favourite mosque is the lovely old Ali Pasha Mosque, with its one main dome and three small ones. It took a hit during the war and now the workmen are inside, whistling as they repair the roof timbers. The man in charge shakes his head and looks up at the place from which the mortars came – the malevolent hills which now look so peaceful and serene in the late September sunshine.

It's only a few minutes' walk from here to what was once the National Library. Standing within its ruined walls, I close my eyes and it's 25 August 1992. The great Moorish-style building, the only one of its kind in Bosnia, constructed during the days of the Austro-Hungarian empire, has finally succumbed to the mortars that have been pounding it all day. Fires burn on all its floors, fanned by winds that blow in through the blasted windows and down from the gutted roof. Books and archives crackle, bits of paper waft this way and that, caught in the hot currents of air that eddy from floor to floor. Later, when it rains, 2 million books and papers – the most precious collection of Ottoman manuscripts in the country – are reduced to a sodden mess. And the person who ordered this destruction? Nikola Koljević – vice-president of the Bosnian Serbs, one-time Professor of Literature at Sarajevo University, author of six books on Shakespeare. Wanting to make sure the treasure was totally destroyed, he ordered the building to be not simply bombed but fire-bombed.

Today, standing in a shaft of sunlight that beams down through the fractured roof girders, I see in the building an enduring beauty, as if the spirit of the manuscripts and books it had once cherished had seeped into the stone of its walls, its arches, its wide staircase, giving to it an immortality all of its own.

The sun sends light angling on to the once-tiled floor, catching the blues and reds of the stained-glass windows, throwing shadows among the pillars and into the remains of the small anterooms, so that the whole scene has the look of a medieval painting spliced with shade and light, rich in Franciscan browns and olive greens. Reflected in the pools of rain on the floor are the criss-cross lines of girders hanging below the gaping, pentagonal roof – a watery image of a world turned upside-down. (On 17 January 1997, five years after he had ordered the destruction of the National Library, and indeed of Sarajevo, Nikola Koljević put a gun to his head and shot himself.)

My dreams here are all nightmares. The waters of sleep that I should be moving through each night turn to stormy currents that leave me feeling uneasy. Outside my window, a river rushes past. If I open the window, I'll be sucked into it. The next night, I put out bread for the birds but they screech and fight over every crumb. The following night I stand in a queue that never moves. I try to edge into another queue but no one will give way. So much queuing and not enough food, not enough room, not enough time. Not *enough*.

But why should I sleep peacefully while the population of Sarajevo – alive and dead – is not yet at rest? In the centre of the city there is a splash of red paint on the pavement by the marketplace, a reminder of the sixty-nine people who were killed one Saturday morning when a mortar, arcing high into the sky in order to wreak the most damage, fell directly upon them.

The dead walk through my dreams and the living through my days. One morning, when all the family are out and Bedra and I are sitting together having a cup of coffee in the kitchen, she tries to articulate her pain and sorrow. I put my arm round her shoulders as she weeps, listening and nodding even though I understand only a few words of what she's saying. She shows me photographs of happy days when her husband and she would take the family to Belgrade for holidays. She has lost touch with her friends there now and she can't understand it. Why? she asks me, tears in her eyes. What did I do to them?

Tom O'Grady, a humanitarian aid worker who came to Sarajevo in the early stages of the war, knows all about the people's pain. 'There's a veneer of normality here: the jaunty look, the cafés, the concerts, the feeling that everything's all right. But it's not. Underneath, there is terrible suffering.' We drive to Gerbavica, one of the suburbs of the city. It's an urban desert like any other – tower blocks of flats, broken pavements, graffiti, though behind each door is a neat home. In Gerbavica, as everywhere else, the population has shifted: refugees have poured in from Goradze and Foca. Tom's Refugee Trust tries to look after the elderly. Many of them are over sixty, war-wounded and confined to their bed or their flat. When things were bad, they drank polluted water because there were no fires on which to boil it: boots, shoes and floorboards had already gone up in flames. Now the Refugee Trust people carry water up twenty floors. 'We're short of food and there are no services,' says Tom. 'The only difference between today and wartime is that there's no shelling.'

We look at another tower block with its windows blown out and its high-rise balconies hanging off. Below it lie broken fences and burnt-out cars. 'This was the front line,' says Tom. It could have been wartime Belfast or Beirut, for this front line is not an anonymous no man's land of barbed wire, dug-outs and gun placements. It's a housing estate such as you'd see on the outskirts of any city. A front line where people got in the way. Many of them fled, but some refused to leave. On an eighth-floor balcony I spot clothes hung out to dry, geraniums climbing round a boarded-up window, an old man sitting in the sun. Above him are another eight floors, empty and blackened with smoke. Tom knows one man who lived on the twentieth floor of an apartment block. The five floors below were uninhabitable but he wouldn't move. Anyway, where could he go? Another day the Refugee Trust rescued an old woman who had lived on her hands and knees for four years in her bullet-riddled flat. She had to learn how to walk again.

Here, at the bottom of the pile, Bosniaks, Croats and Serbs – the ones who stayed – all receive the same help, the same reassurance from the Trust. These people, the oldest, the loneliest, the poorest, the most immobile, all share the same fear that one day, the Trust's familiar Range Rover won't turn up. That is their worst fear . . .

'And then, of course,' says one of Tom's helpers, 'there are all the women who were raped.'

'Raped?' I ask. 'Not these women?' Surely not these women, whose average age is seventy. The helper looks at me with pity. I *still* haven't grasped the true nature of this war.

'The woman in the next flat was raped and she's eighty-seven. Would you like to meet her?'

I shake my head. I can't. I've done enough staring.

'She won't mind.'

'No, thank you.'

One day, out of curiosity, I take a tram from Titova Ulica, along what was Snipers' Alley, to the end of the line and find that it stops just by the remains of the *Oslobodenje* offices. The Serbs pounded it with mortars, not realizing that its design incorporated a nuclear shelter. Now, although the outside walls of its eight floors have been blasted away, its huge central structure still powers upwards. At its base lies a pile of tangled girders, plaster, shattered concrete and glass. Sandbags are scattered round the main entrance and grass has begun to grow up the steps.

Next day, visiting a school for the blind ('We'll reopen,' says the director, himself blind, 'when the children's playground has been checked for land mines.'), I climb up to the top floor and find myself in a room that had been used by snipers. The windows are still boarded up but a small hole has been cut in the plywood to allow the sniper to focus on his target. The director and his assistant stand behind me, waiting.

'Who was here?' I ask the director.

'The Chetniks,' he replied, using the familiar term of abuse.

The squared-cross sign of the Serbs has been painted on the wall in blue and sprayed below it, in red paint, '64% of Bosnia belongs to Serbia.' Beside the word Bosnia has been added another word, in blue, which I can't make out. The assistant is distressed and shakes his head when I inquire. 'Not a good word,' he says. 'I can't translate it.'

I peer through the jagged hole in the boarded-up window and see, pinpointed in the distance, the shattered building of *Oslobodenje*, its size and position a perfect target for the sniper.

Selim Beslagić, the mayor of Tuzla, is famous, for he has wrought the miracle of holding together his town and, in the midst of all the horror and the killing, managed to prevent any serious outbreak of violence between the Bosniak and Serb communities there. For this he has been awarded many prizes, including the Sean MacBride Peace Prize. MacBride – an esteemed Irish lawyer – was, in his own lifetime, a holder of the Nobel Peace Prize.

Although I have failed to make telephone contact with the mayor, I've decided to take a risk and travel to Tuzla anyway tomorrow. The bus leaves at six a.m. To celebrate this decision, I go to the gala concert at Sarajevo's National Theatre. When I get there I find the glass doors are shut and they remain so well after the starting time for the concert. People peer through the glass into the lobby, but no one does anything as discourteous as banging on them. Four years of war has left them patient. Eventually, a side door opens and a man appears to tell the waiting crowd that today, Sunday, the clocks have gone back and that we have all arrived an hour too early. When I walk back to the flat and tell Bedra this, she explains that yes, it's true, but it's for one day only. Tomorrow everything will revert to the old time.

Politely, I query this and explain that where I come from the clocks remain changed for a good six months. Bedra, however, is adamant: it's for one day only. It said so, on the television. As she's obviously misunderstood the whole thing, I let the matter drop and return to the concert.

It reminds me of concerts in Moscow. Everyone is wearing their best clothes, the women elegant, the men in suits, the little girls with shiny, well-brushed hair. One beautiful young man is dressed entirely in white. As usual, I feel grubby in my track-suit trousers, sweater, raincoat and Cape Town boots – though, in deference to the occasion, I have removed the plastic bags. People promenade arm in arm up and down the long gallery outside the auditorium. There are no programmes, just a limited number of photocopied sheets circulating among the audience. Inside the auditorium, a woman invites to me to take the chair beside her. She leans over to ask where I come from. 'You are very welcome,' she says, smiling, when I tell her. Then she whispers, 'You know, this is a good city. We don't hate each other. We never did. Please don't think that about us.' All I can do is nod and smile. Our different languages get in the way. How can I tell her that for me Sarajevo is, and always was, my ideal of the cosmopolitan, embracing peoples and religions with generosity and grandeur? My own city, unique though it is, is largely untouched by other cultures and remains, therefore, sadly unenriched. In Sarajevo, however, Bosniak, Serb and Croat have blended together over the centuries. Islam, Judaism, Serbian Orthodoxy and Catholicism have all made room for each other. (I visited the small Serbian church in Sarajevo one day and lit a candle there – for anyone and everyone.) In fact, it was precisely because of its capacity to accommodate all comers that the city presented such a threat to Belgrade.

The Sarajevo Symphony Orchestra seems small, its numbers depleted, but it plays with grace and is applauded with rapture. Towards the end of the concert people begin to slip away. Is it my imagination or has the conductor speeded up the players? Perhaps he has, for in ten minutes' time the eleven p.m. curfew will be in place . . .

The following morning I get up early to catch my bus to Tuzla and find that Bedra was right after all. The clocks *have* been reset and I have missed it. (An explanation later emerged: the traditional date for putting the clocks back in the former Yugoslavia had been set a year ago. In the meantime, the war had ended and with peace came a move towards greater integration with Western Europe. Time, if not people, could be reconciled. It was decided, therefore, that the clocks should be reset at a later date – to coincide with the rest of Europe. But first they must be changed, as previously decided.) I liked this arbitrary solution and cherished the apparent absence of logic. There are too many comfortable constants in the world.

Next day, at the bus station, I manage to purchase my ticket in Bosnian and, feeling pleased, accost someone else to check which bus I have to catch. They understand me as well! Having a knowledge of Russian is a help, except that I'm a bit lost without the Cyrillic alphabet. Instead, there is a Roman script with dashes and half-moons but sometimes not even those. My little phrase book, bought a long time ago, has Serbo-Croat as its title and sports the red star of the former Yugoslavia on its back cover. I have been advised to conceal it. The language of Bosnia Herzegovina is now Bosnian.

I share my seat on the bus with Vahid, switching quickly to English when I discover he speaks it perfectly. He's studying chemistry at

Sarajevo University and is going back to Tuzla to see his mother and sister.

'Are you from Tuzla?'

'No. Srebrenica . . . unfortunately.'

He must be used to the silence that follows this news. By July 1995 the 8,000 or so Bosniaks in Srebrenica had swelled to 40,000 as refugees poured into the town. When it fell to the Serbs that summer, the exodus began again. Those who could escaped to the forests, where they were hunted down. An estimated 8,000 died. Among those unaccounted for were Vahid's father and fifteen-year-old brother.

Yesterday a family friend showed him a video, taken in happier times, in which he, his father and his brother were playing football.

'I hadn't seen the video before and now I can't get it out of my mind.'

Vahid's girlfriend in Srebrenica had ditched him when the war started to loom.

'She said I was a Muslim. But I said, what's a Muslim? I don't pray. I've never read the Koran. I've never been inside a mosque in my life. The only thing about me that's Muslim is my name. That's enough, she said.'

Vahid was holed up in Srebrenica during the siege and got to know the foreign troops there. 'The Dutch soldiers were terrible. They were young, like me, but all they were interested in were cars and girls. They blamed us for everything. We wouldn't be here, they said, if it wasn't for you people. The best were the Canadians. When my friend was shot in the street, they helped me look after him, but he died very quickly. Then they brought me into their camp and gave me a hot drink.'

I feel helpless in the face of Vahid's monotone voice. I have nothing to offer him. Money would help – but I need what I've got. In Tuzla, I buy him a cup of coffee. He declines my offer of something to eat. To ease my conscience, I tell him to write to me with a list of science books I might be able to get for him, but we both know he won't. Leaving him, I try to steady myself against the emptiness I feel.

The mayor bounds up the steps of Tuzla's town hall, drawing a raft of followers after him, though none of them moves as fast as he does. He disappears up another flight of steps, down a corridor, in through a door, where I catch up with him. He agrees to thirty minutes. Precisely.

Beslagić is a large, square man with a loud voice. He once worked in the local concrete factory. His broad shoulders fill the jacket of his grey suit and his bright, multicoloured tie sends out a signal as exuberant as its wearer. I have a list of questions I want to ask but discard it when I find that his method of answering is to make a speech. It's the old communist way of doing things: I talk, you listen and DON'T INTERRUPT.

Beslagić is a man of Tuzla and the townspeople are right behind him. When some of the refugees from Srebrenica demanded that the Serb citizens of Tuzla should give up their homes to them, since it was Serbs who had created the situation, Beslagić vehemently rejected the suggestion. 'We are all one here,' he told the refugees. 'Our Serb citizens are as much a part of Tuzla as the Bosniaks. *They* were against what was being done in Srebrenica too.'

Every lamppost in Tuzla is festooned with posters bearing a picture of Beslagić. A one-time communist now described as a left-winger, he has no time for the Islam-dominated ruling party and has formed his own, which, creating a coalition of smaller parties, did moderately well in the recent elections.

Energy bursts out of him like electricity, ideas like starbursts. One idea caught fire. The custom in Bosnia, when constructing a house, is to build the ground floor first, then occupy it while the next floor is being built. Last to be done are the doors and windows upstairs, their installation postponed until more money is sent home by migrant workers.

When the refugees poured into Tuzla, Beslagić looked at the Danish government's offer of aid and came up with a deal: the Danes would install doors and windows on all the unfinished houses and in return the owners would accommodate a refugee family upstairs for a year.

Our talk – which is nearly at an end – is interrupted by the phone, and while Beslagić bawls down it I check my notes: he's answered exactly one question. I squeeze in another one about the peace award and he pulls out of a breast pocket three pieces of paper each relating to three different peace awards. He selects the right one, has a run at the name Sean MacBride, stumbles at the first fence but, undeterred, carries on. It's clear he has no idea who MacBride was.

As our meeting winds up, he's on the phone again and then, as I'm gathering my things together, hurtles out of the door. 'I hope you'll visit Ireland one day,' I yell after him, but, like the White Rabbit, he's disappeared round the bend in the corridor.

Back in Sarajevo I have coffee one evening with poet Ferida Duraković and her architect husband, Mirza. They live in an attic close to the centre of the city. It's a comforting room, full of books and pictures and warmed by a glowing stove. Ferida was temporarily away in America two years ago when she suddenly got the urge to return to her besieged city – and to her lover. She flew in on a UN flight, crawled her way through the tunnel and into the waiting arms of Mirza. Their cheerful little siege-conceived baby, Farah, is now nearly one.

Ferida lost all her books – a thousand of them – when she was burnt out of her flat.

'And how did you get this attic flat?'

'It belongs to a friend who went to Belgrade,' she says.

I wonder about this friend. Which is her home now – Sarajevo or

Belgrade? Will she ever return? Will the flat still be hers if she does? It's not a question I care to put to Ferida.

She and Mirza are unequivocal in their praise for NATO.

'The Americans brought the whole thing to an end,' she says, pouring me a glass of white wine. 'The UN could have done but they didn't. The rest of Europe let us down.' She looks me squarely in the eye. 'There was no place for pacifism in this war.'

There is nothing I can say to this. She's right. The UN failed to act strongly and thousands died while some of us chose a comfortless neutrality. Was that a luxury? Is choosing *not* to pull the trigger an indulgence? I have learned from being here that it is definitely reassuring to see a nice, big, heavily armed tank patrolling the troubled streets. My one regret is that none of the tanks or armoured personnel carriers has UN painted on their sides. Had they done, then I would have had no hesitation in pulling the trigger. I say none of this to Ferida. My credo of non-violence is clearly unacceptable to the victims of violence and that is something I have to accept. In any case, Sarajevans are too busy working their way towards a rocky peace to spare time for other people's ideological problems.

I've been hoping to travel to Belgrade. There's a bus leaving every day from the other side of Sarajevo and it takes twelve hours to get there. But somehow the more the journey seems a possibility, the more reluctant I become to go there, although I know that, in the interests of impartiality, I should. So far, although I've heard and seen only one side of the story, I now have little inclination to hear the other. I *know* atrocities have been committed on both sides. I *know* the Bosniaks have provoked the Serbs on occasion. (The final, fearsome attack on Srebrenica grew out of a Bosniak attack on two Serb villages close by.) I understand the fear some people feel about the crusading spirit of Islamic fundamentalism, about the long arm of Turkey reaching northwards ever closer into Europe. But trying to balance it all out, to make all things equal, fills me with weariness. It *doesn't* balance. There is no logic, there are no neat answers in the mathematics of war.

Nikica, one of Tom O'Grady's helpers, offers to take me to where the Belgrade bus leaves, so that I can do a recce. She used to work for the state television station until they stopped paying her. 'They had no money. We were supposed to be paid ten Deutschmarks a month, but sometimes all we got was a packet of cigarettes.' She's philosophical about the international food and clothes aid that arrives round the clock. 'People are proud here. They don't want cast-offs. They'd rather wear their own battered shoes. Some of the stuff you just couldn't use. You see it arriving in Sarajevo all the time in Land Rovers and in smart four-wheel drives. Here comes another safari, we say.' If she puts me in the category of war groupie, she's too polite to say so.

We drive through a neighbourhood blasted by shells and mortars. It had been the Serbs' front line until, under the terms of the Dayton Agreement, it was reclaimed and included again within the boundaries of Sarajevo.

'I was glad about that,' says Nikica. 'My sister lives here.'

We bump up a rocky hill and come to a halt on a barren piece of land from which an unmade road descends towards an army checkpoint. At the side of the road is a woman with a bag round her waist, selling bus tickets to Belgrade. A small group of people waits for the evening bus, women mostly, tired-looking, their goods tied up in cloth bundles. Since this neighbourhood was returned to Sarajevo, the Serbian men, fearful for their future, have gone to live in Belgrade, leaving their women behind to look after the family homes.

The air here feels chilly. No one says anything but everyone stares. Suddenly, I'm on the wrong side.

Nikica asks the ticket woman about departure times. The woman answers and I can hear the coldness in both their voices. I wander away, unconsciously distancing myself from them both, but it's impossible to be impartial. I've spent too long in the company of Sarajevans, listening to their stories of loss. These Serb women, waiting on this desolate hillside, have lost homes and families too, I know. They are part of the equation as much as the Bosniaks. But I find myself looking at them through Nikica's cool eyes. For now, my well of compassion has run dry. I make excuses for my lack of feeling. I am tired, I tell myself. My judgement has been clouded by the sight of so much destruction. I will feel better tomorrow.

I look around the hillside again and the desolation of the scene grinds into my heart. The pale faces of the Serb women stare at me without expression and I know that I will not be going to Belgrade this time.

Bedra and her sister are laughing and chatting in the kitchen as they chop and cut, squeeze and snip. They're bottling fruit and vegetables for the winter – peppers, courgettes and tomatoes, lemons and plums. The window ledges are strewn with drying herbs. A cake has been baked and is cooling on the table. This will be their first winter without war.

I pay my rent to Bedra and give them both a small farewell gift – two linen hankies edged with lace. Bedra has a present for me: a pair of snug slipper socks which she has knitted herself. Tomorrow, I begin my journey home: by bus to Zagreb, then on to Ljubljana, where I get a train to Vienna and finally a plane to Dublin.

The bus leaves for Zagreb at six a.m., going northwards through Tuzla again. It's a journey of about six hours. Bedra has given me some bread and cheese to eat on the way. Half-way along we stop by a roadside restaurant, where everyone gets off for a pee, a smoke or a drink. The restaurant has a carved wooden balcony and a big log fire inside: the sort of place that used to feature on travel brochures for the former Yugoslavia. Outside a man is getting a barbecue ready for the midday customers, stoking the fire, shoving logs under the trussed sheep. While he chats to a friend, he lards the sheep and turns it on the spit, lards and turns, lards and turns, until the sight of the shiny pink flesh slowly cooking makes me think of dead bodies and I look away.

It's a sunny day. The trees are bright with autumn gold, though there's a hint of winter in the air. The road is lined with roofless houses, burnt-out farms, shattered barns. Some people on the bus look. Others chat to their neighbours, used to the sight.

At the Sava river, which marks the boundary between Bosnia and Croatia, we stop and get out. The bridge across the river, Bosnia's main link with the outside world, was blown up and now stands, interrupted, half-way across the wide stretch of water. Soldiers have built a pontoon at its base from which they work, repairing the structure.

The bus passengers scramble and slither down the bank of the river and on to a small waiting ferry. The empty bus is driven down the steep incline and then up a makeshift ramp on to the deck. Behind us a queue of lorries and buses waits to cross. The ferry can take only one large vehicle at a time.

The engine starts up and the ferry, flying the flag of Croatia, churns through the muddy water, pulled across the river on a chain. On the other side a group of people wait. They all have cameras and photograph us as we trudge up the rocky slope of the bank. Keeping my eyes down, I shrink into myself, seeking anonymity among the small group of bus passengers. The people with the cameras are German. They are travelling with a four-wheel-drive loaded with blankets and provisions, part of an aid donation. The word PEACE is painted on one of the doors. Another safari arriving. Their cameras, unselective, see only a group of war-tired Bosniaks, of which I am one. But I know that if I raise my eyes and look at *them*, I will see myself.

ELISA SEGRAVE

Posy: A Portrait of an Expatriate

MAJORCA

Posy lived by the sea. In summer, in the years when I first knew her, she bathed each day below her house at twelve o'clock. If I was already on the beach, I would look up and see her stepping carefully down on to the rocks where there were sea urchins. She always had her two dogs with her. Jeff, the older one, was cream-coloured, with a fluffy coat, curly tail and wide standing-up ears like a papillon. Sydney was a short-haired brown and white mongrel that she had found abandoned on the beach. Once I heard her shout, 'You bastards!' at them.

Posy looked frail and she usually wore white. Her beach wrap was pure white. She had delicate bones, like a small bird, and her elfin pointed face with green eyes was framed with fluffy grey-white hair. She reminded me of the French writer Colette. Her eyes were unusual, deep-set and dark green. They gave the impression of secrets.

My mother said that when she had first met Posy on Majorca, Posy and her friend Connie had tried to walk straight through the plate-glass window of the hotel where my parents were staying. They were drunk. My parents had just bought an old farmhouse and Posy was already living in the area, sharing a house with Connie Thaw. Connie's sister Thelma had been the Prince of Wales's mistress before Mrs Simpson, and Posy too had been friendly with the Prince and Wallis. In the Duchess of Windsor's memoir, *The Heart Has Its Reasons*, the Duchess describes them all holidaying in Biarritz. Posy, 'young, blonde, vivacious and pretty', suggested that they go on a cruise on a cousin's yacht. The Duchess wrote, 'Often the Prince and I found ourselves sitting alone on deck, enjoying the soft evening air . . . Perhaps it was during these evenings off the Spanish coast that we crossed the line that marks the indefinable boundary between friendship and love. Perhaps it was one evening strolling on the beach at Formentor in Majorca.'

Thirty or so years later, having divorced her husband two years before Mrs Simpson married the King, Posy ended up living only a few miles from Formentor. In the mid-1960s it was still an exclusive resort with a luxury hotel and a few very grand houses. One, belonging to a Yugoslav shipping millionaire, was perched on top of a sheer rockface. Now Formentor is packed and in the summer ferries carrying more and more day visitors arrive every half-hour from the Puerto Pollença. On the narrow white beach, with its forest of pine trees behind, are self-service joints selling hamburgers and chips.

But in the 1960s it was unspoilt and so was the Cala San Vicente, only two minutes' walk from the sea, where Posy finally bought her own house. The Cala was then just a small inlet with two little bays full of fishing boats. The first hotel overlooking Posy's beach, which she dubbed 'The Green Latrine', was not built until a decade or so later.

Other expatriates who arrived about the same time as Posy were the Ganymedes, whom my parents had known in Madrid in the early 1950s; the Fowlers – Don Fowler had been American military attaché in Spain; Mariana Angelova, who was Bulgarian and supplemented her income decorating other foreigners' new houses; and a giantess called Queenie von Hertzog, who kept falling over drunk. Out of this group, Posy was the one I liked best. She deliberately made friends with me, despite my being so much younger.

My father also liked Posy. He admired her for her directness, for not being afraid of him and for being able to sometimes complete *The Times* crossword.

My mother said, 'Posy has a masculine mind.'

She then added, 'Posy is evil.'

I didn't take much notice of this, as I thought my mother was being melodramatic. Unlike Posy, my mother did not talk in a straightforward way. And while Posy took a pride in finding out how much things cost – 'Five pounds *per head*!' she would announce, after one of her parties – my mother was not at all practical.

In Posy's garden, with its series of terraces overlooking the sea, stood a statue of three intertwined monkeys. My mother told me that Posy had been brought up in India, where her father had been Advocate General and had prosecuted Gandhi. Perhaps the monkeys originated from there. Posy, however, never spoke about her past, or at least not to me, and other people expressed a similar frustration that she was so reticent about it, particularly since she was talkative, even mischievous, about the pasts of others. No doubt some of her friends would have liked to hear insider titbits about the Abdication Crisis. But in this matter Posy was steadfastly discreet.

In August 1974 my father and I were alone on the island. There was a storm in our valley. Posy came to lunch. She was wearing white again – white trousers and a pure white jumper which she had crocheted herself. At first she was on her best behaviour. Then, after about fifteen minutes, she declared, 'I want my lunch.'

My father replied, 'You'll get it when it's ready.'

While we sipped white wine, I argued with Posy about my father. I said that he had criticized a member of his London club for being what he called a 'Middle European upstart' but would then get annoyed with this man for trying to emulate the behaviour of an 'English gentleman'. I said my father wanted it both ways.

My father sat scowling at us. He couldn't hear much of what we said because he couldn't work his new hearing aid.

Posy, her frail white-trousered legs planted firmly apart and leaning slightly forward – her favourite pose – said to me, 'Your father doesn't like people to pretend to be what they're not. Now, let's see. What *does* your father like? . . . He admires men who fought well in the war.' My father had commanded destroyers in the North Atlantic but never talked about it.

I was privately impressed by the way Posy defended my father, and at that moment I began to like her. I was also intrigued by the way in which she tried to get to the roots of a person's behaviour. I found out subsequently that she was fascinated by murder, what provoked it and how people sometimes got away with it. I was pleasantly surprised as well by the way she treated me as an equal. Although I was nearly sixty years younger than her, she seemed to think my opinion worth hearing.

As we walked in to lunch, Posy pretended that she was drunk. Over the egg mousse, she entertained us by relating stories about other foreigners who owned houses on the island.

The first story was about a Mrs Willoughby, who had choked to death on a piece of meat at her own lunch table in front of Posy. Mrs Willoughby's daughter, who was visiting from England, was also there. The local doctor had insisted on calling the Guardia Civil and they had suggested that she might have been poisoned, either by her daughter, or by Posy, or by someone else in the house. However, the cook had already chucked the rest of the meat away so it couldn't be examined. The Guardia Civil, according to Posy, who was sceptical of everything Spanish, had as usual been incompetent.

Posy's next story was about Mrs Ganymede, who, she said, had come sobbing to her. This seemed unlikely, as Mrs Ganymede was tough and efficient — she let her house successfully throughout the summer to a series of bankers and their wives — and did not seem the sort of woman who easily sobbed. But Posy insisted that she *had*, about the two houses that she and her son Bertie owned next to Posy. Bertie wanted to sell his house to rich German bankers and with the proceeds buy a little farm and plant almond trees. Mrs Ganymede had been in tears, according to Posy, because she feared that in this transaction she would lose money. Posy had told Mrs Ganymede to dry her eyes and had given her some Soberano brandy. She had advised her to stop worrying about property.

Posy's last story was about her own servants, a couple from Valencia. Posy said that the wife had broken her arm. Then she had had a row with her husband, who had threatened to break her other arm. Posy had intervened: 'Yes, I know your wife is a difficult woman, but she must go on cooking. Please don't break her other arm or she won't be able to cook at all.' She herself had then offered to cook one meal a day until the arm mended.

After lunch we sat outside again, watching the storm clouds crowd over the mountains. The mountains were grey and the dark clouds made them black. Posy liked this and mentioned 'The Ride of the Valkyrie'.

When she had finished her coffee and a glass of anis, she said she had to feed her wild kittens, which she had found the week before on the mountain above her house. She was giving them milk with a fountain-pen filler.

'They're so sweet,' said Posy. 'They bring up wind, just like babies.'

Invitations flew fast in Majorca and before she left Posy invited me and my father and mother to lunch the following Saturday. My mother was driving a Renault 5 out from England with a woman friend and would have arrived on the island by then. My father explained that his sister and her husband would also be visiting.

On the day of Posy's lunch party, my uncle and I first drove to her beach to bathe, then we sat in a café. My uncle bought a straw hat in the beach shop, then it was time to walk up to Posy's house beside the pine trees in the baking heat. Her one concession to colour, in a garden which was mostly a series of cascading balconies instead of flowerbeds, was a huge mass of purple bougainvillaea, which sprawled all over her front wall and down the steps. Otherwise, the vegetation was sparse – dry grass with a few large, ungainly cacti. Behind the house was a huge mountain formed of red rock.

My aunt's second husband had been a prisoner in Colditz. He had eventually managed to escape by getting a prison doctor to pretend that he had a stomach ulcer. Harry was a gentle man who never got angry with my aunt, who bullied him. Unlike Posy, with her superior attitude towards anything Spanish or Majorcan, he was enthusiastic about everything abroad. At meals he would ask my mother excited questions.

'I say, Anne, is this fish local?'

'Harry, *do* stop asking if everything's *local*!' my aunt would snap.

At Posy's gate we met my parents and my aunt, who had come in the other car. My uncle asked, 'Rosemary, do you like my new hat?'

'No!' was the predictable reply.

Posy was having the drinks party outside. She asked me *sotto voce*, 'Is that your uncle?'

'Yes,' I replied. 'He was in Colditz.'

Posy then introduced me to the son of the Swiss ambassador to Moscow, who was sitting on one of her pale green chairs. He had skinny white legs, a pouting mouth and spectacles. He looked intellectual. I asked what he did and he replied that he had just taken the Foreign Office exams. I was about to question him about these when my father butted in. The Swiss ambassador's son left me and went and stood by the wall, looking ill at ease.

Posy had already told the Swiss ambassador and his son that she couldn't have them to lunch as well because of her cook's broken arm. So they left, the ambassador saying to Posy, 'See you in Moscow.'

Posy had been invited to stay with him that autumn. My mother, probably jealous she wasn't going herself – she had a passion for Russia – whispered, 'Posy would wreck any embassy.'

We sat down to lunch. Because of the cook's broken arm, and because she genuinely liked cooking, Posy had prepared all the food herself. The main course was curry with sunflower seeds. Several of us exclaimed, 'What an original idea!'

Posy asked us all to help her solve a clue in *The Times* crossword. My uncle suddenly said, 'Stomach ulcer.'

My aunt said, 'That's the first time in twenty years that he's filled in a clue in *The Times* crossword.'

After lunch Posy took me and my mother into her back garden by the washing line to see her wild kittens. I whispered to my mother, 'You know you hate cats.'

But my mother was too much in awe of Posy to say she didn't want to see the kittens. Afterwards she confessed to me that she had found them revolting as they scrabbled up and down the sides of their cage.

We heard nothing from Posy for two days. Then she rang up one morning to talk about the Ganymedes' boat, which my parents were thinking of renting to amuse my aunt and uncle, though my aunt whispered to me that she got seasick. Posy said she had heard that the boat cost twenty pounds a day, which was far too much, and advised them not to take it. She thought my mother was naïve about money.

Then Posy asked to speak to me. 'When are you coming to lunch alone?'

My aunt nervously warned me against being with Posy on my own, but the next day I drove down to the Cala, where I was to meet her. As before, I watched her from the beach as she stepped carefully down to the rocks from where she always bathed. Her thighs were pale and shrivelled and she carried a white towel.

After swimming, Posy drove me back to her house, although it was only two minutes' walk away.

'I do hate walking, don't you?' she said.

'No, I don't,' I replied. 'I like to be near people and observe them.'

'Ah, but you can never tell what they're thinking. And their clothes are so deceptive.'

When we arrived at the house, Posy offered me some wine and then talked again about the Ganymedes. She said that their son, Bertie, was very mean; she had had him to several meals, but when she had finally gone to his place for lunch all she had been offered was a boiled egg.

'Also, he's a homo!' she added triumphantly.

I knew from my mother that Posy had been great friends with a certain French male homosexual on the island. Her pose of being anti-homosexual therefore confused me. I didn't know whether she was putting on a show of respectability because I was young and she didn't know me very well, or whether she always put up this façade. After all, she had been born at the beginning of the century, when these matters were not spoken of.

That day we had our tête-à-tête lunch in Posy's dining room. The pale green table had a glass top and on it were two vases of pink plastic rosebuds. We had fresh sardines, which she had bought herself early that morning from the market in Pollença, and fresh peaches cooked in syrup. (I subsequently discovered that stewed fruit was one of her favourite puddings.) Then we had Brie and Bath Olivers.

Posy was very proud of having acquired the Brie, as she thought everything French was a cut above anything Spanish. There was almost nothing Spanish about her house, except the cook with the broken arm and her husband. Everything else in her house looked French – the spindly furniture, the sparseness of the decor (no heavy dark Spanish chests like those in my parents' farmhouse), the delicate glass and cutlery and the way Posy insisted on no thick Spanish oil in her food. Indeed, no one knew why Posy had chosen to live on the island, as she didn't seem to like anybody or anything Spanish, except for a young couple, Paco and Bianca, both a little older than me, who drove out every Sunday from the capital to have lunch with her, bringing their two children. Posy also liked her bottle of Soberano brandy, which was always on her drinks tray.

Otherwise, she was always complaining about Spanish food, Spanish doctors and the way Spanish cleaning ladies mopped the floor too often.

Posy, however, was in awe of José, the man who worked for my parents, who had spent much of his childhood on his uncle's farm at the top of a mountain in our valley. José had a dignified and stately presence.

'I feel he's like royalty,' she confessed. 'I want to curtsy to him whenever I see him.'

José and his wife had spent several years in Essex, working as cook and butler for an English couple. José spoke respectfully of Posy, calling her 'The Señora' and describing proudly how he helped her each year at the Christmas party she gave for local children. José's own little daughter was among Posy's guests. But despite mentioning this act of generosity, José went on to tell of Posy's meanness. He said that with local shopkeepers, electricians and plumbers she was always suspicious about being cheated. Her attitude to these everyday transactions was an insult to José and his countrymen, on whose island she had chosen to live.

Posy was not unique in this. After all, she and the other expatriates, many of them elderly, had been drawn by the climate and the cheaper cost of living, but had then found themselves stranded in an unfamiliar culture. Even the local language was not Spanish, but a dialect similar to Catalan which was difficult to learn. Perhaps Posy's carefulness over money was a way of trying to keep control.

As for José, his Majorca was a place where once a year in early spring a pig was slaughtered at dawn. Afterwards, all the parts of the pig were used for delicacies such as *sobresada*, a sort of red sausage or salami which my future husband grew to love. José's Majorca was where the local people celebrated the Feast of the Three Kings – *Dia de Los Tres Reyes* – more than Christmas. Some years we stood in the Puerto and watched the Three Kings process on horseback down the winding mountain road from Formentor, followed by various local dignitaries in big cars hooting their horns loudly. There was always one king with a black face, to represent a Moor. The kings then threw handfuls of sweets to the children in the crowd and fireworks were let off. Perhaps Posy found occasions like these primitive, even intimidating. Catholicism – indeed, religion of all kinds – was alien to her. She might not have been pleased to know that the thirteenth-century cross used in the Good Friday torchlight procession was believed to have been thrown up by the sea at the Cala San Vicente, just below her house.

My mother's attitude to the island was also very different from Posy's. She loved the processions, the fiestas, and the belief in the Virgen del Carmen, who was supposed to protect fishermen and whose statue, every summer, was brought out from the church in the Puerto Pollença and escorted around the bay by fishing boats. When I was a teenager, the first time I went to the island, my mother took me into the dusty streets of Pollença in the evening and introduced me to a thin, gypsyish woman with a hard, beautiful face who, my mother said, had made a fortune dealing in property. She was called Juana Cabrer, and my mother whispered that her husband had been shot dead in front of her during the Civil War. The foreignness of this, the sharp green olives we ate, the dark restaurant we sat in with its enormous barrels of wine, seemed far removed from Posy's elegant little dining room.

*

After that summer of 1974 my father died and I did not see Posy again for a few years. Then in July 1979 I invited Andrew, my future husband, to Majorca. Almost at once, I took him to see Posy.

The beach below her house was now dominated by two enormous hotels. Thus the Cala, which in the sixteenth century had repelled at least one invasion by the Moors, had, in the second part of the twentieth century, been taken over by retired English people on deck chairs, mostly from the north of England, reading the latest Jeffrey Archer and plastering themselves with suntan oil.

Posy, however, still managed to create an exclusive atmosphere in her house, only a few minutes away from the crowded beach. She even had a little tablet, made of white china, propped on her dining-room table on which she wrote each course in pencil.

That day, Posy's favourite young Spanish couple, Paco and Bianca, were visiting with their two children. Posy urged us all to take second helpings at lunch, stressing, 'There's *masses* more.' After the two men had followed her instruction, she implied, with a subtle lift of an eyebrow, that they had been greedy.

'I can never decide which one I prefer, him or her,' she said after the Spanish couple had left to drive back to Palma. 'They're both so charming. He, of course, is nineteenth-century. He has impeccable taste in furniture and paintings, but he's hopeless as a bank clerk; his cousin found him the job. And she's so sweet she's like a lump of sugar.'

I told her I was now living in Notting Hill Gate and she mentioned the Rillington Place murders, for which the wrong man had been hanged. Shortly after the women's bodies were discovered hidden in the house, Posy told us, she had made her daughter drive her to 'Christieland', where, she told us without any shame, she had managed to enter the house on a pretext. She had longed to know how Christie had managed to conceal so many corpses behind the wallpaper.

She went on to talk of Jack the Ripper and how he might have been the Duke of Clarence, then she related a complicated saga involving an illegitimate child in Yorkshire, prostitutes in London and ritual murders carried out according to a Masonic rite. Andrew was told to go and look up the Duke of Clarence in Posy's copy of *Burke's Peerage*. While he was out of the room, she whispered to me that the Duke had had a 'Black Room' where various homosexual rites took place. She had been fascinated by the Duke and had gone to visit his grave.

That night in my mother's house I had a nightmare in which I was taunting Posy, knowing she wanted to see me and Andrew again. Then I started asking her politely about novels she had read. Suddenly the car we were in went out of control and we were whizzing round and round as though on the Whip at a fair. In the dream Posy had power over me and I screamed with terror.

Despite my fear of Posy's 'dark' side, or maybe partly because of it, I was fascinated by her. Posy was so unlike my mother. I felt that underneath her naughty gossip, she had a strict regard for truth and didn't shy away from it, as my mother did. I felt that she knew all too well what human beings were capable of, what drove them, and that she wanted to understand their motives as far as possible. During the war, Posy had taken over the running of her husband's factory in Camden Town. It had made spark plugs but she enlarged it to produce ammunition. She later moved the factory to Northern Ireland, where the government was giving advantageous terms, and there she began to manufacture drawing instruments such as compasses.

Posy was insatiably curious about the various personalities Andrew and I encountered that summer, even those whom she had not met herself and was not likely to meet. One was a Peruvian girl, nicknamed Chicken, who, Posy informed us, had recently attacked her mother with a knife.

'Her mother owns a tiny restaurant in the Puerto called the Salt and Pepper and it was there the daughter went for her,' she said knowledgeably, adding that unless Chicken took several pills a day she 'went off her head'.

This 1979 visit was the only occasion on which I saw Posy's bedroom. She had asthma and Andrew and I, passing the two spotted stone leopards standing guard each side of her sitting room, went upstairs to commiserate. Her bedroom was surprisingly bare, except for some very good delicate French furniture. Her sheets were pink and a pink fly-swatter lay on her bedside table. She said it had been given to her by a 'homo' called Jean. (This was the French friend I had heard about.) Posy talked of another male friend, Peebles, who also owned a house on the island. He was Austro-American-German and his wife had died of an infection in a hospital on the mainland after falling off a rock, another example of incompetence, this time in the medical profession, said Posy. The distraught widower had brought round his wife's shoe to show Posy, saying that he couldn't bring himself to throw it away.

Years later Peebles told me that his father had died very soon after his wife and that during that period Posy had been incredibly kind to him, on one occasion travelling the long distance to Palma airport in a taxi to meet him at one a.m. On the way home they found a bus that had fallen off a bridge. Posy had attended to the girl courier who was badly cut.

Although she had some difficulty breathing that day we visited, Posy dismissed our polite inquiries about her health and eagerly cross-questioned us about our social life. She wanted to be the one who introduced us to new people, implying that anyone we met through another source was bound to be inferior.

'Who are you going to see tomorrow?' she asked, as we said goodbye. 'Chicken?'

*

Andrew and I went to Majorca again for a week just before Christmas in 1980. This time we slept in my mother's bedroom. It was plain, with almost no furniture except for a pale green cupboard all along one side, decorated by Mariana, the Bulgarian decorator, and Posy herself. (Posy recounted how she had helped paint on colourful flowers and birds.) Out of my mother's window were fields with fig trees, olive trees and goats with bells round their necks, and grey mountains which changed colour to rose at sunset. At the foot of the hard double bed French windows opened on to a balcony with outside steps which led down to the garden. The only ornament was a large statue of the Virgin Mary in dark wood. A piece of rush matting covered the dark green stone floor.

The room was isolated from the rest of the house, far away from José and his wife. On our first night the French windows suddenly flew open and a hot wind from Africa gusted into the room. I felt we were in a very foreign place.

The life of the expatriates was quieter in the winter months. Some of them occupied themselves by getting involved with the local Anglican church, which held jumble sales, prayer meetings and coffee mornings. Posy was not interested in church functions. Indeed, one of her most dismissive phrases was 'she's very vicar's wife'. In the past she had worked for various charities in England, such as Guide Dogs for the Blind. (She told us that certain members of the public who could see perfectly well sometimes tried to acquire a guide dog by trickery, as they were reputedly so well trained.)

For Posy the winter was an opportunity to see hidden parts of the island. The weather was cooler and there was almost no tourist traffic. Despite her critical remarks about so many aspects of it, she was receptive to the island's beauty. That week in December, she took us to visit an old lady called Mrs Hillgarth, who lived in a large house outside the village of Santa Maria, near the capital. We were a few minutes early, so she suggested we stop at a bar in the village. Posy, who was wearing a smart cream-coloured suit – one of the few occasions when I saw her in a skirt – had a brandy. We stood outside the bar in the winter sun, holding our glasses. A drunk cross-eyed man in blue overalls passed us on his way in, staring.

Posy said, 'Don't tell Mary that I brought you here.'

She explained that Mary was 'Museum' and so was her house. After lunch – Andrew and I had two helpings of each course – Posy criticized the food while her friend was out of the room, saying that it was all of the same colour and consistency. Nevertheless, it was obvious that she liked and admired Mrs Hillgarth, who, she said, was 'a scholar and translator'.

By now we were aware that Posy was not popular with everyone; in some circles her nickname was Poison. One enemy said she needed a dose of vinegar. Nevertheless, despite her mischievous tongue, she was loyal and affectionate towards those she did like. When Andrew and I were married a year later, she sent us an unexpectedly large cheque and when we visited the island again with our two-month-old daughter, she presented me with a pure white baby's blanket which she had crocheted especially. She arranged an outing to a ruined underground church, St Martin of Tours, behind the marshes of Alcudia, a town with narrow medieval streets whose name was Moorish – Al Kudia meaning 'the hill'. We had to skirt round a lake to get to the underground church and Posy lost the way several times. When we finally arrived at the shrine, a Majorcan family had beaten us and were having a picnic, barbecuing meat and burning eucalyptus leaves, which gave off a smell like incense. Posy was annoyed we weren't alone and whispered that she wanted to burst their children's ball with her cigarette. She led us down some stone steps into the ancient church, where there were two pictures carved in stone – one of St George and the Dragon with Christ in the background in drooping robes, seated like a woman, and another of St Martin of

Tours on a horse, with Christ depicted as a beggar beside him. St Martin was supposed to have given half his coat to a beggar.

'No one ever gives everything,' I remarked to Posy, and she replied, 'No, they give the minimum.' In the car she whispered that I was self-sacrificing because I let my husband have the front seat.

Over the next eight years – our son Nicholas was born in 1983 – we visited Majorca every summer after my mother finished letting the house for two months to a man from the Middle East. We also sometimes went after Christmas for a week. Once, when our children were still very young, we were able to stay there for a whole month in January. Posy arranged through her new Spanish housekeeper to send our daughter to a little nursery in Pollença. We took Lauretta, only two and a half, for a look. As the dark-haired children swarmed around her like a shoal of little fish, my daughter with her shock of blonde hair – everyone else in the family is dark – stood very straight. Then she raised one hand. 'No,' she said softly.

I decided she was too young to be with so many strange children when she had only just learned to speak our own language. Posy was annoyed and said she would have to make excuses to her housekeeper.

Although she lived permanently on this small island, Posy still liked to feel she was close to the corridors of power. New books came out regularly from the London Library and she avidly read *The Times* every day. She liked to be be *au courant*, and in the mid-1980s was already talking about AIDS being 'rife' in the Puerto. A book she loved was Geoffrey Household's *Rogue Male*, published just before the war, about a man on the run from agents of a fascist foreign power. She also pressed on us a thriller about Russian and American peace-keeping arrangements in the Sinai. In it, both the American president and vice-president went missing at the same time and a hawk in the Pentagon took over, nearly causing a nuclear war. This was the sort of plot Posy liked. She spoke as though she herself was a diplomat or politician, someone 'in the know'. Perhaps this was why she liked to associate with diplomats, even though she sometimes found their conversation dull.

'See what I mean?' she began, just out of earshot from some Belgian diplomats to whom she had taken enormous trouble to introduce us. 'Borwing [sic] beyond belief!' (Posy sometimes couldn't pronounce her Rs.)

On each of our visits Posy produced more and more people for us to meet, as though she were pulling them out of a hat like a conjuror. 'Who would you like? Mrs Beadle or Mrs Fanshaw? Captain Robertson or Lord Latimer?'

Captain Robertson was a new friend. He had arrived on the island in the 1980s with his wife and been widowed almost at once. They had sold their only house, in Scotland, to settle in Majorca.

'He's wood from the neck up,' whispered Posy, the first time we saw him ascending her steps with his well-trained golden Labrador at his heels, so unlike her own ill-mannered yapping dogs. When he left two hours later she relented, murmuring, 'He's a dear old boy.'

Some years later, when Posy had become friends with him, Captain Robertson drowned in his own swimming pool after a heart attack. Posy tried to get his niece, whose little boy had been the first to spot the disaster, to invite me and Andrew to a cocktail party in the niece's flat in the Puerto and dropped all kinds of hints about it. The niece was determined not to ask us, even when Posy produced a map and cross-questioned her in front of us on how to get there.

Lord Latimer, the ex-chairman of a London bank, was courteous, old-fashioned, modest and was also widowed after retiring to Majorca. Posy was genuinely fond of him and he was one of her most respectable friends. I remember him coming to lunch at her house soon after

Christmas, proudly bearing an English Christmas pudding and brandy butter.

Some of Posy's friendships were stormy. Mrs Fanshaw had been in a concentration camp, and taught English to Majorcan teenagers. Her beloved Alsatian attacked her pet parrot and, in trying to save it, Mrs Fanshaw herself had been bitten badly on the arm. Posy had her to stay while she was convalescing, but then fell out with her after an argument over Posy's servants' day off. She was later reconciled with Mrs Fanshaw.

Then there was Bettina, whom Posy nicknamed the White Dove. As a young woman, Posy told us, the White Dove had been involved in a scandal in a Hungarian hunting forest, while on a romantic weekend with her lover, who was married and part of the Prussian royal family. He was found dead that weekend.

'It was all over the papers at the time,' said Posy and, referring to the White Dove's beauty, added, 'If I were a man, I'd be attracted to her.'

The White Dove was shy and didn't go in for social chitchat. She preferred petting Posy's new puppy, whom someone had found in a ditch and brought to Posy's house.

Another victim of Posy's insatiable curiosity was the White Dove's cousin, Princess Isabel, who was both French and German. She visited the island one summer and Posy took her out alone to a restaurant. Posy returned disillusioned.

'Princess Isabel believes in government by an élite. I've no time for that. It's antiquated and undemocratic,' she told us the next day.

As I grew older, I began to see Posy herself more clearly: her kindness to those she liked, her almost childish desire to shock – 'Who cares if Albertine's "*disparued*"? I wished she'd "*disparued*" years ago when I read it,' she announced during a discussion on Proust; the way she pretended to be more in control than she was; and, most of all, her refusal ever to be bored. One evening, when in her late eighties and with a recurrence of asthma, she insisted on coming down to the Puerto late at night with me, Andrew and Paco to sit in a café, where she bought us a bottle of bubbly. We all watched Bertie Ganymede walk along the promenade, his face like a shiny brown nut, to join a descendant of the would-be King of France and other members of the international set in the most fashionable café that summer.

'They look so relaxed but actually they're all sick with worry about who's going to end up paying for the drinks,' Posy observed.

Paco had left his wife and was embarking on a series of brief love affairs. Posy took a great interest in these, and offered advice. About the first girlfriend, who was a single mother from London, Posy reported, 'I haven't met her, but Bianca saw her in the Puerto and she said she reminded her of margarine. Margarine! That's all I can tell you.'

Although by the end she was nearly blind, she never referred to her physical weaknesses and never gave up her fascination with other people. On one of the last occasions I saw her, she was enthusiastically inviting a Lady Glanville, who had just arrived with her husband to live on the island and who had been a professional ballroom dancer, to 'come and have a cup of char' after having a haircut in Pollença. I had supposed that, having lost so many old friends, Posy might be lonely, but after Lady Glanville had left Posy explained that it was she, not Posy, who had complained of loneliness.

Posy died, in a chair in her own house, the same month that my marriage ended and my mother, now widowed for fifteen years, finally sold her farmhouse. That September in 1989 was the last time we ever went to Majorca as a family. I learned subsequently, when I met Maria, her housekeeper, who had been with her that day, that Posy had died quickly and peacefully, and that before the doctor arrived she had made up her face and put on powder.

*

There are still aspects of Posy that puzzle me. I think I was right, in my early twenties, to notice her secrecy. About the time that I met my future husband, my mother met a Mrs Vereker and more or less fell in love with her. Posy dubbed her 'Mrs Veryqueer'. Mrs V gave herself airs – her husband had been what she called a 'dip' – and was disliked by almost everyone for her incredible rudeness. Posy stood up to her.

'She was Mulliner's daughter. He designed Rolls-Royce engines. She claims everyone's been on top of her, even the King of Siam, and he's a notorious homo.'

Mrs Vereker disliked children and once at the dinner table asked why on earth anyone should have a thermometer in the house. Posy hissed, 'You're not a mother!' and when Mrs V later moaned that she wanted to die, Posy scolded her. 'You may *think* it but you musn't *say* it.'

'Why? It's true. I want to die.'

'Because it's embawwassing, and there's no reply.'

After Posy died and my mother developed Alzheimer's – 'You're going to have a lot of trouble with your mother!' Posy had prophesied – a woman who had been with my mother and Mrs Veryqueer to Majorca reported that soon after their arrival my mother had gone up to visit Posy and had returned to the beach in a state of ecstasy.

'Posy has told me there's another way of life!' my mother had declared. The strange business with Mrs Veryqueer had then gone full steam ahead.

Recently, I returned to Majorca. I had become friends with Lyn, a Canadian woman of my own age to whom Posy had introduced me, saying, quite rightly, that she was 'a honey'. I drove to Posy's house on my own and walked up the stone steps, almost expecting to still see the two slim spotted leopards which used to be on either side of her sitting-room. A man came out and I tried to explain that I wanted to go inside as I had known the previous owner. But he spoke only

German and although I tried English, Spanish and French I realized it was hopeless and turned away.

I thought of Posy when I first saw her, stepping carefully into the sea off the rocks at the Cala, her two dogs at her heels, her pure white beach robe on the step behind her.

Lotus Season

CAMBODIA

The day before I arrived in Phnom Penh, there was an attack outside
the National Assembly. Four grenades had been thrown into a demon-
stration organized by the Khmer Nation Party; the demonstrators
were protesting against judicial corruption. As my flight was
announced at Bangkok airport, I made a quick call to my sister in
London. 'Tell Mummy I'm OK, will you?' I said. My mother sleeps
very little, even less since my father died three years ago; she lies
awake at night listening to the radio. I was concerned that she might
have heard about the massacre (as some journalists were calling it)
on the World Service, then imagine that I had been injured or killed.
If I – a Westerner – had been hurt, it might have been headline news.
As it was, I don't think the attack even made the British papers,
despite the fact that 150 people were badly injured and nineteen were
dead.

I arrive at Pochentong airport on the last day of March 1997. I haven't
seen my Cambodian friend Sotho for almost five years. I have no way
of knowing if she has even received the fax which told her that I was
coming to Cambodia. I worry that she won't be at the airport. I am
anxious that I will not recognize her. I also worry about Princess
Bhopary Norodom, the granddaughter of King Sihanouk. The princess is an additional, unwelcome complication. A Cambodian friend

in London with close links to the royal family has kindly arranged for her to meet me with a car. Now I'm afraid that Sotho will be offended that the princess has come to meet me and think that I don't want her there.

Sotho and I have communicated erratically over the past five years. I have sent messages and occasional letters via people who were going to Cambodia, and the odd postcard from wherever I happened to be. Some years ago a Frenchwoman who had set up an orphanage in Phnom Penh brought me a beautiful antique brass Khmer teapot which Sotho had sent as a present. My letters to her are usually rather stilted, because I have to write them in French and that restricts me (though somehow it doesn't when we talk). The more time goes by and I don't see her, the more difficult it becomes to write.

Six months ago, in October 1996, I received a letter. It arrived out of the blue, written from Kuala Lumpur, where, it seemed, she had some business – which, in itself, was a startling piece of information. She wrote, '*Je vais attendre de nouveau de pouvoir repenser au moment où tu peux venir. Ne fais rien, annonce seulement ton arrivée . . .*' As I read these affectionate, tentative words ('I will wait once more to be able to think of the moment when you can come. Don't do anything, simply announce your arrival . . .'), I realized that I could no longer delay going to Cambodia. As soon as I had booked my ticket, I sent a fax with the date and number of my flight.

At Pochentong, Sotho's elder daughter, Kulikar, is waiting at the gate. There is no sign of the princess. Kulikar takes my passport, the completed visa application form and a twenty-dollar bill and hands them to a uniformed man behind a high desk; she speaks rapidly in Cambodian, so speeding up the whole slow process. While we are waiting, she tells me that her mother has been ill, that she has had an operation, just three weeks ago.

'Oh, no,' I say. I think that she is going to tell me that Sotho is dead. 'Is she all right?'

'Yes,' says Kulikar, 'yes, she's all right now. She has had cancer.'

As I hear the word 'cancer', I feel my eyes fill with tears. The thought, not just that Sotho has been seriously ill and I have known nothing about it, but that she could have died and I would have found out only by coming to Cambodia, is terrifying. I don't know why not having known seems so dreadful. What could I have done thousands of miles away in England? But I keep thinking that I should have known and, more importantly, that I should have come earlier, that I shouldn't have left it so long, that, if I had come sooner, perhaps Sotho wouldn't have got cancer.

'She's waiting in the car. She can't walk very well,' says Kulikar.

I met Sotho in 1990 when I went to Cambodia to research a book. No one had turned up from the Ministry of Foreign Affairs to meet me at the airport (in those days, travel was much more difficult and journalists had to be accompanied by official guides and interpreters). I was standing, sweaty, anxious and with no clear idea of what to do next, when a pretty, elegantly dressed woman in her early forties asked if I needed help. She recommended a cheap hotel, the Asie, and took me into town in a yellow bus.

In the days that followed, we became friends. We were roughly the same age and managed to transcend the usual barriers of language, culture and experience. Our friendship began perhaps out of mutual self-interest – loneliness, need, curiosity – but then we found that we liked each other, got on and could talk as if we had known each other for years instead of mere days. She was fascinated, not only by my possessions (clothes, cosmetics, personal items, including tampons, which she had never seen before), but also by what I told her of my life: of my long-term boyfriend who didn't want to marry me and our make-ups and break-ups, about my cats and the way I earned my living. And, over and above what she could tell me about Cambodia, I found that I could ask her anything and be sure of a truthful and illuminating answer. We trusted each other. Our friendship made me realize how much I missed my friends at home, particularly women friends with whom I could speak freely, when I was away; our friendship made all the difference to my time in Cambodia.

But I haven't seen her since I was last in Phnom Penh in 1992. My book about Indochina was published that year and since then my life has changed. I have also written a book about the Caribbean; I have turned forty; I have been forced to accept that I am not going to have children; I have left London to live in the country, have left the country and returned to London; I have taken a job because I could no longer afford to write full-time; I have lost the job. *Insomma*, as the Italians say, I have moved on.

Sotho's life has changed even more. When I first met her, she was working for the Ministry of Tourism. She had very little money – twenty dollars was a fortune. Like everyone else in Cambodia, she was still recovering from what Cambodians call 'Pol Pot time', when the Khmer Rouge controlled the country, from 17 April 1975, which they proclaimed 'Year Zero', to 7 January 1979. This period, as every Cambodian over the age of twenty knows, lasted exactly three years, eight months and twenty days. Now Sotho has her own business, organizing tours for foreign, mainly French and Japanese, tourists and making travel arrangements for many of the NGOs (Non-Governmental Organizations) based in Phnom Penh. She employs six or seven people; she owns two brand-new, air-conditioned mini-buses; she has a fax machine, a mobile telephone, a refrigerator, a fluffy white lapdog; as well as KL, she has been to Bangkok, Singapore and Paris. As a sideline she deals in antiques, bric-à-brac that she has found in Tuol Tom Pong market or in Siem Reap; hotel decorators, of whom Phnom Penh is suddenly full, come to buy from her. She writes, '*Mon petit commerce va très bien.*' Yes, she is very successful, but, along with the prosperity for which she has worked so hard over the years has come sadness and hardship. She lost more than half her family to the Khmer Rouge. Now she has cancer.

Sotho was born in Cambodia in 1947, five years before I was born in Singapore, where my father, a diplomat, was stationed. Her father and her mother were both Sino-Khmer – born in Cambodia, but originally from Fukkien. She was the third of seven children, three boys and four girls. Her father spent his life working for foreigners, mainly the French, and she grew up on the rubber plantation at Chup, near Kompong Cham, in central Cambodia, which the French had built in 1927. The family lived a comfortable bourgeois life, with plenty of privileges. Every day they were given two big loaves of bread and could order butter and jam, and cloth – calico and poplin – to make clothes. Sotho's parents wanted her to marry a Chinese man, preferably a Fukkien Chinese, but she met and fell in love with a pilot from Air Cambodge. This handsome man, with his classic, dark-skinned, Khmer good looks, wooed her with copies of *Vogue* and *Paris Match* which he brought back from Paris. Her father made her wait a whole year before he relented and said, 'If you want to marry him so much, go ahead.'

Forty years ago Cambodia was a cheerful, peaceful little country ruled by Prince Norodom Sihanouk, who had succeeded in gaining independence from the French in 1954 (Cambodia had been a French protectorate since 1863). Sihanouk was determined that his country should remain neutral and stay out of the Vietnam War; to this end, he had broken off diplomatic relations with the United States in 1965. In early 1969, the Americans, convinced that the National Liberation Front guerrillas of South Vietnam were taking refuge over the Cambodian border, began to send B-52s on bombing missions over Cambodia. Meanwhile, dissatisfaction with the corruption, favour-swapping and patronage of Sihanouk's rule led, in March 1970, to a successful right-wing coup; this had been instigated by the army and the urban middle class, and is now widely believed to have had the tacit support of the United States. The Americans intervened, deposed Sihanouk and installed General Lon Nol at the head of the country.

Cambodia slid slowly into chaos. Lon Nol's government was extremely corrupt and shored up by American aid. Between February and August 1973 the Americans launched a six-month intensive bombing campaign, during which they dropped 257,500 tons of bombs on Cambodia – nearly twice as many as they had dropped on Japan during the Second World War. The guerrillas, whom Sihanouk had nicknamed the Khmers Rouges (*khmer* simply means Cambodian and *rouge* was a comment on their political leanings), gained increasing control of the country. People were starving. The Americans pulled out at the beginning of April 1975, leaving the field clear for the Khmer Rouge, who emptied the cities and drove the people, like pack animals, to the countryside.

In 1975 Sotho was twenty-nine. Kulikar was two. Sotho had a job in the administrative section of Air Cambodge and was studying law in her spare time. Her elder sister was married to a general in the Lon Nol army. Her father was the accountant at the rubber plantation and factory at Chup.

When the Khmer Rouge marched into Phnom Penh, Sotho, her husband and her daughter were taken to the countryside, to Kandal province, just south of Phnom Penh. In January 1976, nearly nine months after the Khmer Rouge take-over, Sotho's husband was imprisoned. She was allowed to visit him three times and then not again. Months later she learned that he had been killed. Meanwhile, her eldest brother died at Tuol Sleng, the converted high school where the Khmer Rouge interrogated and tortured people; her elder sister was killed, too, during this period, along with her husband, the general. Sotho's father also died. She never saw his corpse. She only heard about his death from a cousin: he was taken away on a *charrette*, a wagon. All that remained of him were his clothes.

During the day, like everyone else, Sotho worked in the fields. Kulikar, who was too small to work, was cared for by the elderly women, who also did the spinning and weaving. The women were often hungry and would get the children to steal food. Sotho was terrified, because she knew that if her daughter was caught stealing, Kulikar would be killed, even though she was too small to know better.

One day Sotho was bitten by a scorpion. Feverish, she was taken to what passed for a hospital. As she lay, delirious, on the filthy floor, with only an old, dirty *krama* (the traditional Cambodian cloth that serves as scarf, turban, towel and even hammock) to cover herself with, she dreamt that she was in the hospital in Phnom Penh where she had given birth to her daughter. '*J'ai rêvé de mon mari qui m'avait portée dans ses bras jusqu'à la salle d'accouchement et des draps blancs où j'ai accouché de Kulikar*.' She had been very much in love with her *mari*, her husband, who had carried her in his arms from the delivery room. I guessed from things that she had said that hers had been a happy and passionate marriage. She once told me that her husband had been born under the sign of the Dragon and that he would joke that, as a result, he was '*très puissant*', which has the double meaning of 'powerful' and 'potent'.

One afternoon in late 1978, while Sotho was out working in the fields, a couple of cadres came to talk to her. They said, 'Angkar [the mysterious all-powerful organization to whose rule the individual had to submit completely] wants you to remarry.' She knew that she could not refuse outright and answered, 'The time is not yet right. The country is not profitable. It is better to wait.' But they wouldn't listen to her and she was taken in a cart drawn by a water buffalo to a village ten miles away, where she met her future husband. He was the camp cook who had seen her and chosen her to be his bride. He belonged to the Khmer Rouge but was not, according to Sotho, a 'killer' or even a bad man, just coarse. They were married – which, under Pol Pot, involved making a vow to Angkar rather than before one's parents and one's community – two months before the Vietnamese arrived in January 1979. Sotho said that the nights were the worst and that she could remember nothing about the wedding night. A year later, she gave birth to a second daughter, whom she named Vaddhana, meaning 'progress'. The marriage did not last. Sotho was so shamed by this union that she brought Vaddhana up to believe she had the same father as her sister, the dashing, *puissant* Air Cambodge pilot. Her elder daughter, Kulikar, knew the truth.

Today Kulikar is a competent young woman who speaks almost fluent English. She has an Australian boyfriend who works for an NGO and whom she plans to marry soon. Vaddhana, having sat her *baccalauréat*, has refused to continue her studies. Instead she has trained as a beautician and works in a boutique.

The airport is crowded and very hot. As I stand in line waiting for my visa, Sotho comes very slowly into the Arrivals Hall. She can barely walk and is leaning heavily on Kulikar. She seems tiny – but then Cambodians are tiny people. I can't tell if she is smaller than she was. She looks incredibly fragile, like a china doll, as if she will break into little pieces at any moment and with any sudden movement. She says, '*Je ne pouvais plus attendre.*' She could not wait. I put my arms round her. I am at least a foot taller than her. We are both crying as if our hearts will break. For the rest of my time in Cambodia, whenever Sotho and I are together she holds my hand as a child might.

At first sight, Phnom Penh seems unchanged from five years ago. It is still a dusty, amorphous city of scrappy buildings and anonymous concrete blocks, each looking as if it had been barely completed before being taken over by ten very poor families. None of the buildings appear to have been decorated, or even painted. I have never known the Phnom Penh so beloved of foreign correspondents in the 1960s and early 1970s, with its 'flower-scented streets', its 'indolent charm' and 'schoolgirls in white blouses and blue skirts pedalling past with dazzling smiles, offering garlands of jasmine to have their pictures taken'; I never saw the city of broad boulevards and graceful colonial buildings that was, in the words of one nostalgic writer, a 'perfect fusion of French and Asian cultures'.* So I cannot really imagine what I have missed.

When I first went to Cambodia in 1989, Phnom Penh was a grim place – though undoubtedly better than it had been under the Khmer Rouge. A former Vietnamese ambassador to Bangkok who went in with the so-called Liberation Army in 1979 compared the city they found to Oran, the Algerian town which is the setting for Camus's *La Peste*, saying, 'There were rats in the streets, corpses everywhere.' Ten years later there were rats but no corpses – at least, not that I could see. Nor was there hot running water, street lighting, rubbish clearance, a reliable supply of electricity.

Today, in 1997, Phnom Penh *still* lacks these amenities, but now there are literally dozens of new hotels and restaurants, most of them with generators to supplement the erratic electricity supply and guarantee the air-conditioning, without which most Westerners seem unable to function. It takes me two weeks to find my old hotel, the Asie, because it has changed out of all recognition. Sotho says it has become a brothel. It now has a vast neon façade, a restaurant and a barber's shop.

These days you can eat extremely well in Phnom Penh – French, Italian, American, Russian, Tex-Mex, Thai, Indian, Japanese, Malaysian, Vietnamese (reflecting the huge influx of foreigners) and Cambodian. Food is cheap, too, by Western standards. In the gleaming Bayon supermarket on the Boulevard Monivong, there is every kind

* These quotes are taken from *River of Time* by Jon Swain.

of imported delicacy, from Russian caviare to Australian beef, English biscuits and American ice-cream, but the special Vietnamese sauces come from California rather than from across the border. There is an old, bitter history of enmity between the Cambodians and the Vietnamese which even the arrival of the self-styled Liberation Army in 1979 did little to alleviate, but perhaps I am reading too much into the origins of these jars.

Phnom Penh has become a get-rich-quick city, full of foreigners hoping to cash in. One afternoon in the Hawaii Hotel, where I am staying, I meet a portly Nigerian; he is visiting from Hong Kong, where he is in the export business. 'I'm here as a tourist,' he says unconvincingly. 'Can we go out for dinner one evening?' That morning he had been to visit the 'Killing Fields', the former 'extermination camp' of Choeung Ek where 8,985 corpses, victims of the Khmer Rouge, were found, many headless, many of naked women and children.

'Are you going to Angkor Wat?' I ask.

'What's that?' he asks.

I explain.

'I am if you are,' he beams.

There are more *motos* than *cyclos*. They rush around town at high speed, spewing carbon monoxide, while their passengers perch on the back, clinging to the *moto* driver. I prefer *cyclos*, which proceed at a more leisurely pace and remind me, probably subliminally, of being in a pushchair. Phnom Penh must be one of the few cities in the world where there are more than enough taxis (or their equivalent).

New shops proliferate. Opposite the Hawaii I can see the Happiness Haircut Shop, the London Tailor and the Cowboy Selling Modern Clothing & Shoes. These, to Westerners, jokily named businesses exist throughout the Third World, outlets for the aspirational, but in Phnom Penh today you can also buy clothes by Armani and Hugo Boss. Years ago I purchased an old automatic Omega wrist watch for forty dollars from a man with a stall near the central market. It has been going strong ever since; I never take it off. Now I could buy – if I could afford it – a brand-new, state-of-the-art Longines or Rolex or Patek Philippe, or even another Omega, from anyone of myriad jeweller's shops stocked with foreign goods. The television in my room has four or five channels, at least three of them showing the US Open golf tournament. But the most common items for sale in Phnom Penh are videos, video games, generators and mobile phones. Everyone, but everyone, has a mobile phone.

It is strange to see Sotho whip out her mobile and punch in a number in Paris or Taipei. As we drive along – very slowly because of the poor roads and because, in her frail state, everything hurts – suddenly, deep in her handbag, the phone rings, and I listen to her chattering away in French about groups of ten or twenty tourists who will shortly be converging on Phnom Penh and demanding tours to Angkor and luxury accommodation. Somehow, for me, these telephone conversations in a foreign language with someone very far away epitomize all the changes that have taken place in Phnom Penh.

When I remark that so much has changed, Sotho says, '*L'amitié n'a pas changé.*' No, but she has. Terrifyingly. The cancer has shrunk her, aged her, and the pain from the operation has caused her to bend almost double. She walks – hobbles actually – with one arm pressed to her abdomen, as if she is holding in her guts to prevent them from spilling out.

Below the surface, however, many things in Phnom Penh are just the same. Sihanouk's return was supposed to herald a new dawn for Cambodia. He was going to make everything all right, heal the wounds and unite the people. Six years later, the same old infighting, the same old corruption, the same old poverty are still in evidence. On the morning of my departure for Phnom Penh a report in the *Bangkok Post* claims that Pol Pot is 'alive, well and commanding troops in Amlong Veng', and that he and his deputy, Ta Mok, have taken control of the troops to stop them defecting to the government. Sotho tells me that corruption is rampant, '*une vraie anarchie*'. The roads both inside and beyond the capital are still in a dreadful state of disrepair. Sotho says that sometimes they are mended but then the rains come and, as there are no drains, they are wrecked again immediately. Around my hotel there are great mounds of rubbish, and the streets smell sour and rotten. People sleep in hammocks, slung from buildings or lampposts over the pavements. Pavements? Worse than the streets, these are composed of broken slabs of masonry, puddles of fetid water, piles of garbage. Throughout Asia poor people conduct their lives in full view of the world, but conditions on the pavements of Phnom Penh are those of the worst sort of slum. It is hard to believe that the standard of living of most Cambodians has improved. The hospitals certainly haven't improved. Sotho's cancer was ovarian; she had to go to Bangkok for the operation, because in Phnom Penh the facilities do not exist to treat any type of cancer. She is lucky that she was in a position to borrow 4,000 dollars, the cost of her surgery, from the bank.

In the central market there are still mounds of gold and silver and precious stones: sapphires from the mines in Pailin in the west of the country, an area which is still controlled by the Khmer Rouge; rubies from Burma; and pale, watery emeralds from India. It used to be known as *le marché jaune* because it contained so much gold. The air around the flower stalls is redolent of tuberoses and the lotus blossoms are being swaddled into tight bunches wrapped with hemp, their stems stiffened with fine wire to prevent the heavy heads of the flowers from drooping. Buddhist New Year is only a few days away and people are making their preparations. I buy an elaborate flower arrangement, swathed in orange cellophane (orange is the Buddhist colour), and then walk to the Bayon supermarket for a tin of imported chocolate biscuits to take to Sotho. The lid of the tin shows an English

Victorian family enjoying a lavish tea – scones, crumpets, three different kinds of cake – in front of a log fire. I hail a *cyclo* and ride down to where Sotho lives, near the river and opposite the National Museum. I have learned, from frustrated experience, that not a single *cyclo* or *moto* driver in Phnom Penh knows the whereabouts of the National Museum, a large and beautiful building near the Royal Palace. Even though Kulikar has painstakingly taught me how to say 'National Museum' in Khmer and written it down in Cambodian snail's-trail script, still the driver doesn't know where it is. So now I just ask for 'FCC' (the Foreign Correspondents' Club, which is nearby) and we both know where we are.

Sotho places my offerings on a makeshift altar just inside the front door of her house, next to small piles of fruits, cosmetics and tinned and dried foods. There they will stay until after New Year. The tinned and dried foods are there because she does not feel well enough to cook. Then she tells me that she still dreads New Year, because it falls just before 17 April, the day that the Khmer Rouge took power. Upstairs, in Kulikar's bedroom, there is a photograph of a handsome man in uniform. It is her father, the Air Cambodge pilot. In Vaddhana's room there is no such photograph. Sotho eventually told her the truth about her parentage but says that Vaddhana does not accept it.

We climb aboard one of the air-conditioned minibuses and go to visit Vaddhana in her boutique. On the way Sotho tells me that it gives her a strange – and not particularly pleasant – feeling to think of her daughter doing manicures and facials. Vaddhana's boutique adjoins a beauty parlour and is on the corner of one of the broad boulevards that run through the city. Vaddhana is wearing tight bell-bottom hipster jeans in thick lime-green corduroy and a skimpy striped top. On her little feet are white patent-leather sandals with three-inch platform soles and her toenails are painted light blue. Her dark hair has been given red highlights and has been lightly permed;

the perm is a cheap one and it has made her hair frizzy and dull (Sotho has also had a haircut, tint and permanent wave, courtesy of Vaddhana; the results are not brilliant). Vaddhana sports bright orange lipstick and heavy 1960s-style black eye make-up. As a little girl, she was so beautiful it took my breath away (in one of Sotho's letters she wrote, '[*Vaddhana*] *devient de plus en plus belle, ce qui me fait très peur*'). Now she looks dreadful, like one of the Spice Girls, but then my English goddaughter, of about the same age, looks rather the same. The boutique is stacked with hideously garish clothes – just like those that Vaddhana is wearing – which, Sotho says, the young of Phnom Penh rush to snap up as fast as Vaddhana can get hold of them.

This is the first time I have seen Vaddhana since my arrival. She doesn't seem particularly pleased to see me; as a child, she always hid her face in her mother's lap and refused to speak to me. Now, as Sotho pushes her forward, she bows her head and puts her hands together in the traditional greeting, the *sampeah*. She does not, however, thank me for the present which I brought her from London, a sleek, shiny, white shoulder bag from a trendy, mirrored shop in Knightsbridge. I spent some time choosing it, at least twenty minutes, discussing with the young shop assistant whether it was likely to please a sixteen-year-old. 'Yes, she'll love it. They're the latest thing,' she told me. Irritated by the memory and Vaddhana's present gaucheness, I ask her if she likes her present. Vaddhana hangs her head and nods. When she was little, she always preferred whatever I had given Kulikar. Not on this occasion. This time, Sotho tells me, Kulikar wishes that I had brought her a bag like Vaddhana's instead of the scarlet 1950s-style vanity case which was her gift. I promise to send her one when I get back to London.

Vaddhana's behaviour now is annoying, bordering on bad manners, but it is hard to be cross. I remember the photograph above Kulikar's bed and the absence of such a photo in Vaddhana's room. I think how difficult it must be for her to understand the way things are, to accept the difference between herself and her sister, a difference which, through no fault of hers, has the potential to affect the course of her life, and I feel a sense of overwhelming pity for her.

We leave Vaddhana and proceed slowly out of town to a restaurant on the banks of the Mekong. The countryside is ravishing: the pools are brimming with lotuses, the water buffalo are wallowing in the mud and the sun is shining. Sotho and I eat our lunch – wafer-thin pancakes stuffed with bean sprouts and herbs and some kind of spicy minced meat – in a deserted restaurant. We are the only guests; the restaurant is one she uses for her tour groups and quite expensive. She will not let me pay. After lunch, we walk – hand in hand – to the pagoda.

Sotho begins to talk about her illness. The hospital in Bangkok and the operation evoked memories of Pol Pot time and of the earlier, happier time when her husband carried her in his arms from the delivery room for Kulikar's birth. For three nights after the operation she had dreamt that she was lying in the mud in the ricefields, searching in vain for her house, sure that she *had* a house with stairs up to a second floor. This, to me, makes a kind of horrible sense: an operation is an ordeal, just like childbirth, the pain of which is made bearable only by the prospect of the baby. Torture and surgery are the two sides of the same coin. Sotho had not felt able to talk to anyone about these nightmares, certainly not to Kulikar or Vaddhana, because she felt that it would be too upsetting for them. Though Kulikar was a mere baby during the Khmer Rouge period, Pol Pot remains a bogeyman to Cambodian children. Finally, Sotho asked Kulikar to light sticks of incense to the Buddha and the nightmares stopped.

During the following weeks I develop a theory that Phnom Penh now is – superficially at least – how it used to be in the good old days, when the war was on and when foreign correspondents loved it so.

Sipping a pastis in the Foreign Correspondents' Club, a wonderful old colonial building with high ceilings and big, wooden fans and deep chairs, I think, 'This is how it used to be': expats, pretty native girls, reasonable Western food, cheap drink. South-East Asia is a great place for a *man*. In the evenings, over a pizza at Happy Herb's down by the river on Sisowath Quay, I see the young male NGOs with their delicate Cambodian girlfriends and feel an odd sense of *déjà vu*, a sense that I have no right to feel, in that the former Phnom Penh is something I have only read about. The *Lonely Planet* guide describes Herb's as 'as close as you get to a Phnom Penh institution'. It has been open for only two years. Are people already forgetting the past?

Sotho's brother thinks they are. One evening we drive out to see him. He lives on the outskirts of Phnom Penh, in the countryside, in a beautiful wooden house. He is a professor of archaeology and spent the Khmer Rouge years in Paris. Sotho says, '*Mon frère ne sait pas comment vivre au Cambodge.*' Certainly he is angry and upset. He says, 'Not only have people not progressed, they have *regressed*. Ten days ago there was a massacre. Nobody is talking about it now.' The *innocence* that apparently characterized the city in the past has gone.

I notice that many houses in the countryside bear hand-made signs which read FOR RENT or FOR SALE. 'Why are all the signs in English when we are far from the centre of town?' I ask. '*C'est la mode*,' Sotho says, laughing, and adds that it makes her brother furious.

Angkor is the spiritual heart of Cambodia. It was Angkor which inspired the Khmer Rouge. Their policies were intended, in theory, to 're-create' the past greatness of the Angkor period ('If we can build Angkor,' declared Pol Pot, 'we can do anything'). But by using forced labour to construct a network of canals, in imitation of that which existed at the time of Angkor and harnessed the monsoon waters to create a constant water supply, one which supposedly provided for 'the permanent irrigation of ricefields', Pol Pot actually dragged the country back into the dark ages. Most of the 'intellectuals', including the doctors and anybody who spoke a foreign language, either fled or were killed.

Angkor is also now the touristic heart of the country; it is the reason most foreigners want to visit Cambodia. 'Did you see Angkor Vat [pronouncing the "w" like a "v" as in German]?' tourists ask – most of them have heard its name even if they don't know what it is. And Angkor is the one real opportunity that Cambodia has to make some money. A day pass to the temple complex costs twenty dollars. But it is worth it. A woman in Saigon once told me, 'Nothing we have can compare with Angkor,' and of course she was right. Nothing that anyone has can compare with Angkor.

I fly to Siem Reap, over the vast milky-brown expanse of the Tonle Sap, the Great Lake, whose waters, fed to bursting point by the Mekong, miraculously reverse during the rainy season and start to flow north. Sotho is too unwell to come with me and I am travelling with Philip Jones Griffiths, a Magnum photographer who covered the war and now spends much of his time in Cambodia. You can get there by boat but the journey takes hours; sometimes the boats sink. As we fly over Angkor Wat, which is visible from the sky, Philip tells me that a Malaysian development company, YTL, has plans to turn it into a theme park with boat races and water-skiing on the moat, *son-et-lumière* and re-enactments of events from the *Ramayana* in the ruins. Philip says that, if this actually happens, he will join the Khmer Rouge and blow up the whole place.

The last time I was here, I stayed at the Grand Hôtel d'Angkor, formerly the Grand Hôtel des Ruines, a large, shabby, cream-stucco edifice built, presumably by the French, in 1937. The UN troops were here in full force and a number of them were billeted at the hotel. Today the Grand Hotel is covered with scaffolding, as the entire roof is about to be replaced. It has been acquired by the Singapore

Raffles Group, which will revamp it until not a trace of the old place remains. Sotho has got me a room in a medium-priced hotel, the Bayon, on the banks of the Siem Reap river. It is the end of the dry season and the river is low but, none the less, full of small boys splashing and laughing, rinsing their *motos* and their cattle. In the past, in the intense heat, I have envied these bathing children, but now the water looks so polluted that I don't feel a pang. The hotel has a garden by the river's edge all decked out with fairy lights in honour of New Year. I sit here, drinking a cold beer and reading. It would be heaven if it weren't for the insects. Sotho has bought a small piece of land in Siem Reap and plans to build a little wooden house – for her old age. At least, that *was* her plan.

A man at the helm of a conveyance made of a sort of pram attached to a motorcycle takes me round town. It is the only such vehicle in the place and I feel like the Queen sitting high up in my open carriage. People ask, 'Your first time here?' I have been here several times before and so the correct answer is 'No.' However, Siem Reap looks so different that I feel I should answer 'Yes'. There are many new hotels and restaurants and dozens of souvenir stalls and shops. We pass one with a long, vertical sign which reads:

ANG
KOR
WAT
SOU
VE
NIR
SHOP

In the market I buy an egg-shaped stone made of some mineral which glows like a sunset when you hold it up to the light. I ask what the stone is. 'Egg stone,' comes the answer, which leaves me none the wiser. I also buy a hundred 10mg tablets of Valium, which cost 18,500 *riel*, about eight dollars, and a small book of English–Khmer popular proverbs.

Angkor is now as busy as a Middle Eastern bazaar, with dozens of hawkers competing in the sale of souvenirs and cold drinks. As visitors get out of their cars, the salesmen swoop, chattering like magpies. 'You buy cold drink from me. Only one dollar. You buy film. You buy souvenir. Very cheap.' It is exhausting. I think nostalgically of my previous visits, when there was no one else here. Now, if the hawkers don't get you, the beggars will. The broad, sandstone causeway which leads to Angkor Wat is lined with begging victims of land mines. One is a middle-aged woman who has lost both arms. She looks away, as if ashamed, as I stop to give her a dollar. Amputees with prostheses usually wear wellington boots over them.

As we walk towards the central temple complex of the most perfect building in the world, it begins to pour with rain. Within minutes we are soaked to the skin. We take shelter and ten or so small children appear, out of the grey stonework, like the spirits of Angkor, to look at us. They bring bunches of lotuses and other flowers. The monks in their saffron robes seem to float by; they move as if by divine right. The moat is liberally carpeted with lotus blossoms. When the rain stops, after an hour of downpour, the air is clear and luminous and most of the tourists have gone.

We drive back to Siem Reap, where I find that I am chilled to the bone by the rain. I walk to the row of shops opposite the hotel and buy an extra-large T-shirt. It has a painting of Banteay Srei temple on the back. The following morning we are to go to Banteay Srei.

It is my first visit to the tiny, exquisite temple which was vandalized by André Malraux in the 1920s. The future Gaullist Minister of Culture visited Cambodia in 1923 and made straight for Angkor, where he had planned to plunder 'some little-known, overlooked or forgotten shrine in the jungle'. He wanted antiquities to sell to

American museums. The remote, tenth-century, rose-pink sandstone temple of Banteay Srei seemed ideal. The Cambodian authorities caught up with Malraux and arrested him. He was sentenced to three years' imprisonment but never actually went to jail.

All through the Khmer Rouge period and afterwards, it was impossible to visit Banteay Srei. It is one of the outlying temples, about twenty-five kilometres from Angkor Wat; the road was strewn with land mines and there was also a danger of attacks from Khmer Rouge soldiers. A British mine clearer, Christopher Howes, was abducted in Siem Reap with his Cambodian interpreter in March 1996. He is still missing. Unless you had an armed escort and were able to pay a small fortune, you couldn't even consider going there. And even if you were able to pay for protection there were no ultimate guarantees: in late 1994 an American woman tourist was shot and killed there; her armed guards fled.

Today it is possible to make the trip for forty dollars a head. A very young soldier accompanies us. He sits up front next to the driver. He has a gun and looks as if he knows how to use it. When we arrive, even though it is early, we see that a great many Cambodians have got there first; they are visiting in preparation for New Year, happily photographing each other. They want to have their photograph taken with me. I am happy to oblige, though I know I must appear enormous next to them, even more enormous than in fact I am. I feel safer in Cambodia than anywhere else I have ever visited. How can one be scared in a country where one is twice the size of everyone else?

After the vastness of Angkor Wat, the smallness of Banteay Srei comes as a surprise. Its *petitesse* commended it to Henri Parmentier, head of L'École Française d'Extréme-Orient in Hanoi (whom Malraux consulted before his expedition); he also admired the sheer perfection of its buildings. We wander through the ruins, which create a sort of hall-of-mirrors effect: doorway upon doorway, as if you are seeing double or triple; bas-relief after bas-relief, until you are almost dizzy. Much of the stone is blackened; some is green with lichen, and in places the original rose has turned beige, then orange and finally grey. Over half the *apsaras* – the celestial dancers – have had their faces gouged, or half-gouged, out. The garudas, the *hommes-lions*, the mythical creatures which are half-animal, half-god, are all damaged. Malraux isn't the only one to have left his mark on Angkor. Every site has been vandalized, if not by the Khmer Rouge, then by looters who have hacked away at the statues and carvings to satisfy the demands of eager collectors. The police have done nothing to stop it. Rather they colluded with the thieves. The Conservation, where such items as are recovered are kept under (often ineffectual) lock and key, is now policed by a special force.

In the end, I am not sad to leave Siem Reap. I wonder if I will ever return. Every time I come here I find myself wondering if I will come back; but the formal perfection of Angkor Wat is hard to resist. Sotho sends the car to Pochentong airport to meet me and a note saying that she does not feel well enough to leave the house. In Phnom Penh it is terribly hot, with the kind of oppressive heat you get only in cities. The combination of intense humidity and imminent departure produces a sensation akin to premenstrual tension. I feel swollen and anxious. That evening, outside Happy Herb's, the young mine victim, who has had both his legs blown off at the groin, is waiting patiently in his usual place. And as usual I give him a packet of Camel Lights and a dollar. Unlike some of the beggars in the market, he neither pesters nor menaces, but then he is not exactly mobile.

I see Sotho, briefly, twice more. She is angry with Vaddhana, who stayed out, without permission, till after midnight on New Year's Eve, running round Phnom Penh with her friends. She also feels terrible; her insides hurt and she tells me, again and again, that she is having major problems going to the bathroom. She is normally so fastidious and reticent that I know she must be in terrible pain to confide such details. Soon she will go to Bangkok to consult the specialist there. I tell her that it will take time for her body to heal, that she must be patient and rest. She says she will try but her anxiety is too great. She hopes to go to France in the summer but doesn't know if she will be well enough.

On the morning of my departure, I go to Tuol Sleng. This is in the nature of a pilgrimage, or possibly as penance. I do not expect to enjoy myself. It is just as I remembered it. Here are the torture rooms with the rusting bedsteads to which the prisoners were chained; here are the leg-irons and the handcuffs; here are the instruments of torture; here are the twenty-year-old bloodstains. Here are some paintings of massacre and torture scenes; they were done by Heng Nath, who survived his time there. Here are the lists of the victims who were exterminated daily and the lists of those who were arrested daily. Here are the photographs of the victims, young, old, male, female. Sotho's elder brother, whose face I do not know, is among them.

At home in London, I receive a fax from Sotho. '*La situation politique ne va pas très bien, cela va beaucoup affecter notre business. Tout le peuple Khmer vive actuellement dans l'inquiétude et l'incertitude.*' Anxiety and uncertainty remain the order of the day and Sotho's business, built up so painstakingly over the years, is threatened by the continuing unrest. I go to the shop in Knightsbridge and buy a shiny bag, like Vaddhana's, for Kulikar. The bag comes in red, yellow and black, as well as white. Kulikar has asked for a black one. In a chemist I buy a vial of Vitamin E oil for Sotho to rub on her scar. The oil is supposed to help the healing process. I pack up the bag and the oil and send them via a friend to Phnom Penh. I wonder if they will arrive safely.

In my little book of proverbs, I find four proverbs on friendship:

A life without a friend is a life without a sun.

Misfortune tests the sincerity of friends.

A friend is proved in distress.

Everything is good when new, but friendship when old.

But the proverb that sticks in my mind is one that stipulates, 'Fear not the future, weep not for the past.' I ask myself, in Cambodia, is that possible?

IMOGEN STUBBS

The Undiscovered Road

NORTHUMBERLAND

Be grateful for the freedom
To see other dreams . . .
Learn to free yourself from all things
That have moulded you
and which limit your secret and undiscovered road.
BEN OKRI

The girl in her lap is also the girl in her heart.

The teacher had suggested they spent more time together, 'bonded' more; talked of her sitting alone in the playground staring at the sky; a strangeness – maybe the new baby . . . her workload?

She had been appalled. Not wonder-gazing but strange.

She had resolved on a journey – just the two of them – to her roots. To their roots. She had spoken of things she had not thought about for a long time: of a lake surrounded by high trees; of an old muscovy duck with a monocle of birthmarks; of a deserted railway station hemmed in by blackberry bushes with fruit as sweet as chocolate; of standing waist-deep in cow parsley drinking from a tin; of a landscape scorched by heather with real fresh air and water you could drink from a tap.

The girl had listened blankly.

'I think I'd better bring my Gameboy.'

They are dressed and ready by six. The mother is so hot that her hair sticks to her head. She is wearing thermal everything – they are going north. The girl is wearing her ballet skirt and Pocahontas slippers. She eats five Yum-Yum doughnuts for breakfast, recognizing that her mother is on some kind of guilt trip. Under her arm she clutches her teacher's much-cherished bear, entrusted to her for the weekend as a test of responsibility. Her irresponsible mother, envisaging another wrist-slashing lecture from the teacher, begs her to leave Old Ted at home. She refuses.

As the taxi driver holds the door for her she turns in consternation. 'I think we forgot the nit comb.'

The taxi ride to King's Cross is not peaceful.

'The other day I only had Geraldine James in the cab, didn't I? You know, *Jewel in the Crown*. I told her – I said – you don't do yourself any favours with the roles you get, know what I mean? I mean, she's quite pretty in life and all that . . .'

The girl tells him that in Cornwall she was sick in a taxi.

At the station they ask for two second-class tickets to Newcastle for a grown-up and a five-year-old. The ticket seller takes issue with this.

'She's not five.'

'She certainly is.'

'She is not five.'

'I am five.'

He presses his shiny face right up against the window and growls, 'Under-fives travel free.'

The girl is bewildered. Her mother explains that lying is not always wrong – not when you are being so blatantly ripped off, and if it leaves you more money for sweets and comics.

The girl is doing the human body at school. She does not want the *Puppy* magazine with a free plastic cocker spaniel called Sparkle. She wants the *How My Body Works* magazine with a free plastic intestine. She is in lecturing mood, and when she speaks she tucks her hair behind her ears: 'About germs. All night and day they never sleep, they never cook. They don't have lunch. They just eat off their adventures. And they are baddies, because germs push all the food out of your mouth and you're sick – like in Cornwall.'

There is no room at all in second-class. They sit on their bags in the corridor next to a drunk man in a tie that looks like open-heart surgery. He reads the back of the girl's magazine: 'Right – guess how many smell particles there are in a footprint. Give up? Two hundred and fifty billion. Easy Peasey Lemon Bloody Squeezy.'

They are passing a huge pyramid teabag. The mother is wondering if it represents end-of-the-millennium desperation for novelty or a real breakthrough. She is wondering why she let herself be browbeaten into bringing Old Ted in her rucksack instead of *The English Patient*.

The girl leans across their bags and kisses her.

'I love kissing you.'

'That's because you have an affectionate nature.'

'No – it's because there's too much spit in my mouth and it gets rid of some of it. You know – saliva – where the germs live.'

She is remembering a story her mother told her. A man she feared was in love with her had come to tea. When they were in the garden she heard him come up behind her and say, 'I love you – and my mother and father love you.'

As she turned to say, 'I'm fond of you too, but . . .' he went on, 'But our yew trees simply can't compete with yours.'

*

The door opposite them opens, releasing an avalanche of wet loo-paper like dirty snow. They move into first-class.

It is now more vital than ever that the girl is four.

She is finishing off a burger, which came with a free wind-up mini-burger.

'How old are you?'

'I don't want to be four, it's babyish.'

'I've already explained . . .'

'Only if you'll play characters with me.'

Oh, God, no. Anything but that.

'Right. I'll be Old Ted, only I'm called Hannah and in true life I'm actually Barbie and Ken's dog, OK? And you're the hamburger. So what's your name going to be?'

Around them are men in suits with laptops and a symphony of mobile phones. They look at the girl as though she were a crash in the stock market. When a phone rings it is a great ego rush for its owner. He is suddenly a star on the nine-thirty King's Cross to Aberdeen. They are drinking awe-inspiring quantities of coffee because a nice subservient man in a waistcoat brings it round and it is free. One man is already so hyper that he only occasionally deviates into sense: 'All I have to say is one thing. Firstly, it is as good a time as any to make the transaction. Secondly, in the long term it is likely to be a probable 100 per cent no-risk situation vis-à-vis reduction of assets. And thirdly – and most importantly of all – '

There is a long pause.

'Um . . . I'll have to get back to you on that one.'

In a pathetic attempt to look interesting, the mother begins a sketch of the girl, who is trying to sleep. She makes her look like a croissant with hair.

'We're not Rembrandt, are we?' says the ticket inspector.

She hands him the tickets and attempts to regain some dignity.

'A man's reach should exceed his grasp – or what is heaven for?'

'I am four!' pipes up the girl. 'I am four! Four I am! Just for today.'

'We're four today, are we? Happy birthday.'

'Say any name and I can think of a song with that name in it. Give up? "Happy birthday to you, blah blah blah. Happy birthday, dear Amadeus . . ."'

Amadeus had been a possible name for the baby – a postnatal aberration perhaps. And perhaps certain.

Anyway, your man goes off with that real corker under his belt.

A pasty-faced girl goes past in luminous green and orange. She is wearing platform shoes that would be great for puddling paddy fields in China. Behind her a tiny child with a crew cut opens a dirty handkerchief and marbles cascade to the floor – ochre, violet, ruby red . . .

'Pick them up, you stupid little git!'

To her credit, picking them up herself would not only be life-threatening – it is simply not a possibility without dismounting. The boy manages to retrieve most of his treasures but abandons the crumpled handkerchief. As he goes, it opens up like a white flower coming hastily into bloom.

They are outside Peterborough crawling through countryside that might have been drawn with a ruler – a touch of colour, yes, but as the girl might scribble idly with a crayon before tearing her drawing to pieces. There are trees huddled together like things awaiting extermination. You have to want to see the wonders, the mother is thinking, or you see only that the rot's set in.

The train has slowed right down due to 'the encumbrance of high winds in this vicinity', and they are quite literally being overtaken by a lady on a bicycle wearing an aquamarine headscarf. Not a ripple disturbs her head and the trees are megalith still.

The girl is sleeping and as she sleeps she makes little mewling sounds. The mother writes something in her sketchbook.

> perfect your fragile life
> bees, shadows, fire, snow,
> silence and foam combining
> with steel and wire and pollen
> to make up your firm and delicate being

The words belong to Pablo Neruda.

At Peterborough a man gets on and sits opposite them. He has huge teeth which rest on his lower lip and Eric Morecambe glasses. In his pocket is a book called *Let it Flow.* Within ten minutes it is made known to them that he is a cab driver who is also a shaman and clairvoyant. He has a very pronounced cockney accent. All of a sudden he gets a 'visualization' which, along with 'divination', is his forte.

'A contract of some description within the next month. And does "Richard" mean anything?'

She has a transsexual workout instructor called Rikki – though he preferred Dolores at eyelash-dyeing parties.

'See what I mean? Contract – it's hard to put things togevver – maybe it was "contact". See what I mean? Let it flow – it comes into your head and you – must – strike – while the – iron – is – hot. I try to open up to it, you see – read people's minds. Sometimes I 'ave to draw the curtain down myself because at times you see things – 'specially in ladies' heads – that ladies wouldn't like you to see. You see? Innermost thoughts an' all that . . .'

Thrill is certainly jostling with thrill on this trip.

He gets off at York, leaving behind an irate ticket inspector, four empty lager cans and a divination: 'What I can say to you is this.

Many opportunities are passing at your disposal, but your abilities is slightly lackin'.'

Uh huh . . .

'In other words, don't try for the moon . . .'

After York, the landscape starts to look freehand and heavy green; more as God intended, somehow. Though countryside seen through the stilled frame of a sealed window might as well be countryside seen on television.

'Chimpanzee takes snapshot of lion.'

It is a headline and it has caught her eye.

'Brilliant, isn't it?' says the hyper businessman. 'You can't beat the Tory rags when it comes to April Fools.'

Once the concept is explained to the girl it is the source of endless amusement: 'I just saw an igloo. April Fool!'

'Oops! I dropped Old Ted out of the window. April Fool.'

She is scouring the papers for other possible gems.

'Why I really love the Spice Girls by Brain of Britain.'

'Swampy – eco-warrior to contest constituency of Blackley in General Election.'

'Liverpudlians feel they are an oppressed minority.'

'Gary Lineker to buy Leicester for £50 million.'

'Embroidery – the new Rock and Roll!'

She has a feeling none of these qualifies.

'By an accident,' whimpers the girl, 'my orange juice spilt down my dress.'

The mother's heart is suddenly caught off guard. She is remembering when she had been to see her mother in hospital and there had been orange juice spilt down her nightie but no one had bothered to clean it off. It had been the beginning of the most unforgivable indignity.

'April Fool!'

They had the same eyes – like young trout deep down in a clear river.

'Oats and beans and barley grow,' blurts out the loudspeaker – this presumably started life as 'Next stop Newcastle upon Tyne.'

They get off the train to the unmistakable sound of the singing whale, last heard at a natural-birthing class in Clapham. On the opposite platform is a man with an army haircut blowing into a rubber pipe which is attached to the small end of a traffic cone. He is playing 'I am Sailing' by Rod Stewart.

Rather surprisingly, the girl wants to know about the statues above the station exit. 'Well . . . the one with the beard is King Edward or George or someone, and that one looks kind of Roman – maybe he built the roads – no, maybe he is Hadrian, who built the Wall, except he had a beard . . .'

The girl has wandered off in search of a snack. She finds her near a stall selling flowers dipped in turquoise dye. She is stroking a really manky-looking stray.

'What a country,' the mother says larkily. 'Even the dogs are going to the dogs.'

A huge gobbet of spit arrives at their feet. The girl perks up: 'That's saliva – where the germs live!'

In between the stall-holder and some daffodils is a dog-bowl marked BEAUTY.

They are looking for the car-rental office. Every street seems to lead to the shopping mall. In front of the entrance to the Atrium, a small crowd has gathered around some staggeringly incongruous street artists. They are swathed in white sheets and their faces are white. They move in slow-motion. A woman has one doll strapped around her waist and one doll with its legs around her neck. They too are faceless and white. On her head is a doll with its arms raised, as if in fear or delight. Next to her is a man with a sort of table on his head covered in corn, and a third man wears a headdress like a gnarled tree covered with cobwebs.

They are students from Newcastle University and the idea is stolen from an Indonesian ceremony called 'Infinite walking to the for ever'. The whiteness signifies a flock of geese with the world on their heads; babies and babies mean ongoing life; the table of rice fields means sustenance; the umbrella tree means shelter and law; and flowers and fire mean the sacred spirit – only she isn't there, she's gone to the loo.

Their audience consists mainly of young mothers with bare legs and cigarettes, and children in *Star Wars* T-shirts. Everyone is amused or moved in some way. A man with lovebites, or a very unfortunate skin problem, puts fifty pence in their box: 'It's amazin' what you can do wi' a couple of toilet rolls and some sticky-back plastic . . .'

Someone asks if they are part of the Labour election campaign.

A woman takes out a sandwich and suddenly they are sluiced by seagulls.

The man behind the counter in the car-rental office is wearing sunglasses and a waistcoat that looks like sperm under a microscope. He is surrounded by posters of semi-nude couples drinking cocktails and sunbathing on beaches. The foam is coming out of the back of his chair. Unfortunately, the car promised over the phone is not available. Fortunately, they do have one other car. Unfortunately, it is rather more expensive. The cosmopolitan girl yawns and asks if Northumberland will be more like Turkey or Antigua.

They are caught in Newcastle's one-way system for forty minutes. New Newcastle seems to have exchanged mystery for confusion. The city has been wallpapered with Channel 5 posters. One of them advertises a film described as a 'slamdunk of a movie'. It's certainly one way round the problem of selling garbage.

They finally escape on the Jedburgh road, leaving behind a blur of concrete and denim and daffodils.

The mother is explaining that her grandmother was born and married here – her mother was born and married here, she was born and married here – in the same church over at . . .

> 'Oh, it's a GREAT GREAT
> BRILL BRILL
> MEGA MEGA SKILL SKILL
> to have a friend like JESUS
> yeah it's a . . .'

Whoa.

Where had she learned that?

'Church.'

She isn't aware her daughter has ever been to church.

Did she learn about God?

'Sure.'

The girl is bouncing up and down with happy-clappy Old Ted. 'Guess how he made the world. Give up? First snow, then April . . .'

'Maybe God isn't a "he" – ' the feminist lamely flickering within her ' – maybe God's a "she".'

'Of course God's a he.'

'Why "of course"?'

'Because, Mummy dummy, God is a boy's name.'

There is a nonplussed pause.

'First snow, then April – then what?'

The girl looks at her incredulously. 'The human body, of course.'

*

She is thinking her daughter to be a poet. She is thinking about a bit of poetry in which God is a chicken but can't remember who wrote it. She says it out loud, and when she speaks she tucks her hair behind her ears.

> 'Because the Holy Ghost
> Over the bent world
> broods with warm breast
> and with ah!
> bright wings.'

The girl leans her head to one side and smiles: 'Yes – I like that.'

She looks a little bovine, perhaps because she is chewing gum. And the mother decides she would like to tell her about Bonnie and Shirley.

When she was the same age as the girl, her grandmother lived in an old grey mossy house on a lake surrounded by woods. In the holidays they would travel up from London to see her in an old van and it would take fourteen or fifteen hours. When they arrived, Peg – who they are on their way to visit in Wooler – would look after them. And she would buy them sweets from the Co-op travelling van, because the house was in the middle of nowhere and there were no shops and even though it had its own railway station the trains no longer stopped there. There were ducks and roosters and hens, and they would collect the warm eggs for breakfast. But best of all were the two cows, Bonnie and Shirley. Early in the morning, she and her brother would creep into the milking shed that felt warm although it wasn't warm, where Peg would be sitting like a harpist milking the cows, and she would tell them stories about their mother when she was little. And sometimes they would try milking the cows – burying their faces in the heaving warm brownness, watching the huge noisy tongues going up and down the salt licks like red waves on white sand . . .

'Shall I tell you something?' says the girl. 'Indian people – when they are chewing gum – they don't talk.'

She is losing her interest. Fragments, then – snippets.

There was a boathouse with a rowing boat for picnics and fishing and diving off . . .

There was a ruined castle where they played kick-the-can, and where once they met a man with a lion cub in his arms . . .

In winter they would sledge down the hill on to the frozen lake and if the ice cracked it made a sound like a gunshot. And in the mornings there would be footprints on the ice of deer and foxes, and sometimes unidentified marks that looked like bear prints . . .

Once there had been a night-time skating party with flaming torches and Northumbrian pipes and a fiddler, and meringues that were chewy like toffee. And someone had made a snow unicorn. And someone had proposed to someone at midnight by the bulrushes where the swan would later make her nest. And it had suddenly all seemed so clear and still – as though the universe were holding its breath. She had seen it through the window, kneeling up on her camp bed, wishing the night would never end.

She had experienced a 'moment one and infinite' – she realized it now . . .

The girl says she wishes she was young again.

They are on a very straight road coming into Morpeth. The mother feels just about equipped to deal with a lecture on the Roman history of the area.

The girl has already done the Romans at school – they lay down a lot and drank beer and ate bunches of eggs, and when they weren't doing this they made roads in very short skirts like the Spice Girls.

*

She turns on the radio.

She finds a programme about the writer James Baldwin. They are playing an old recording in which he is talking about the phrase 'to find out', and saying what a thrilling, what a life-enhancing, idea it was.

And surely it was. God – so much of life nowadays was met with a shrug or a sneer. But now she is worrying about her ability to respond viscerally to anything any more. Earlier, when she had said, 'Isn't it beautiful?', it had sounded like an empty phrase, voiced only to reassure herself that she was still a sentient creature involved in the world – not a skimmer.

They have stopped in Morpeth to buy something for Peg's dog. They are in a pet shop buying a chocolate-flavoured doggy kebab, while inside the mother is undergoing a Wordsworthian crisis. The girl thinks it would prefer one of those Hunchback of Notre-Dame dog chews. The shopkeeper points out that they are in fact rabbit- and turkey-flavoured doggy sporrans. Heck – it's an easy mistake to make.

As they leave they pass two dogs.

'Those,' confides the girl, 'were two of the most alarming dogs ever.'

'Why?' asks the mother.

'I don't know, do I?'

In the window of an old-fashioned ironmonger's that sells everything from water butts to Tuscan-style crockery they see a 'Wunderbag': it has a place for pens, a place for lipstick, a mirror, a memo pad, a place for credit cards, a calculator and much, much more. The girl is five and she cannot imagine making it through another day of life without one.

The lady taking the money tells her she is a lucky wee lassie. The girl ponders.

'For my fifth birthday I got a Lady Diana with twenty-four outfits – but all the hats looked like vegetables.'

A vicar who has been browsing is leaving the shop empty-handed. At the door he turns back: 'Would you let me know, Mrs Walker, if anyone else is interested in that bain-marie?'

As they get into the car, the mother sees a shop bearing her mother's maiden name. Suddenly she feels like a tutelar of the place. She is somehow connected to this town by her clan. It is an emotional bonding that defies Pay and Display machines and discarded burger wrappers; it is a real moment of feeling. And when she looks at the map – Cambo, Alnwick, Rothley, Longframlington, Scots Gap, Netherwitton – she recognizes them all as characters in her life, as part of her identity, and her heart fills up so quickly.

They drive on towards Wooler. Ahead of them the land is dark purple, but the sea to the right is lit up. There is so much sky, and different weather in all directions. Above them an enormous wave is about to crash on to a blue beach.

'Two times two equals four,' yaps the girl delightedly, not once lifting her head from the calculator.

The shadows of the clouds are now moving across the fields like so many armies. The mother also did the Romans at school. All she can remember is that the armies formed 'tortoises' – huddling together with their shields held above and to the side of them and then advancing. She wonders if they practised this during tea-breaks from their road-building. She wonders if any of them got a bit giggly.

All across Rothbury Moors the heather and gorse are in full bloom, like some sort of shattered inviolability breaking into song.

'About nature,' says the girl, looking across to the Cheviot Hills. 'On the other side of the lovely blue gentle line – in the soft area where all the colours are – beyond that, beyond the mountains, is another country where God lives.'

Just off the A697 in Eccles.

'If you snip the air with scissors,' asks the girl, 'does it hurt God?'

The girl is eating vast amounts of chocolate. They are passing a field of black cows with brown and white calves.

'What are those cows mad about?'

'They're not mad.'

'Oh, OK. When I push my fingers in my eyes they go bonkers – then I see butterfly wings.'

It was extraordinary, the mother is thinking, that Shakespeare had been so right about everything – even that.

'I am a great eater of beef,' says Sir Andrew Aguecheek, 'and I believe that does harm to my wits.'

'OK, Mummy. About technology . . .'

The girl got hyper when she had chocolate. Nevertheless, the teacher was obviously even more impressive than the mother had thought.

'About technology. Number one – making rabbits . . . actually, no, let's play guess-the-tune. I'll start.'

The girl is crazy about old musicals, so it must be one of them.

' "Younger than Springtime"?'

'Nope.'

' "Moses supposes . . ."?'

'Nope. Silly answer. Give up? It's "Barney" – the one about divorce and everything:

> I have a friend, he's just moved in,
> he comes from Alabama,
> and the person that he lives with is
> his dear old sweet old gramma.'

Barney, the didactic purple dinosaur adored by the moral majority and children everywhere, had not originated in Britain. The British could, at least, be proud of that.

*

Somewhere between the Empire and the National Front, patriotism had become a dirty word. The mother is hoping it is still all right to love your country. In countryside like this, in a sunset like this, she couldn't help feeling a sense of 'England, my England'. Here. Now. 'At the still point of the turning world – ' just before the caravan park outside Wooler.

'Look at the sunset.'

But the girl is worrying that she had forgotten to do up her seat belt.

'Quickly – before it disappears. Look at it reflected in the river – orange and green and pink. Look how the water swallows the colours in its ripples, and then they resurface as bright as before but trembling . . .'

The girl is incensed: 'Barney says you have to wear a seat belt – which would you rather disappeared, me or . . . or . . .' Maybe she is overdoing it, but she is in floods of tears.

And so they find themselves at sunset, standing by the river – hand holding hand, holding and being held – both of them in a reflective mood. And high above them a whaup dances to its own private grief – calling through the wilderness for its lost soul, yet never finding it. Or so it is said.

Peg had just returned from a walking holiday in Australia. She was under five foot and over eighty. Her hair would be in tight dark curls like Shirley Temple, and she would be wearing ski pants and chrysanthemum-red lipstick. There would be tea laid out with every sweet thing imaginable and paste sandwiches – enough for fifteen people. And she would insist on waiting on them like a servant, even though for the mother she was more than the best part of her family. At Christmas she had 107 presents to buy for her real family. She didn't have a dog.

*

They are sitting down to tea. She had brought them a silly little gift from Australia but it had been confiscated at Customs. It was an official Australian mosquito trap.

Every present she herself has ever received, every postcard and every photograph, is in the room, and each object tells a story and together they make up her life. Amongst her treasures are china Scottie dogs; painted pigs and angels; plastic kangaroos; Spanish dancers; there is a carving of a shepherd; a crocheted swan; there are pictures of sheepdogs and Bonnie and Shirley and the Queen and Prince Philip; there is a lucky Scottish grouse-foot brooch and a wooden book on which is printed the Lord's Prayer; there are two clay crosses, 'In Memoriam' and 'Carpe Diem'; and there are photographs and photographs. The girl is drawn in.

'Who's this?'

'That's my mother's mother – your great-grandmother.'

'She looks nice. I didn't even get to see her.'

'Well – she died . . . because people do. And Peg used to look after her. And that's my mother and father, your grandparents, getting married – under those swords because he was in the navy. Do you see, it's the same church where we got married, when you were a bridesmaid and wore your red Doc Martens . . . and that's Nana, Peg's mother . . .'

The girl has found a clown that plays music while acting drunk. It plays 'Oh my dear old organdy'. Suddenly, giddily, the mother is swung back to when she was six – she is sitting in bed with mumps and her grandmother is reading from a book called *Candyfloss*. It is about a little doll with red hair and an organ-grinder. Her grandmother sings 'Oh my dear old organdy, organdy . . .'

*

'For heaven's sake you've hardly eaten a thing! Have one of these. Apparently they're very nice – they've got butter icing in them. Do I take it you don't like chives?'

There is a picture of Holy Island. They are remembering when she and her brother once went there with Peg. At Eglingham, on the way home, they had stopped at a pub. Inside someone was singing 'Danny Boy' in a deep baritone voice. The singer turned out to be an incredibly dishevelled mynah bird – it was the most exotic thing they had ever seen. It spoke in broad Northumbrian, except to the curate ('Good evening, Thomas. How are you today, Thomas?'), and it could make the sound of the slot machine and the bus pulling up outside.

As she takes away the perishables, Peg talks of an incident the night before that made her feel old. She had been watching a special report from Sarajevo on the news and must have nodded off without realizing it.

'My book was still on my lap and I had my glasses on. Well . . . I heard them talking about lesbians – they were arguing, you see, so their voices were raised – and I thought, goodness, there must be bigger problems to sort out in Yugoslavia than that. But, of course, it wasn't the same programme. It was one of those late-night rude ones for young people.'

They are looking at photos of her walking holiday in Australia. The first four are blue taken from different angles – Hockneyesque.

'Yes, that was Gary trying to get a photo of the plane arriving.'

Peg has never had any trouble with fitness. When she was young they had to walk four miles to school and back – from Ellingham to Seahouses. Her father was a shepherd on thirty shillings a week. She passed her exams, but she needed nine pounds for books and they could not afford it. At fourteen she worked on a farm, milking cows – her father and her brother had serious influenza, her sister had a burst blood vessel, her mother had asthma. She was given a tiny cottage in exchange for milking the cows and that was all – no wages. Her aunt, who lived not far off, used to send down bones and they would make soup with the bones.

The mother is thinking about the girl's Wunderbag. She is wondering how you make a child understand how lucky it is, and how you isolate ineffable moments of happiness – moments to feed off for the rest of your life.

Later, Peg had joined the Land Army and ended up working with her sister on a farm by a lake. Her sister had married and moved south, but Peg, with the sole responsibility for her mother, had begun a lifetime in the service of one family.

'We're sort of relatives . . .'

'No. You are my dear, dear employers.'

She is telling the girl about the prisoners of war with whom she worked. There was a horrible one, an SS trooper – Karl somebody, six feet seven inches – an enormous brute of a man.

'We were coming over the bridge – I've never forgotten it – and he reached down into the water – like that, quickly – and pulled out a great big eel. And it was lashing around his arm, you know, and squeezing like that . . .'

The Italians were nice. It was very hard for them being in a country with such awful weather. One of them had a cousin who had a glove factory in Manchester, but they weren't allowed to correspond. So she had written to let the cousin know how he was.

'By God, if this great hamper didn't arrive. Stuff we'd never even seen! There were oranges and bananas. There was olive oil. And a beautiful pair of gloves – pigskin, I believe. But your granny was always terrified that we'd be found out. Sabotage, you see – telling them where POWs were. It was a serious war crime.'

At first Peg and her mother had lived in the waiting room of the deserted railway-station house. They had cooked in the fireplace, with coal thrown to them by passing engine drivers in exchange for mushrooms and blackberries. Sometimes they would stop for a cup of tea – 'trouble on the line'.

The girl is determined not to go to bed. Peg tells her that her mother used to walk off on her hands whenever she was told to go to bed.

'I'm going to handstand off the sofa.'

'No, you certainly are not . . .'

Too late. Her legs hit a shelf and myriad little ornaments hit the floor. Amazingly, only one thing breaks – a sheep drinking champagne with 'CongratEWElations' written on its side.

'Never you mind one bit – it's only a silly trifle I won at the fair in Corbridge. It was that last week your grandaddy had on leave before Sicily. But didn't we have ourselves an ower grand time . . .'

At the age of twenty-one he had survived the First World War and won a Military Cross in Gallipoli. And then, twenty years later, he and his brothers had been called upon to go back to war. He had been shot in Sicily in 1943, and by an extraordinary twist of fate he was taken to a casualty clearing station where his brother-in-law and best friend was the commanding medical officer. And he had died in his arms. One of his brothers had also been killed and another came home with Parkinson's disease – 'his young son could carry him under one arm at the finish'. Their mother's hair had gone white overnight.

They had sent back his uniform still bloody and Peg had put it straight into a trunk in the attic. She had never shown it to his family.

*

When her dear employer had remarried – a member of the high church – she had instantly fallen out with him.

'Your church hasn't got a Christian attitude at all – it is a hypocritical church.'

In shock he had brought Canon Blackburn to convert her.

'And how do you come to that conclusion, young lady?'

'Jesus said, "All denominations are welcome", but you treat us like heathens when we come to your church – we cannot take Communion and so forth. You come to our church – Presbyterian – and whoever you are you're made welcome to join the Lord's supper. "Other sheep I have which are not of this fold . . . and they will be one flock and one shepherd."'

The Canon had stared at her for a while. Then he said, 'You are a funny little person', and left the room.

When the girl is finally in bed, they have a glass of wine and talk about Peg's mother, who in later years became very senile. One morning Peg had come down for breakfast to find Brillo Pads spread with butter and marmalade.

'Nana – I cannot eat those, they're wire . . .'

'You're far too nice, gabbit. Don't be so fussy.'

Another time Peg was bathing her in front of the fire in the hip-bath. The late-night news was on the television.

'Put that thing off – I am not having that man looking at me.'

'He cannot see you.'

'He can so.'

Just as she had quietened down and was off to bed, a BBC voice said, 'Good night.' She was out of the room like a shot.

In the end Peg had been obliged to take her to work. In the house she would tie her to a chair with a shawl and, because Nana had to have something to do, she would give her string to untangle.

Late at night, Peg would sit tying knot after knot after knot.

When she milked the cows she would have to shut her in the loosebox. One time her employer had said, 'Don't do that – I'll keep an eye on her.' Peg had warned her, 'Mind, she's as fly as a box of monkeys.' And true enough, within seconds, she had gone.

They found her in the boathouse just standing staring into the water.

They are sleeping in Peg's bedroom. On the mantelpiece is a picture of Nana as a girl with a laughing face.

The mother lies in bed and her thoughts are rambling.

When she was a child, grandfathers were men who had been killed in the war – and her generation felt a direct, rather sombre responsibility to them for that sacrifice. But it was different now. Now was all about . . . what? About 'finding happy', that was it really for young people, 'finding happy'.

And to achieve this they seemed to be sloughing off the burden of history to move more freely into the next century, armed with those two great disconcerters, arrogance and technology.

It was all happening so quickly.

And her generation was being consigned to 'not relevant' as rapidly as nostalgia was being traduced as sentimentality.

And it was all happening so quickly.

She draws in a big breath.

She picks up a 1952 edition of *Country Fair* in which her grandmother is featured and which has been lovingly kept by her dear, dear servant:

A rosette for E. M.
She comes of North Country Quaker stock, but according to one friend grew into a cross between a Salvation Army lassie and a Chorus girl . . .

The article goes on to talk about her success as a playwright, one play running in the West End for over four years. It does not mention that once her husband had been killed she could no longer write.

> Today she is to be found either farming, writing, gardening, making jam, washing up, reading, arguing, milking cows, feeding pigs or cooking for a family – always high busy, yet always bubbling over with fun . . . The charm of E. M.'s plays is that they have the magic that enables us to look at ourselves with affection. In them the author does not laugh at the audience; instead she makes the audience laugh at themselves, and, moreover, laugh immoderately. Which means, of course, that her plays do not and never will date.

Which meant, of course, that today her plays were totally unknown. The royalties were now about £32.50 a year – thanks to various WI groups in Gibraltar. There was a large posed photograph of an elegant woman in a tweed suit.

> And on seeing this picture, you must agree that we're good choosers. E. M. is surely the very model of what a country wife ought to look like.

The overwhelming feeling emanating from the face in the photograph is that it knows some bollocks will be written underneath it.

In the same magazine her grandmother had contributed an article about the joys of barn-dancing:

> If you want to see a number of people of all ages getting the greatest amount of fun and exercise out of the smallest outlay of cash, go to a village dance.

What had happened to dancing in the late twentieth century? It was a joy that had been taken away from so many people over a certain age. Grown-ups were condemned to jiggling about self-consciously while a pitying Rastafarian played 'Yellow Bird' on an electronic glockenspiel. It wasn't joyous – it was horrific. When the girl was old enough a machine would probably do the dancing for you. It was all happening so quickly.

Her parents had met at a dance when her mother had just come down from Oxford. And so she had never really had a career – but it was different then.

She is falling asleep thinking about her own student days, when having children was less certain than having a career, because 'fulfilment' was to be achieved only in terms of that career. It seemed funny now – all that feminist excitement, and all that fear too. It was frightening to wear make-up, or to be taken out to dinner, to feel broody. It was unthinkable to marry. And now, many of her friends were unable to have children because of their age or clingfilm or something. Who should have listened to whom? Had it all happened so quickly?

The girl wanted to marry. She wanted to marry James up the road, with whom she did ballet. They weren't bothered with careers or children, but were definitely going to have a white rabbit called Wendy . . .

After a huge breakfast, the mother and the girl are going into Wooler to buy some picnic things for their trip to Holy Island. The girl has a little toy from Australia that tweets like a bird. She keeps it in her hirt pocket and presses it gleefully. When she finally takes it out, she says that it's like a bird has flown out of her heart.

The grocery door is covered in notices:

> Wooler Leek club holding coffee morning.
> Hipshake – dance to the rhythm and beat the blues. At the local filling-station.

Everyone in the grocery smiles at them. They seem to be the only people actually shopping.

'I cannot drag him away from that metal detector,' complains an elderly woman with a chesty voice. 'It's kept him from his First Aid classes two weeks running. I said to him, if I keel over in Wooler High Street all of a sudden and need artificial insemination – a fat lot of use you'll be to me with that metal detector.'

Many of the shop windows contain surprises: the optician's is full of knitting patterns and baby clothes, and Wooler Music Centre has some painted chickens on a bit of string and a pair of castanets and that is all.

They enter the second-hand bookshop and come face to face with a mounted badger's head. Before they can reach the books they have to negotiate their way past a hip-bath, a pile of clogs and a big lampshade with Bing Crosby on it.

She takes a pile of books out of the bath: *Victorian India in Focus*, *Oh for the Borders*, *The Honey-bee: An Analysis*, *Abyssinia* . . . Her mother had always said that books were 'wings to fly with'. She picks out a rather frail, dusty book about the First World War. 'To be a man will continue to demand a courageous heart, as long as mankind is not quite human.'

It cost less than *Zag the Great and Zig the Big*.

On the way back they pass two women in the doorway of a bakery.

'Did you enjoy it Saturday night?'

'No – I came out soon after you . . .'

'It was horrible, wasn't it?'

'It was disgusting. See ya . . .'

As they drive to Holy Island along the Belford road Peg fills the landscape with stories: 'That's Warrenton – one of my cousins died in that cottage . . . and over there, at Cockenhaugh Hill, the other shepherd's wife went into labour and had to be carried three miles on a gate – Dulcie, lives in Wooler now. And d'you see that bush? A young woman was murdered in that bush . . . Oh, and just over that hill is the Bluebell, where they have very nice sausages . . .'

They have their picnic by the causeway, waiting for the tide to go down. In front of them are large stone blocks that had been put there to prevent enemy vessels from landing on the beach. Other than a solitary ice-cream van, there is coarse grass or water as far as the eye can see.

'Mind – it's got very commercial here.'

It is quite unbelievably blustery on the island. They all link arms and it feels a bit less windy. Outside the castle a mother is arguing with her son.

'You are not seeing inside the museum and that's final. And if you want that ice-cream you'd better start bloody behaving yourself.'

Eventually they take refuge in the Holy Island gift shop. Among the relics on offer are portable mini-fans; plastic Viking helmets; koala bears playing cellos; porcelain 'I love you, Mum' dinner bells; and wooden spoons with nuns on them.

The island is famous for St Cuthbert, a shepherd boy from the Lammermuir Hills who became a bishop of the island and was canonized for being pure and ascetic. The good news for modern-day pilgrims is that St Cuthbert is now available in glow-in-the-dark plastic.

Peg treats them to tea in the café. A young waiter dressed in a silk shirt takes the order. The moment he has gone, a waitress asks, 'Is Scot serving you OK?'

Behind her an older woman goes up to Scot.

'You look awful in that shirt. As soon as you're done, take it off.'

When Scot brings the tea, he has kindly brought a hot chocolate for the girl and a saucer of milk for Old Ted. In a whisper Peg is revealing that the gift shop was selling shells shaped like breasts and bottoms.

'They were very good, mind. Extremely accurate, and very well crafted.'

They cross the causeway and drive back towards Wooler. Twenty minutes into the journey, a distraught girl says she has lost Old Ted. They drive back over what is possibly the longest causeway in the history of the world. Scot, in a different shirt, searches high and low, until the older woman says 'coleslaw' to him in a threatening manner and he has to go.

Back in the car the girl has found Old Ted and has gone to sleep.

On the way home Peg tells a story of how one winter, at the crossroads near Netherwitton, a hiker had stumbled across the frozen body of a man. He had rushed to the nearest farm and breathlessly conveyed the news to the farmer, who was sat in front of the television.

'Aye, that'll be Auld Ted. I'll hie him doon to the hoose on the mucker soon as I've finished the match.'

They are saying goodbye to Peg as she sets off for her allotment. When her dear employer had died it was as if a bird had flown out of her heart – she does not want to return to the lake-house.

On the way to Rothbury, it is the mother's turn to people the journey. She points to various houses, telling the girl about a great-aunt who decorated Easter eggs by dyeing them with onion skins and petals; about a great-uncle who collected tin soldiers that lived in ranks, in a state of readiness, on the bedroom carpet. They pass the nursing home where she last saw her favourite, most eccentric relative. When she had been to see her she was slumped with her nose pressed against Thomas the Tank Engine on the television, refusing to eat. When they had tried to feed her she had turned aside muttering something about elm trees.

'She hears arias in tomatoes,' the doctor had said, 'but she doesn't know two times two.'

Only a year before, they had spent a hilarious drunken evening together searching for one of her prosthetic breasts, which had eventually turned up in the freezer.

She was the funniest person the mother had ever met – but now she couldn't remember a single thing she had ever said.

At her funeral she had tried to read 'Dear Lord and Father of mankind', but had broken down on 'Drop thy still dews of quietness'. People had been rather shocked and put it down to her being pregnant. And in some ways they were right – she could not bear the fact that everyone had to die. When her grandmother had died, she had written a poem which her mother had kept.

> my god my god
> my luvly god
> i liv with you forever
> you liv with me forever
> we liv we liv
> we liv forever
>
> gods arnser
>
> man you dont liv forever
> we do
> we dont.

The girl is singing a made-up song.

> 'In the light of the moon
> where the dish and the spoon
> sat where the bong tree grows
> where the flowers twitch and a wicked witch
> has a poggle in her nose.'

*

The girl wants to know if horses can fly. The mother tells her the story of Pegasus.

'He could fly?'

'Yes.'

'In true life?'

'In true life in mythology.'

They are coming into Rothbury. The old-fashioned garage is still there, with pumps that have the shells on them. And all the wonderful hardware stores. And the sweet shop where she had seen her first ever bearded lady. And the cottage hospital where she was brought into the world by her great-uncle, who, many years before, had held her grandfather in his arms.

Everyone looks so friendly. She wants to stop people and say, 'Did you know my grandparents? My parents? They were something, weren't they?'

There are primroses around the war memorial. It becomes obvious that the girl believes that all wars are fought by men in red jackets and large black furry hats, who live in kennels outside Buckingham Palace.

They are opposite the church where she has attended so many christenings and weddings and funerals. At one wedding the hymn numbers had been different on either side of the church – and 'For the beauty of the Earth' had competed with 'Lord of all hopefulness', with neither side willing to capitulate. One Easter the organist had been ill and the vicar's wife had been volunteered, together with their son's electric piano. She was put in a very dark corner of the church and while she was under-scoring 'O Lamb of God', she had inadvertently missed the 'organ' button and pressed 'disco'. She had then worked her way through 'samba', 'jungle' and 'tubular bells' before abandoning it and rushing into the vestry.

*

She takes the girl to the cemetery, where many of her family now live. It is opposite the hospital where she was born. The girl is enchanted by the green glass stones on some of the graves and throws balls of freshly mown grass. When they reach her grandmother's grave, she hurls herself down, somewhat melodramatically, and says, 'Poor Granny, she didn't even know me.'

They end up in the sweet shop.

While she argues with the girl about her desperate need for a Mr Potato-head, the shopkeeper confirms that there had been talk of dumping radioactive material just beyond Rothbury, but he thought it had been abandoned. And yes, the bearded lady was his aunt.

On the door is a poster saying, HELP US DEFEAT TERRORISM. Even here. Even so.

As they walk along the High Street there is suddenly a heart-stopping roar and the earth trembles. A low-flying military jet skims the town. No one around them appears to notice. The girl drops her ice-cream stick – the joke question on it is illegible, but the answer is 'toothless squirrel'.

As they go into the Co-op to buy a picnic tea, they see a crowd. They are mainly women, with vegetables leaning out of their baskets. They are looking down helplessly at an old Labrador lying quietly on the pavement with blood trickling through its faded gold and grey. The dog is looking apologetically to where an old lady stands, bewildered, still holding the lead. Their eyes meet like an old couple.

The girl gets very tearful.

'Will it be all right?'

'Oh, yes, it's going to go and live in heaven.'

'Heaven in the cemetery or beyond the mountains?'

'Whatever.'

'So my grandparents will have a new dog as well as a new gold-fish?'

'Whatever.'

'A dog's better, because I couldn't stroke my goldfish or even sleep with her.'

She opens her Wunderbag and takes out the chocolate-flavoured doggy kebab, which she has wrapped in tissues. She puts it very gently on the pavement near the dog, just in case.

They drive across the moors in silence. The mother is biting her lip because she suddenly feels so very sad.

The girl senses this and touches her arm. Just as they arrive at the lake house, she says, 'I know, Mummy, when we've had our snack, we can hunt for remains. What do you say?'

'Remains of what?'

'Remains of when you were young, of course.'

When I was a little girl I used to go to a house in Northumberland and there were two dogs, two cows, twelve hens, five ducks, two swans, and there was a lake surrounded by high trees. Amongst these trees were tiny mossy streams, and sorrel and blueberries. We would put our feet in the lake and cram in mouthfuls of sorrel and blueberries, until the juice ran down our legs. And there were long branches stretching over the lake that we would sit on, and bounce in and out and in and out of the water. And we would see fish swimming among the tall bulrushes that rose like Excaliburs out of the lake. Sometimes we would split their brown velvety pods with sharp stones, and a stuff would come out like the inside of a pillow and fall like a dust of light on the water. In these quiet, quiet woods there was a ruined cottage that smelt of the wet bark of trees and we would collect pine cones to make fires in the fireplace, and cook sorrel and blueberry soup in old tins, and we would draw pictures of each other on the walls using the ashes. And one summer evening, when we had discovered a strange man asleep in the cottage, we had hidden in the trees outside and spoken very loudly in phoney German accents in the hope of frightening him away. And there was a rowing boat, which we would take to the middle of the lake to fish from; and when we were too hot we would dive overboard, being careful to avoid the reeds, and grin at the fish swimming happily underneath. And when we sang, it would echo around the woods and away up to the ruined castle, where we sometimes would play a game called Allies versus the Enemy.

I had not been back since my step-grandfather had suffered a stroke, unexpectedly remarried and later died. A sign had appeared on the gate saying, BEWARE OF THE DOG. But now it was empty. It had been well looked after and some things were untouched, owing to National Trust rules. The cowshed was unchanged – even the muck seemed to have been preserved – and the smell was still the smell of the cows.

We tiptoed round to the front of the house, ran down the slope and sat by the wretchedly old wooden jetty to eat our picnic. My daughter stripped off her clothes and put her feet in the lake, and we lay back on the spongy lawn that smelt so sweet, with the sun shining on us and the earth underneath us.

'I can hear the daisies growing,' my daughter had whispered, 'and I can touch the sky like a pigeon – rroo coo rroo coo rroo coo. What is sky?'

'A big lake.'

'And our breaths float up and make it cloudy.'

'White sails of a galleon ship.'

'White tablecloths in the wind.'

'Mmm.'

'Flap, flap, flap.'

*

Not strange after all but wonder-gazing.

Suddenly a woman had come storming down the slope. When she saw who we were her face had softened. She was perfectly polite, asked after the family and gave us permission to stay and walk around the woods. She was finally leaving the house – it had got too much for her.

The thing that had meant the end of it all had now become benign.

The little seats made out of logs were still inside the rhododendron bush. Many of the trees were dead, but the sorrel was rampant. My daughter crammed some into her mouth and kicked at the earth that used to be a stream. Everything was dry and the floor was sharp with pine needles. She needed a piggyback because there were so many brambles. Nature seemed to be reclaiming her own – trees had fallen, bushes overgrown – and it was impossible to walk around the lake. My daughter was a bit scratched and a bit frightened by the slapping of the water which accentuated the hush.

It had all suddenly felt unfriendly.

We walked up to the castle. It was just a pile of grey stones with some sheep nestling behind, out of the wind. But there were some new-born lambs gambolling in the bracken, and my daughter laughed and laughed.

We went back down to the lake-house. Where there had been raspberry canes there was concrete, and where there had been a henhouse was a neat flowerbed. The table-tennis house on legs, that had smelt of the 1940s, was gone. The railway station was gone. Ernie Bell the stationmaster was gone, together with Ernie Bell's rhythm band. The ballroom on the lake – long, long gone. There were no more animals. It was quite lifeless.

Yet the potential was still there to set a child dreaming.

SARA WHEELER

Requiem

BANGLADESH

I pushed the swing doors of the adult education centre in King's Cross and looked through the rain to the far end of the car park. No Ford Escort. It was a characteristically bleak November evening in London, the puddles on the tarmac reflecting the sulphurous glow of streetlights and the air thrumming with traffic. I pulled my raincoat tight and huddled against the wall.

My head was leaning against a kingfisher-blue sign inscribed, 'Kingsway College for Adult Education, London Borough of Camden'. What a dread phrase it was, 'adult education'. A repository of unfulfilled hope. Two small rivulets trickled inside my collar, and I began reciting Bengali conjugations in my head, to take my mind off the rain: *ami bhalo achhi, apni bhalo achhen, tumi bhalo achho.*

I had enrolled for a term of evening classes in beginners' Bengali to prepare for a trip to Bangladesh, but as I stood in the rain and clenched my teeth against the cold all I could think of was how much I loathed the boring classes and, worse, how I didn't want to go to Bangladesh at all.

It was like this. Two years previously I had spent seven months in Antarctica, gathering material for a book. Ever since, sitting behind a desk at home, inside my head I had remained on the ice sheet. The project was finished, but I couldn't leave Antarctica behind.

So I sat down and worked out what place on earth might be the polar opposite of the South Pole.

Nobody lives in Antarctica, but Bangladesh is the most densely populated country on earth. Antarctica conjured up ice-cream-cone mountains, but when I thought of Bangladesh I saw the rotting corpses of children floating in the sewers of Dhaka. Except for a waitress who got herself knocked up on a Russian whaler and gave birth in Antarctic waters, no child had ever been born below sixty degrees south. And whereas Bangladesh is on the Tropic of Cancer, Antarctica was very cold indeed.

I decided to put it all behind me and, triumphant, bought an air ticket to Dhaka. Fuck the ice.

So now it was particularly galling that my heart wouldn't follow my plans. My fantasy life had always been realized by travel; I had grown to rely on it. This time, it wasn't happening. The trip to Bangladesh, so thoughtfully conceived, wasn't turning out to be an expression of my inner life at all.

A car horn beeped and I saw Peter peering through the windscreen wipers of my Escort. Peter was a tall and irascible Canadian who had been based in London for thirty years. We had spent the past six months living in each other's houses. I was still blaming everything on Antarctica, but I was beginning to wonder how much he had to do with it.

Tucked neatly into the crotch of Asia, Bangladesh consists of silty lowlands squeezed between north-east India and the western border of Burma. It is the size of England and Wales and almost entirely flat. It is a protean land, constantly reshaped by water rushing off the Himalaya, and as much as 70 per cent of the country is submerged at any one time. The overwhelming majority of its 112 million people are Sunni Muslims, making Bangladesh the third-largest Islamic nation in the world.

I arrived in Dhaka during a tropically thunderous night. The whole city smelt like a cabin lit by kerosene. The streets were pricked not with the beams of headlights but with the woozy glow of kerosene lamps swinging from the undercarriages of elaborately painted cycle rickshaws. None of the rickshaw wallahs spoke a word of English, so I ended up in the wrong place all the time. My attempts at speech met with limited success. I had unconsciously expected Bangladesh to be like India, where English-speakers are ubiquitous; but it wasn't like that at all. I was annoyed to recognize such a nasty little colonial assumption lurking under my cosy liberal carapace. Hindi had never taken root as the national language of India, whereas Bengali is as much a part of Bangladesh as the monsoon rains. What Bangladeshi needed to speak English?

The more a building had cost, the more hideous it looked. The architectural language of Dhaka said, 'Nobody here cares about buildings.' The only thing most people had the energy to care about was survival, and I was amazed at the resourcefulness and ingenuity I observed on the streets. One family had set up a production line on the pavement cleaning old nail-varnish bottles. The first man was squatting in front of a small mountain of empty or half-empty bottles, the cracked flagstones around him splattered like a Jackson Pollock canvas. When he had removed as much of the paint as he could, the man passed each bottle to his brother, who soaked it in a bucket and handed it to a small boy who plunged it into another bucket, that one exuding clouds of vapour smelling of ammonia, and so it went on until the last person, who presided over a gleaming pile of clean nail-polish bottles. Once a day these were loaded into a bicycle basket and another boy pedalled them all away, clinking furiously.

In the rich residential districts of north Dhaka I saw a slimming clinic and, in the early morning, small groups of joggers in saris and sneakers.

*

In Dhaka I thought of home too often. I felt as if I were a prisoner inside my own head instead of a free spirit in a foreign land. After all the travelling I had done, I was confused to find myself the victim of homesickness and disembodied anxieties. I had so many preconceptions about what I was able to do – about my adaptability, resilience and independence; was I losing the markers and maps of my own moods?

Perhaps, I decided after a week or two in the capital, the countryside might shake me out of this slough. One morose evening, trapped in a grim hotel room, I formed a rough plan to travel by train up to the top of the country and slowly work my way down to the bottom.

At the main station I arranged the first leg of the journey in less than an hour, an achievement little short of an Old Testament miracle by Indian standards. In India I would have looked forward to a seven-hour wait in a queue followed by a tortuous conversation with the under-manager responsible for that particular branch line about why the train I wished to catch had been temporarily taken out of service on Tuesdays, Wednesdays and Thursdays. At the end of it all, I would have discovered that the train had been replaced by another which departed at the same time and on the same days as the first one but which, because it was a temporary train, was reserved from a different station.

Bangladesh was not a little India. Once again, my preconceptions were muddled and wrong.

With the ticket in my pocket, I telephoned Peter.

'Hello!' he said enthusiastically.

He had been in the bath; he was standing in the top hallway, dripping. I saw the light filtering through the leaves of the plane tree outside his bathroom window and falling on the tiled floor; the pools of water he would have spilled; and the hardback book open at the side of the freestanding green bath, pages slowly sucking up water.

The conversation was punctuated by the echoes and delays of

antiquated technology, and they reinforced my sense of displacement. After we had chatted about my trip and his news, a pause filled the line.

'Nothing's happened,' I said.

'Good!' he said, even more enthusiastically than before. He seemed uncharacteristically sure of himself. Then he said, 'That means we're going to have a baby, doesn't it?'

The train ground out of Kamalpur station in the middle of Dhaka and rocked its way past miles of huts jammed against the track, all in a state of advanced dereliction and boiling over with people. I was sitting in the first-class carriage, and an obliging steward ferried through china cups of milky tea. An hour later, the slums yielded.

The emerald rice paddies were gilded with rivers and Gothic in their fecundity. Women were stooping, men sitting on their heels and children tottering under enormous wicker baskets. Drying saris garlanded the bushes. A single boat cracked the pewter surface of a stream.

My eye persistently alighted on pregnant women. They were working in the fields. I wondered if there were so many because Bangladesh is such a populous country, or whether I really was pregnant and some kind of magnetic force made them leap out at me. I found myself longing for certainty. I wished I could do a pregnancy test, but purchasing such an object was beyond the resources of my Bengali and they probably didn't exist east of Delhi. I stopped smoking, anyway.

Peter's happiness and certainty seemed so remote. I vaguely resented it: the baby – if there was one – was here, with me, not in north London, safely installed with a telephone to hand. Yet when I looked at the women toiling and bulging, I felt no sense of identification, no uplifting emotion about the universality of motherhood. I didn't feel anything at all – although something was different. I was lonely. Yes, that was it. If this child existed, I wanted to be with its father.

I had assumed that the onset of motherhood would be like a foamy wave of emotion, not a slow unfurling of uncertainty. It was on my mind all the time as Bangladesh uncoiled, but when I turned my attention to it, it slipped away, displaced by drongo birds, jackals and emaciated dogs. I was awash with emotions that I didn't understand, and when I tried to work them out, they ran away from the traps I set. The inner landscape was more alien than the one outside the window, and I was afraid that what lay ahead was the most foreign territory of all.

When the train stopped, blind beggars groped along to the open windows. I fell asleep in the middle of the day and was woken by a shiny elbow stump prodding at my cheek. The amputee was carrying a tin bowl in her mouth. Beyond the station, a row of men were lathering themselves on the steps of a brick tank, and behind the tank a proud old palace was quietly decaying.

The region that became Bengal flourished as early as the ninth century BC. It consisted of a disparate collection of states, most of which, by the fifth century BC, had been permeated by the spread of Aryan culture. The states were united once or twice, and the influence of Hinduism and Buddhism see-sawed until the twelfth century AD, when Islamic invaders conquered the whole region. The Muslim Moghuls stimulated a golden age in Bengal, and in 1608 the great empire moved its capital to Dhaka.

The next invaders, the British, went on to make Bengal the heart of their Indian empire. In 1912, however, they shifted their capital across the country to Delhi, and thirty-one years later an apocalyptic famine killed between 3 and 5 million and almost crushed the spirit right out of Bengal. At Partition, in 1947, East Bengal became East Pakistan, half of a brand-new Muslim country, and the majority of its

Hindus fled west to India. In 1971, after a brutal civil war, East Pakistan won its independence from its western wing and became Bangladesh – land of the Bengali people.

A Bangladeshi over fifty-one was born Indian, and anyone between fifty and twenty-seven was born Pakistani.

I got off the train at Srimangal, in the heart of tea country. An itinerant ear doctor was cruising for trade along the platform, a tray of sinister implements suspended from his neck. It was dark, and the medieval lanes around the station were dancing with candle-flame.

I had arranged to stay in a guest house on a tea estate, and a man turned up to collect me in a rickshaw.

The next morning, I walked around the terraced hills. They were quilted with squat tea bushes and whirring with insect wings. The roads and tracks slicing through the hills were spotted with squads of pluckers – all women – walking barefoot to work in faded saris, the baskets on their backs held by a cord tied round a cloth top-knot. They carried their lunch in scarves, hanging over their shoulders like swag bags. Plucking is a feudal job, handed down the generations. A few men roamed the terraces with scythes, chopping at the jongli bushes.

Bangladesh's 158 tea estates are all located up in the north-east. Fifty per cent of their produce is exported. As these hills don't yield tea of an especially high quality, it gets drunk mainly in Jordan, Pakistan and Russia. The producers are grateful, too far down the economic totem pole to expect to sell to the West. While I was in the north-east, the English-language newspaper the *Daily Star* ran an alarming editorial about 'gangs of organized toll extortionists in the tea gardens'. The phenomenon it went on to describe, in which local gangsters forced tea producers to hand over hefty and regular payments, thereby effectively fixing the price of tea, was a typical example of the way the Bangladeshi economy functions. *Mahajons*, a kind of Mafia, run half the country. The government collects almost no taxes and the state control that does exist is hugely elastic.

I reminded myself that Bangladesh is a new country – it came into being the year I entered secondary school and only eight years before Margaret Thatcher became Britain's prime minister. No wonder it had such a Wild West feel about it. No wonder too that it remains vastly reliant on foreign aid and that the smart districts of Dhaka bristle with the acronyms of the agencies that dish it out. Crippling bureaucracy and endemic corruption coexist unhappily in Bangladesh among the murky politics of aid, and a sizeable tranche of aid cash returns to the donor country in consultancy fees. The big idea of the economic sector is currently microcredit (lending to poor people, either individually or in small groups), and new schemes do cast a weak ray of hope on to apparently intractable problems.

But it is weak. Calcutta might have earned a place in the geographical imagination of the West as a cipher of disease and despair, but rich Bangladeshis go to Calcutta for medical treatment. Most depressing of all, whenever the country shows signs of struggling to its feet, another cataclysmic national disaster, usually a flood or a cyclone, knocks it back down.

'Congratulations on coming to Bangladesh!' said a jolly man in a business suit, slapping me on the back. I was walking around a tea-processing plant. The leaves were being oxidized, and the air was thick with a moist and pungent aroma. When I emerged from the factory part of the plant, I collided with a gaggle of suited men. Despite the considerable heat, the one who had congratulated me, apparently the only English-speaker, was wearing a hat like a woolly profiterole.

He explained that he and his henchmen were on a joint government–UN-sponsored child-labour commission.

Children were toiling all over the tea estates. Minors worked everywhere in Bangladesh.

'Does the government want to put a stop to child labour, then?' I asked.

'Oh, yes, very much,' the man said with a large smile. 'If they are under twelve it is very bad.'

The Lawachara evergreen and semi-evergreen tropical rain forest, folded deep within the tea plantations, had by some stroke of fate escaped the deforestation ravaging most of Bangladesh. The canopy swished with the beat of bird wings, screaming capped langur monkeys darted among the mahogany trees and I even saw a hoolock gibbon, a beguiling cocoa-brown creature with white eyebrows, tapering fingers and bright eyes. It was impossible to get away from people, though, there or indeed anywhere in Bangladesh. Knots of them lurked on the loneliest path. To compound the problem, since white faces were a rarity, everybody was terribly interested in me. I was pleased that people tried to talk to me, and I sensed that I was never in danger, but I grew tired of being followed around.

I had discovered that the loss of language can be a great stimulant. It was as if I were turning in on myself, retreating into a private world of memory and imagination. I wanted to be left alone with this feeling. Obsessed with shaking people off, I found myself stepping smartly behind teak trees to give a curious companion the slip.

Women were more covert than men in their efforts to shadow me, their voyeurism handicapped not by solidarity but by social convention. It was surprising, at first, to learn that in Bangladesh both the prime minister and the leader of the opposition were women; but both took on almost hereditary roles, the PM as daughter of Sheik Mujibur Rahman, the quasi-legendary 'founder of the nation' (he was assassinated in 1975), and the leader of the opposition as the widow of Ziaur Rahman (the president assassinated in 1981).

For ordinary women, imprisoned within problems of their own, these figureheads are remote. Although the dowry has been banned by law, it still exists on the ground – even the continuing dowry, which must be paid regularly, like rent. Violence against women is a huge and largely unaddressed problem in Bangladesh, and it includes the popular pursuit of throwing acid into the face of one's ex-girlfriends. Men apparently can't stand the idea of other men taking up with women they once thought of as their property, and the handy solution is to disfigure the women, thereby rendering them unmarriageable.

After four days on the tea estates I caught a train due south to Chittagong, second city and first port. The journey took all day, past an uninterrupted succession of bony oxen, rickety ploughs and drongo birds squatting on rotting telegraph poles. The train eventually crossed the Karnapuli river and entered the city via a suspension bridge. According to Ptolemy, in the second century AD Chittagong was one of the finest ports in the East. It swapped hands many times – the Muslims and Arakanese, in particular, tossed it between them like a beachball.

I found a hotel; it was leprous with corrosion and smelt of mouldy vegetables. The next morning, on the pavement outside my window, I watched a man and a woman rolled up in blankets trying to catch more sleep while three toddlers, who had other ideas, pulled the coverings from their faces. All three children had suppurating eye infections.

This image, unlike the pregnant women in the fields, made me panic. I thought about my own putative baby, shocked at the responsibility I had undertaken. My anxieties were magnified by the squalor all around me; my baby's destiny was not, of course, a childhood on the streets of Chittagong, but I could no longer apply logic to my thoughts.

*

In the afternoon I walked to the Memorial to the Martyrs of the Language Movement, an ugly concrete affair draped with a flag and a few desiccated wreaths. On the street below people were burning rice husks under Primus stoves. In 1948, a year after Pakistan came into existence, Urdu, spoken throughout the western half of the country, was designated the national language, despite the fact that no one in the eastern wing spoke it. On 21 February 1952 Bengali-speaking students at Chittagong University marched in protest and five were killed. The event is held up as a significant moment in the evolution of the independence movement and cherished in the national psyche as proof of what Bangladeshis can achieve, despite their destitution.

As the train line ends at Chittagong, I caught a bus 100 miles south, down the narrow band of Bangladesh adjacent to the Burmese hills.

I got off at a town called Cox's Bazar, the beguiling name acquired from its eighteenth-century Dundonian founder. The beach there was allegedly the longest in the world. The Bangladeshi coast is entirely exposed to the Bay of Bengal, and in Cox's Bazar trucks were patrolling the main street issuing cyclone warnings from loudspeakers. The last cyclone killed 100,000 people. A week after it struck they were still hooking bodies out of trees.

Most of the people on the streets of Cox's Bazar were tribals with Tibetan features carrying babies peeping out of pink woven slings. They had come down from the hills to buy and sell at the market. The hill tribes mostly practise slash-and-burn agriculture (*jhum*), despite the fact that the government has tried to ban it to prevent further erosion of the hill tracts. Relations between the tribals and the government are strained. The day before I arrived two activists belonging to Shantibahini, a loose collection of tribal peoples struggling to protect their culture and achieve some kind of political autonomy, had been arrested outside my hotel by the security forces and charged with the possession of arms.

Cyclones notwithstanding, Cox's Bazar is the main holiday resort for middle-class Bangladeshis, and they all clamoured, when I appeared on the beach, to have their photograph taken with me. This was a paradox. Bangladeshis almost invariably displayed the pride characteristic of a young country. 'We are not poor mentally,' a rare English-speaker encountered on a train had been anxious to reassure me. Yet they were terribly influenced by what they perceived to be the glamour of the West. It was the zenith of sophistication to return from your holiday with snapshots of yourself idling with a white-skinned person, and in the cities the people depicted in advertising hoardings were suspiciously fair. But I didn't mind posing for their pictures.

I went back to Chittagong by bus and on to Dhaka by train, as I had decided to travel down to the Gangetic delta on a Rocket paddle steamer, and these departed from the capital. The Ganges officially becomes the Padma when it enters Bangladesh and the Brahmaputra is renamed the Jamuna; half-way down the country they join to become the Meghna. This river moves 400 million tons of earth a year and regularly rearranges the map. As for the magnificent seven remaining Rockets, built in Calcutta in the 1920s, their paddle wheels are powered now by diesel engines.

The Rockets travel four times a week between Dhaka and Khulna, a twenty-four-hour trip. I had booked a first-class cabin on the top deck. It opened on to a carpeted dining area in which a group of saturnine Bengalis were permanently hunched over pyramids of steamy rice.

I spent most of my journey sitting outside in a cane armchair as the Rocket chugged sedately down the Meghna. Hundreds of small boats puttered past, and anguished calls to prayer drifted across from the banks. Great rafts of bamboo were being floated south. Schools of Gangetic dolphins leapt among pale mauve pontoons of water hyacinth, and riverine gypsies tethered their covered boats to coconut palms in search of customers for their herbal medicines. I was intermittently ministered to by a steward in a crisp white jacket and dirty turban. He brought tea and biscuits, and said, 'Good morning, sir', very softly whenever he approached, whatever the hour of day or night.

Once, in the evening, I crept down to the lower decks. People were sprawled everywhere – hundreds of people. Right at the bottom, soldiers were lying on their backs around the engine, huge black boots at their sides and guns tossed against the railings.

In the morning, flotillas of small boats emerged out of the mist, the oarsmen, standing, sunk within tightly wrapped shawls.

By the time I reached Khulna, I was sure I was pregnant. I felt fine. A little weary of rice and watery curried vegetables, but fine. Now I was certain about something, and that helped dislodge my inchoate anxieties. I wanted to call Peter very badly, but no international telephones were working. 'Line is failure,' said a bored attendant at the STD telephone booth next to the Rocket terminal.

I found a hotel next to a derelict jute factory. For many years, yellow-flowered jute was Bangladesh's main export, and there is still a Ministry for Jute, and a jute exchange. Jute flourishes in the humid climate of the Gangetic plain and has been the main cash crop of wetland smallholders since about 1700. It is harvested during the floods, and to cut the plant farmers dive down to the base six or eight feet under water, using the stalk as a guide. Bangladeshi jute divers are said to be the most skilful swimmers in the world. The emergence of synthetics has resulted, as usual, in shrinking demand and falling prices, effectively strangling the industry.

*

I was making my way to join a pleasure boat setting off for four days in the waterways of the Sundarbans, a dense mangrove forest along the Bay of Bengal embracing the greatest tidal delta in the world. I had discovered the existence of this strangely un-Bangladeshi excursion in Dhaka and arranged to join a group of eight passengers and six crew. It was only a few miles down to Mongla, the port where we were due to embark, but all travel in southern Bangladesh is circumscribed by ferries (these invariably turned out to be primitive and overladen rafts), and they are usually broken, paralysed by *hartals*, Bangladeshi-style strikes, or simply clogged with queues. As a result, the trip took half a day and I was three hours late, though this wasn't nearly as late as everyone else.

The Sundarbans forest covers 2,300 square miles, two-fifths of which are in India and three-fifths in Bangladesh. The forest is largely impenetrable on land and too dense for occupation. It is criss-crossed, however, by a complex network of waterways, and these we were scheduled to chug through, observing the fecund wildlife and enjoying the peace – a rare commodity in Bangladesh.

The boat, *MV Chhuti*, had ten small cabins arranged around the lower of two decks, all facing outwards. Bathroom facilities consisted of two toilets in the bows, two shower cubicles and two public washbasins. The crew bunks and galley were crammed below decks and the top deck was reserved for lounging around.

The other passengers eventually turned up and boarded noisily. I soon learned that they did everything noisily. They were middle-class professional families from Dhaka, the ringleader a doctor in his fifties with a Mephistophelean smile. This man addressed me throughout the trip in a language tantalizingly close to English. He would begin a dialogue with enthusiastic optimism, realize that the sentiment he wished to express was beyond his capabilities, and promptly leave the sentence he had begun languishing in the syntactical desert, trunkless as Ozymandias. None of the others spoke a single word of English.

Disobliging tides meant that *M V Chhuti* was unable to leave Mongla before morning. We anchored opposite a row of prostitutes' thatched huts, the incumbents' business confined to tanker crews. The night was punctuated by the low elephant grief of ships' horns.

We set off before dawn and from the top deck I watched flocks of egrets rising from the mangrove swamps.

Mephistopheles had brought his father, wife, a son of about ten and a teenaged daughter, the latter evidently extremely inconvenienced by the presence of her parents, who seemed to annoy her a great deal. She had smeared turmeric on her face to make it brighter, a process I saw her repeating in front of the cracked mirror above one of the washbasins each morning. I wondered if she had her eye on a member of the crew, as the prospect of meeting eligible young men in the heart of the Sundarbans was as remote as it would have been in the Gobi Desert.

The forest consisted of densely packed sudari trees, a type of mangrove yielding wood suitable for telegraph poles and paper pulp. Due to tidal shifts and the high salinity of the waterways, the Sundarbans constitute a strange and wonderful ecological hinterland. Spotted deer, rhesus monkeys and wild boar proliferated on land, crocodiles slunk along the river banks, primeval horseshoe crabs with rotating proboscises roamed the beaches and the birds seemed almost limitless in their abundance and variety. The kingfishers alone had apparently transmuted into hundreds of different species, each iridescent flash entirely different from the last. Tan-winged Brahmini kites followed the wake of our boat, themselves pursued by white-bellied sea eagles, and pied mynahs rose from the banks in small clouds.

The further west in the forest you go, the more saline the waters become, with the result that the trees are shorter on the Indian side and there are fewer birds. Bangladeshis are very proud of that.

At meal times conversation stormed to and fro across great platters of sloppy vegetable rice and fried fish. Mephistopheles's aged father never partook of this food, apparently eating alone at another time in some secret location, but while we were at the table he remained in the corner of the cabin on the lower deck in which we dined, emitting what I took to be the occasional Shavianism. Mostly my companions ignored me, but occasionally, I suspect out of boredom, they turned their attention to the strange habits of foreigners, further subdivisions of the species apparently being considered unnecessary.

I was trapped among a small crowd on *MV Chhuti*, but it was a contained and familar crowd. They began to blend in with the mangroves and the hum of the engine, and I began to loosen up.

The Sundarbans are the home of the man-eating Royal Bengal tiger.

The government claims there are 450 of these elusive creatures left in Bangladesh, but experts put the figure nearer 200. The last census on the Indian side came up with a total Indian population of 250, but this too could be optimistic. The Royal Bengal, smaller in size and brighter in colour than northern tigers, has evolved in isolation, and what makes him such a mysterious beast is his selective predilection for eating people. In particular, he likes the Bangladeshi honey collectors, who arrive in the Sundarbans late in the season.

The tiger is deeply embedded in local mythology. In Bangladeshi villages abutting the Sundarbans the tiger god, Daksin Ray, receives regular offerings and people there are careful to refer to the beast as 'uncle', avoiding the Bengali word for tiger in case it provokes the spirits of the forest. Some of these small communities have lost men so frequently that they are known as *vidhaba pallis*, tiger-widow villages.

The mythology of the tiger settled on our boat. We all dreamt about him and I was frequently aware that the others were talking about him over meals, even though I couldn't understand what they were saying. I often heard a hissed call of '*bagh!*' (tiger) from the top deck, and we would all rush up and lean over the railings, straining our eyes to see him.

But we never did. Once we spied fresh pad prints emerging from the water and a pair of red-wattled lapwings beaking around in a pile of spoor.

The best time to be on *MV Chhuti* was otter time. For generations, in the lonely backwaters of the Sundarbans otters have been trained to chase fish. Very early, before the monkeys wake, a spectral fishing vessel emerges from the dawn mist and a pair of otters, harnessed and squeaking, dive through the milky-chocolate water while four men, standing up in a gondola-shaped boat, manoeuvre nets attached to six-foot bamboo poles. When they aren't working, the otters live in a wicker cage strapped to the stern of the boat.

If the otters didn't come, before *MV Chhuti*'s engine began to throb the only sound was the incantation of the old engine-man reciting the Koran on the lower deck. I never heard him speak apart from his prayer sessions, but he was a hieratic presence on board our boat.

Besides the otter fishermen, the only other people in the Sundarbans were itinerant grass cutters collecting thatch, and a small community of men and boys who came each summer to fish conventionally. They lived their lonely and uncertain lives in a compound of thatched huts, roofs reaching the ground, and slept on tiger-proof platforms. The cracked earth of the compound was spread with coir mats on which the boys had laid out thousands of fragile silvery fish.

One afternoon our cook bought crabs from a pair of fishermen who pulled in alongside *MV Chhuti* and we ate them on the top deck. Islamic law bans the consumption of shellfish, but among our little party the rule seemed to apply only to those over thirty.

We landed alongside a natural jetty at dusk and I walked in the chequered shadow of the trees, the sky flared with coral and each mangrove frond perfectly defined in the tropical light. There was no undergrowth in this forest, just hundreds of thousands of fibrous stalactites, the root system of the mangroves. I felt calm in those few days, as if I saw things more clearly. My old life seemed to be peeling away like a label from a bottle. I was able to think coherently, for the first time, about my baby. It was as if my centre of gravity were altering, like a tidal shift in the great waterways of the Sundarbans.

NOTES ON CONTRIBUTORS

DEA BIRKETT is a writer and broadcaster. She is author of *Jella: A Woman at Sea*, which won the Somerset Maugham Award, and, most recently, *Serpent in Paradise*. She was awarded a Winston Churchill Travel Fellowship to join an Italian circus. She grew up in the southeast of England and now lives in London.

GINNY DOUGARY has lived in Kuwait, where she was born in 1956, Sydney, New York and London. She is the lead interviewer for *The Times* magazine and the author of *The Executive Tart and Other Myths*.

LESLEY DOWNER was a Japan specialist until she discovered Africa. She has written several books about Japan, including *On the Narrow Road to the Deep North*, which was shortlisted for the Thomas Cook Travel Book Award. In 1991 she wrote and presented a series on Japanese cooking for the BBC and is now a journalist.

SHENA MACKAY was born in Edinburgh and lives in London. She has three daughters and two grandchildren. She has published two novellas, seven novels and three collections of stories, and edited two anthologies. Her books have won many awards, and *The Orchard on Fire* was shortlisted for the 1996 Booker Prize. This year Jonathan Cape publish her novel *The Artist's Widow.*

SUZANNE MOORE is currently a columnist for the *Independent* and has contributed to many national newspapers. *Head Over Heels*, a collection of her essays, was published in 1997. She lives in London with her two daughters.

KATE PULLINGER is, for the time being, an armchair traveller who writes fiction, most recently a novel, *The Last Time I Saw Jane*, and a collection of short stories, *My Life as a Girl in a Men's Prison*. She is Canadian, lives in London and longs to get away.

MARY RUSSELL is an Irish writer who divides her time between Dublin and Oxford. Her travels have taken her to, among other places, Sudan, Lesotho, the Republic of Georgia and the Finnish Arctic. She is author of *The Blessings of a Good Thick Skirt* and *Please Don't Call It Soviet Georgia*. For relaxation, she plays squash and poker. She has two granddaughters.

ELISA SEGRAVE lived in Madrid until she was three. She is the author of *The Diary of a Breast* and *Ten Men*. She has published short stories and articles and is now writing a third book.

LUCRETIA STEWART was born in Singapore and spent much of her early life in the Far East. She is the author of *Tiger Balm: Travels in Laos, Vietnam and Cambodia* and *The Weather Prophet: A Caribbean Journey*, which was shortlisted for the 1996 Thomas Cook Travel Book Award.

IMOGEN STUBBS was born in Northumberland and grew up on an old sailing barge in west London. She read English at Oxford and went on to become an actress. She is married to the director Trevor Nunn and they have two children.

SARA WHEELER is a London-based travel writer whose last book, *Terra Incognita: Travels in Antarctica* was a bestseller. Her son, Wilf Wheeler, was born seven months after she returned from Bangladesh.

Visit Penguin on the Internet
and browse at your leisure

- ◆ preview sample extracts of our forthcoming books
- ◆ read about your favourite authors
- ◆ investigate over 10,000 titles
- ◆ enter one of our literary quizzes
- ◆ win some fantastic prizes in our competitions
- ◆ e-mail us with your comments and book reviews
- ◆ instantly order any Penguin book

and masses more!

'To be recommended without reservation ... a rich and rewarding on-line experience' – Internet Magazine

www.penguin.co.uk

READ MORE IN PENGUIN

In every corner of the world, on every subject under the sun, Penguin represents quality and variety – the very best in publishing today.

For complete information about books available from Penguin – including Puffins, Penguin Classics and Arkana – and how to order them, write to us at the appropriate address below. Please note that for copyright reasons the selection of books varies from country to country.

In the United Kingdom: Please write to *Dept. EP, Penguin Books Ltd, Bath Road, Harmondsworth, West Drayton, Middlesex UB7 ODA*

In the United States: Please write to *Consumer Sales, Penguin Putnam Inc., P.O. Box 999, Dept. 17109, Bergenfield, New Jersey 07621-0120*. VISA and MasterCard holders call 1-800-253-6476 to order Penguin titles

In Canada: Please write to *Penguin Books Canada Ltd, 10 Alcorn Avenue, Suite 300, Toronto, Ontario M4V 3B2*

In Australia: Please write to *Penguin Books Australia Ltd, P.O. Box 257, Ringwood, Victoria 3134*

In New Zealand: Please write to *Penguin Books (NZ) Ltd, Private Bag 102902, North Shore Mail Centre, Auckland 10*

In India: Please write to *Penguin Books India Pvt Ltd, 210 Chiranjiv Tower, 43 Nehru Place, New Delhi 110 019*

In the Netherlands: Please write to *Penguin Books Netherlands bv, Postbus 3507, NL-1001 AH Amsterdam*

In Germany: Please write to *Penguin Books Deutschland GmbH, Metzlerstrasse 26, 60594 Frankfurt am Main*

In Spain: Please write to *Penguin Books S. A., Bravo Murillo 19, 1° B, 28015 Madrid*

In Italy: Please write to *Penguin Italia s.r.l., Via Benedetto Croce 2, 20094 Corsico, Milano*

In France: Please write to *Penguin France, Le Carré Wilson, 62 rue Benjamin Baillaud, 31500 Toulouse*

In Japan: Please write to *Penguin Books Japan Ltd, Kaneko Building, 2-3-25 Koraku, Bunkyo-Ku, Tokyo 112*

In South Africa: Please write to *Penguin Books South Africa (Pty) Ltd, Private Bag X14, Parkview, 2122 Johannesburg*

READ MORE IN PENGUIN

A SELECTION OF OMNIBUSES

The Cornish Trilogy Robertson Davies

'He has created a rich oeuvre of densely plotted, highly symbolic novels that not only function as superbly funny entertainments but also give the reader, in his character's words, a deeper kind of pleasure – delight, awe, religious intimations, "a fine sense of the past, and of the boundless depth and variety of life"' – *The New York Times*

A Dalgliesh Trilogy P. D. James

Three classics of detective fiction featuring the assiduous Adam Dalgliesh. In *A Shroud for a Nightingale, The Black Tower* and *Death of an Expert Witness*, Dalgliesh, with his depth and intelligence, provides the solutions to seemingly unfathomable intrigues.

The Pop Larkin Chronicles H. E. Bates

'Tastes ambrosially of childhood. Never were skies so cornflower blue or beds so swansbottom ... Life not as it is or was, but as it should be' – *Guardian*. 'Pop is as sexy, genial, generous and boozy as ever, Ma is a worthy match for him in these qualities' – *The Times*

The Penguin Book of New American Voices
Edited by Jay McInerney

'Traditional, well-crafted, poignant tales rub shoulders with ones from the inner city which read like bulletins from a war zone ... At their best [these stories] shake you up, take you some place you've never been, and dump you into some weird life you've never even imagined' – *Mail on Sunday*

Lucia Victrix E. F. Benson

Mapp and Lucia, Lucia's Progress, Trouble for Lucia – now together in one volume, these three chronicles of English country life will delight a new generation of readers with their wry observation and delicious satire.

READ MORE IN PENGUIN

A SELECTION OF OMNIBUSES

The Penguin Book of Classic Fantasy by Women
Edited by A. Susan Williams

This wide-ranging and nerve-tingling collection assembles short stories written by women from 1806 to the Second World War. From George Eliot on clairvoyance to C. L. Moore on aliens or Virginia Woolf on psychological spectres, here is every aspect of fantasy from some of the best-known writers of their day.

The Penguin Collection

This collection of writing by twelve acclaimed authors represents the finest in modern fiction, and celebrates sixty years of Penguin Books. Among the stories assembled here are ones by William Boyd, Donna Tartt, John Updike and Barbara Vine.

V. I. Warshawski Sara Paretsky

In *Indemnity Only*, *Deadlock* and *Killing Orders*, Sara Paretsky demonstrates the skill that makes tough female private eye Warshawski one of the most witty, slick and imaginative sleuths on the street today.

A David Lodge Trilogy David Lodge

His three brilliant comic novels revolving around the University of Rummidge and the eventful lives of its role-swapping academics. Collected here are: *Changing Places*, *Small World* and *Nice Work*.

The Rabbit Novels John Updike

'One of the finest literary achievements to have come out of the US since the war . . . It is in their particularity, in the way they capture the minutiae of the world . . . that [the Rabbit] books are most lovable' – *Irish Times*

READ MORE IN PENGUIN

A SELECTION OF OMNIBUSES

Zuckerman Bound   Philip Roth

The Zuckerman trilogy – *The Ghost Writer*, *Zuckerman Unbound* and *The Anatomy Lesson* – and the novella-length epilogue, *The Prague Orgy*, are here collected in a single volume. Brilliantly diverse and intricately designed, together they form a wholly original and richly comic investigation into the unforeseen consequences of art.

The Collected Stories of Colette   Colette

The hundred short stories collected here include such masterpieces as 'Bella-Vista', 'The Tender Shoot' and 'Le Képi', Colette's subtle and ruthless rendering of a woman's belated sexual awakening. 'A perfectionist in her every word' – *Spectator*

The Collected Stories   Muriel Spark

'Muriel Spark has made herself a mistress at writing stories which seem to trip blithely and bitchily along life's way until the reader is suddenly pulled up with a shock recognition of death and judgment, heaven and hell' – *London Review of Books*

The Complete Saki

Macabre, acid and very funny, Saki's work drives a knife into the upper crust of English Edwardian life. Here are the effete and dashing heroes, the tea on the lawn, the smell of gunshot, the half-felt menace of disturbing undercurrents ... all in this magnificent omnibus.

The Penguin Book of Gay Short Stories
Edited by David Leavitt and Mark Mitchell

The diversity – and unity – of gay love and experience in the twentieth century is celebrated in this collection of thirty-nine stories. 'The book is like a long, enjoyable party, at which the celebrated ... rub shoulders with the neglected' – *The Times Literary Supplement*

READ MORE IN PENGUIN

A SELECTION OF OMNIBUSES

Italian Folktales   Italo Calvino

Greeted with overwhelming enthusiasm and praise, Calvino's anthology is already a classic. These tales have been gathered from every region of Italy and retold in Calvino's own inspired and sensuous language. 'A magic book' – *Time*

The Penguin Book of Lesbian Short Stories
Edited by Margaret Reynolds

'Its historical sweep is its joy, a century's worth of polymorphous protagonists, from lady companions and *salonières* to pathological inverts and victims of sexology; from butch-femme stereotypes to nineties bad girls' – *Guardian*

On the Edge of the Great Rift   Paul Theroux
Three Novels of Africa

In *Fong and the Indians*, Sam Fong, a Chinese immigrant in a ramshackle East African country, is reduced to making friends with the enemy. Miss Poole runs a school in the Kenyan bush in *Girls at Play*, and in *Jungle Lovers*, the fortunes of a dedicated insurance salesman and a ruthless terrorist become strangely interwoven.

The Levant Trilogy   Olivia Manning
The Danger Tree • The Battle Lost and Won • The Sum of Things

'Her lucid and unsentimental style conveys the full force of ordinary reality with its small betrayals and frustrations but, at the back of it, images of another and more enduring life emerge' – *The Times*

The Complete Enderby   Anthony Burgess

In these four collected novels Enderby – poet and social critic, comrade and Catholic – is endlessly hounded by women. He may be found hiding in the lavatory where much of his best work is composed, or perhaps in Rome, brainwashed into respectability by a glamorous wife, aftershave and the *dolce vita*.

READ MORE IN PENGUIN

A SELECTION OF TRAVEL BOOKS

Hindoo Holiday	J. R. Ackerley
The Innocent Anthropologist	Nigel Barley
South from Granada	Gerald Brenan
The Road to Oxiana	Robert Byron
An Indian Summer	James Cameron
Granite Island	Dorothy Carrington
The Hill of Devi	E. M. Forster
Journey to Kars	Philip Glazebrook
Journey Without Maps	Graham Greene
South of Haunted Dreams	Eddy L. Harris
Mornings in Mexico	D. H. Lawrence
Between the Woods and the Water	Patrick Leigh Fermor
Mani	Patrick Leigh Fermor
A Time of Gifts	Patrick Leigh Fermor
The Stones of Florence *and* Venice Observed	Mary McCarthy
Calcutta	Geoffrey Moorhouse
Among the Cities	Jan Morris
Spain	Jan Morris
Sydney	Jan Morris
Travels in Nepal	Charlie Pye-Smith
The Kindgom by the Sea	Paul Theroux
The Pillars of Hercules	Paul Theroux
The Marsh Arabs	Wilfred Thesiger
Behind the Wall	Colin Thubron
Journey into Cyprus	Colin Thubron
The Lost Heart of Asia	Colin Thubron
Ninety-Two Days	Evelyn Waugh
Third-Class Ticket	Heather Wood
The Smile of Murugan	Michael Wood
From Sea to Shining Sea	Gavin Young